Sam Huff and the Gunner.

Their Incredible Journeys from Coal Camp No.9 to the Hall of Fame

by Seseen Francis

Published in the United States of America by:
Francis Publications
PO Box 503
Fairmont, WV 26554

ISBN 978-0989738224

First Edition

Prologue

In the 1930's, No. 9 was just one of many coal camps in the rugged hills of northern West Virginia. The close knit community of a few hundred men and women – immigrants from many lands and those born here – lived in coal camp rows of houses, toiled together, and raised children while living their dangerous lives. Among those living here at the time were a five-year-old kid in elementary school and a young man just out of high school. Their homes were "a dirt road apart", just a few hundred feet from each other. Incredibly, both of them would somehow find a way from this place to be recognized among the greatest football players of all time. Both were inducted into the NFL Hall of Fame. This is their story.

Coal Camp No. 9

Katherine Huff knew the sound of trouble. The sound was the silence. All at once the pumping pounding beat of the coal mine tipple just over the hill had stopped. She stood still. Silence.

She swept her son, Sam, up in her arms and then opened the screen door. It banged closed behind her. Chickens squawked and scattered as she quickly stepped off the porch. She walked steadily – not in a panic, but in a prayerful march toward the mine portal.

She had done this before – dozens of times. Each time it had been a false alarm – trouble, but no tragedy. She wasn't alone. As she walked she could see other women coming from the rows of houses that lined the hillside. These women, too, had grown accustomed to the sound of their life.

In a moment Maria Coceano came to Katherine's side and joined her. Up ahead a dozen other women had begun to make their way to the rim of the hill overlooking the portal. Eta Gatski, with two-year-old Mary Louise in her arms, was hurrying to catch up to Katherine and Maria. Soon there was a large crowd of women, twenty or more, from the houses that supplied the labor for the Number 9 mine in a slow caravan along the short road to the portal.

Katherine took a deep breath. The smell of coal dust was strong – its taste bitter. Now she noticed the weight of her son. She set him down. He walked quickly beside her as they approached the mine entrance.

Miners had already begun to emerge from the mine. By their calm, the women collectively breathed a sigh of relief.

Katherine took a cautious step down the dirt bank closer to the miners hoping to hear their conversation. The words kept falling on top of each other. Another deep breath. She knew everything was okay. She looked for her husband, Oral.

Ben Bennett, a mine foreman, seemed to be getting most of the attention. "Nothing wrong," he said. "Just a bad pump."

Katherine saw Oral and went to him. Little Sam held onto his mother's dress to keep up with her and stumbled. Katherine held tight to his hand and lifted him to his feet. "Robert Lee, hold on to me!"

Sam gripped his mother's hand tight. He knew when he heard his birth name "Robert Lee" that he had better pay attention. His mother and dad only called that out when the moment was urgent. His name had become Sam, short for "Sambo", given to him by his big sister Mickey because of his always dirty face reminding her of Little Black Sambo from first grade reading. Now everyone called him Sam except…

Oral wiped the back of his hand across his mouth – then spit out the grit. "Getting some water down there – bad pump. Maintenance will fix it for tomorrow."

As Oral turned to walk toward the house, Katherine picked up Sam and followed, their footsteps grinding in the coal dust, sounding like the crunch of snow on a cold day – a rhythm to the playful clank of a lunch bucket as they headed for home.

Frank Gatski, a seventeen-year-old tough kid becoming a man, was one of the last to emerge from the portal. He smiled through the grime on his face – a smile that belied the place – the Tarzan-like features were framed by his blonde hair dirtied by coal, which hung from beneath his hard hat. The dirty coal-stained coveralls he wore couldn't hide the muscular body beneath. His erect stance made him seem even taller than his 6 foot 3 frame. Even taller especially in contrast to the stooped and hunched figures of some of his co-workers. Nothing scared this kid – except his dad and mother.

Unlike almost every other miner, young Frank liked the work. He saw it as a game. He wanted to load more coal faster than everybody else – and he did. The older guys just looked at him and smiled. The young kid who they thought simply was full of crap – trying to be tough, suffering from young exuberance – but Frank didn't care. He was going to be the best at whatever he did.

Eta saw Frank and walked over to him. "You okay, son?"

"Yeh," Frank replied.

"Where's your father?'

"He's taking care of the horses. He's okay. Ain't nothing wrong, Mom."

Eta studied Frank. "You look mad."

"Yeh, I am mad!"

"Why? You're safe…"

"Oh, Mom, I was gonna have my best day – I already loaded ten cars – better than anyone else."

She reached up and touched his face. "Now you're talking like your dad. Always the best, huh?"

Frank turned his head way, a little embarrassed at his mother's touch, "There's dad," he said.

Louis Gatski brushed his hands as he walked toward Eta and Frank. He smelled of the horses he tended, an odor that mingled with the smell of coal dust and axle grease. The stable boy job was what he had done for years. His work was vital to the whole process of getting the coal from deep underground. After miners would loosen the coal with picks, and shovel it into the cars, it was up to his horses to pull the cars to an area where the electrical trolley system would take over and pull the load the remaining distance to the surface.

Louis valued his job, knew how important it was, and like everything else he did, he took great pride in it.

He took off his gloves. "No trouble" he said in his thick Polish accent.

His wife smiled, "Yes, thank God," she said as she made the sign of the cross.

Louis nodded, "Aye- we'll be back tomorrow."

"We better be," snapped young Frank.

Louis looked up at him and shot him a stern look.

Frank explained – "Well, I had been doing real good. Heck, I loaded ten cars already and...."

"Don't worry, son – you'll have plenty of time to load your coal. Huh, someday you might just get sick of it"

Frank's smile lit up again, "I don't think so, Papa."

The crowd of miners and their wives and children mingled and talked as they drifted back to their homes. The sounds of different languages and dialects – and bad English – fell on top of each other. There was the West Virginia twang of the Huff's, the Polish of the Gatski's, the Italian of the Coceano's...there were English, Arabic, Spanish, Italian, German ... all going at once – a cacophony of many tongues rising in the air meshing with the rhythm of the tramping footsteps going home.

The sound of a car in the distance coming toward the crowd forced everyone to the side of the narrow road. The ambulance from Leazer Funeral Home had been alerted that there was trouble at No. 9. The funeral home ambulance always came to assist in helping the injured, if there were any. The ambulance turned up dust as it went by and slowed to a stop near the mine entrance. Ben Bennett walked to the driver. "Everything's okay – but still mighty glad you came"

"We got the call – we always come, you know – just in case," the driver said.

"I know," Ben replied. "Just a water pump problem. It'll be fixed tonight."

"Where's Louis Gatski?" the driver asked.

""Right up there," Ben said. "Anything wrong?"

The driver reached to the back seat and picked up the newspaper. "Thought he might like to see this. It's about his son, Paul. He got his picture in the paper – playing football at West Virginia Wesleyan."

Ben took the paper. He read the headline. "Paul Gatski on All-Conference Team ". He looked up. "That's great. Can I have the paper to show...?"

"Sure," the driver said.

Ben hurried to catch up with the Gatskis.

"Louis, here's some good news about Paul. Look, his picture." Frank stepped in front of his father, took the paper from Ben's hand and read "Paul Gatski, West Virginia Wesleyan tackle was named to the 1938 WVIAC All-Conference team announced today."

Louis smiled broadly, "Hey, that makes me real proud."

Frank asked, "Can I keep the paper?"

Ben nodded, "Sure can."

"Paul is coming home tonight. We'll celebrate!" Eta said.

Ben had a better idea, "Frank, bring Paul to the bar when he comes. I'll buy you a beer."

As the Gatski's turned toward home, their friends gathered close to them in a slow walk as they heard the good news about Paul. Oral Huff said, "I knew that boy would make a name for himself." Ms. Coceano, in her broken English, asked, "What is this…?" Mrs. Abraham explained in her Arabic-ladened English, "It's a big football t'ing."

As they walked away, each family left the caravan when they came to their small house among the rows of houses that were lined up on the ridge above the mine.

In No. 9, you couldn't tell one house from another, … except for the Superintendent's house – which was situated on its own large lot away from the rows of houses occupied by the workers. The coal company built them all within an easy walk to the tipple and the mine portal. The houses were low-cost and identical – one story, frame, four rooms, which included two bedrooms, a kitchen, and a dining room, a coal stove, an outside pump for water, and behind several feet away, an outhouse.

Every lot was about twenty by forty with about ten feet between each house. Some families would personalize their property with a garden, which could help feed a family – a chicken coup where they could gather eggs in the morning. Some even kept a cow for milk.

Eta and Louis Gatski were married in 1912. She was seventeen; he was twenty-seven. They got busy raising a family, and in rapid succession four boys were born; Benny, Paul, John, and Frank. Then in 1936, fifteen years after Frank was born, out of nowhere, came a daughter, Mary Louise. Eta Gatski was forty-one, so the birth of the child was a total surprise – and a delight.

By that time, Benny had married and moved to his own home in nearby Grant Town; Paul was attending West Virginia Wesleyan College; John was home after two years in the Coast Guard with plans to enlist in the Marines; and Frank was a high school senior planning on working with his dad at the No. 9 mine.

The four Gatski boys served as fathers to little Mary Louise; for sure she never wanted for protection.

Across the road, a few houses away from the Gatski home, Oral and Katherine Huff were raising their young family; two pre-teen daughters, Martha and Mickey; seven-year Donald and their youngest, Sam, who was just five.

There weren't more than five cars in the entire coal camp. No one needed one. Work was right there – and the company store on the property supplied everything – and without question – everything a family needed. The tab kept at the store for each family was reconciled each payday so that a worker may not actually have realized cash – but instead simply resolved his debt to the company. On payday, the Company would deduct rent for the house and the amount of the tab at the store – and give them a check for the balance. It usually wasn't much! Yes, "They owed their soul to the company store."

Of the five automobiles in No. 9, the Gatskis had one, the result of the interest in cars of four grown boys and Louis' ability to keep the car in repair. The Model T Ford was an easy fix for someone who had access to company nuts and bolts and belts. Louis could fix anything – and he had become one of the unofficial repairmen of the coal camp. Lawn mowers, bikes, swings, sooner or later, ended up in the Gatski's small front yard.

My Brother the All-Star

The news was all around No. 9 and Farmington about Paul Gatski.

Nobody was prouder than Frank. He sat down on the bed. He looked up at the newspaper clipping he tacked to the wall. He asked himself, "Could I do that, too?" Then he laughed at himself. It was absurd. He had decided a year ago when he graduated from high school to not go on to college. His mother wanted him to go to Fairmont State College, just ten miles away, but he wanted to go to work in the mines with his dad. Football wasn't on his mind anymore. After all, he had only been an average high school football player – a tall, skinny kid, six feet tall and about 160 pounds, who couldn't even make the first team. There was little question that college recruits would be anywhere near Farmington High School looking for him.

He had decided to follow his father and brothers into the mines. It was what everybody did. It was the best money around, worth about eighty cents for every ton of coal he could load – and he could load about as much as anybody in the entire camp. In the last two years, the kid had a growth spurt that transformed him into a man – 6 foot 3 and 220 pounds – and it was all coal loading muscle.

The wind blowing through the window rattled the newspaper clipping. Frank wondered, for a brief moment about his future. His imagination began to take over. He was still just seventeen. He had constantly grown bigger and stronger. Could he find a better life for himself by going to college? As far fetched as it seemed, he wished he could play college football. Then his shoulders sagged. It was ridiculous, of course. How in the hell could that ever happen?

Ten School Rivalry

Farmington is located in Marion County, in the northern part of the state. Marion is one of West Virginia's smaller counties - only thirty miles from one end to the other. The county seat of Fairmont is located in the eastern half of the county. In the 1930's it had a population of 25,000. The city is divided by the Monongahela River, which flows north to Pittsburgh where it joins with the Allegheny to form the Ohio River. One side of the river is West Fairmont, the other side, East Fairmont. Each has its own school, a Class A school, the largest category of West Virginia schools with more than 600 students. Of course they are fierce rivals in all sports and everything else academic.

Several small towns dot the county. The largest of these is Mannington located in the western half of the county just 14 miles from Fairmont. Mannington had a population of 3,000 with a high school whose enrollment was also large enough for a Class A classification.

Five other small towns are clustered around Fairmont and connected by winding U.S. Route 250 or its tributaries of roads less traveled. From Fairmont it is just a mile to either Barrackville or Rivesville; seven miles to Farmington and Monongah; and ten miles to Fairview.

Each town existed primarily for the coal mine that was right there or nearby. Nearly everyone in these towns worked in the mines or in a company directly connected with the industry, such as a mine equipment repair outfit or a mine supply house.

Near each of these towns were even smaller communities like Idamay, Carolina, Rachel, No. 8, and No. 9 – all coal camps – that grew up right beside the mine portal. The communities or camps were named after daughters of the mine owners or just simply took on the number of the company mine.

All of the small towns – Barrackville, Rivesville, Fairview, Farmington, and Monongah – were just a short drive, or long walk from each other. And each had a high school, all rated Class B, because of low enrollment. And each had a football, basketball, and baseball team – and even a band!

They were Barrackville Bisons, The Rivesville Rams, The Monongah Lions, The Fairview Indians, and The Farmington Farmers. Yes, that's right. FARMERS. One would wonder how farmers might fare against bison, rams, lions, and Indians...

There were two other high schools in the county St. Peter's and Dunbar, both located in Fairmont. St. Peters, a Catholic School, did not have a football team, but did participate in basketball and baseball; Dunbar, the Negro school, competed in football and basketball against other Negro schools around the state.

It is quite remarkable to consider that in the short fourteen mile stretch from Fairmont to Mannington there were ten high schools! TEN. The intensity of rivalry was a foregone conclusion!

The closeness of the towns made for fierce competition. Players who went to different schools developed friendships through playing on the same summer baseball team, or because their parents worked at the same coal mine or factory or by attending the same church. There was a lot of pride at stake when you were going to see the opponent at Sunday mass after the big game on Friday night.

Farmington, Four Block Town

Farmington, population 500, was just a four-block town. In all directions there was a coal mine – No. 9 was about two miles away; east of Farmington; Idamay was a mile to the west; another mile beyond that was Carolina; Rachel was two miles north and Barrackville No. 7 was four miles south.

Farmington was lit up at night by four 200-watt incandescent street lamps – one on each corner – and Leisure R Inn, Ben Bennett's gathering place, where everyone went to talk, complain about the game, or shoot a game of pool. The neon sign buzzed a warm welcome to guys coming from the mine and on their way home from work in the mines where they could rinse away the black grit of an eight hour shift with a Carling Black Label or an Iron City or a Duquesne or a Pabst Blue Ribbon.

The Leisure R Inn on Main Street was just a few feet from the perceived dead center of town – where Main Street intersected with Mill Street and where there was the" thriving" business section of Farmington that included Manchin's Grocery Store, Farmington Market, Triangle Market, Parrish's Pharmacy, Toothman's Hardware, Bock's Clothing Store, Joe's Café, the U.S. Post Office, and the West Virginia State Liquor Store.

Ben Bennett wiped his bar clean. His hair was still a little wet from the bath he had just taken after his shift at the mine. He being the owner of a bar to mining, but he didn't want to give up his seniority at No. 9. That pension, he figured, would come in handy someday.

Ben felt the stiffness in his back as he slid open the door of the beer cooler and leaned in to pull out an Iron City. He snapped off the cap and set it in front of one of his regulars. Nick Jones didn't even have to ask for the beer. As soon as he came through the door, Ben went into action.

Then so did Nick. In no time, the bottle was empty.

A small wooden cased RCA Victor radio sitting on the shelf behind the bar droned out the news for five minutes every hour. In between the newscast, country music played softly – giving life to the quiet conversation.

The sound of Nick setting the bottle down on the counter was all Ben needed to return to the cooler and pull out another Iron City.

As he did, his attention was drawn to the sound of the radio. The music had disappeared – and Gabriel Heater was giving out the news. Urgency was in his voice – and Ben noticed. He turned toward the radio to listen. His jaw tightened. Then he turned toward Nick.

"Who is this Hitler?" Ben asked. "Sounds like he wants to take over all of Europe - first Austria, now Czechoslovakia."

Nick finally spoke, "Can't trust Germany. I was there in the war. Don't want to go back – but I would if I had to. Hell, all of us might have to go – President Roosevelt's talking about…"

The slamming of car doors and loud voices outside stole away Ben's thoughts and made him brace for a jarring entrance. He was right. The door swung open fast and banged against the wall. Six young men in a mood – crashed in, their loud talk drowning out the sound of the radio.

Ben smiled. It was the Gatski's – the four brothers along with a couple of strangers – and it looked like they were having fun. Then he nodded the acknowledgement that they were celebrating and football star Paul Gatski was in the middle getting all the attention from brothers Frank, Benny and John and the other two guys.

Ben reached out to Paul. "Hey Paul, congratulations – let me buy everyone a beer." As the guys found a table Ben reached beneath the counter and pulled out the newspaper. "Been reading about you." Then he looked up "We're all damn proud."

"Thanks, Ben, that means a lot." Pointing to one of the strangers, Paul said, "This is my roommate at Wesleyan, Doug Kline and this is his friend, Richard King. He goes to Marshall College in Huntington. They're going home for Christmas. They're stopping here for dinner with us." Ben shook hands with both of them.

Richard King said, "The truth is he needed a ride home and I'm the one with a car."

"That's part of it," Paul said. "So when Frank said to come down for a beer on you, bet you didn't think I'd bring half of No. 9 and visitors besides."

"It's okay. I'll treat anybody you want to bring. We don't get that many college football stars around No. 9, you know – All-Conference and ..." Ben picked up the paper for reference, "and two All-Opponent teams, St. Vincent's and West Virginia State..."

"Ah, it's nothing – small college."

"Don't matter – it's great!" Ben looked around at everyone. "Six beers. Iron City?"

He returned to the cooler, slid open the door and pulled out six beers, quickly opened them and returned to the table.

While everyone downed their beers, the conversation around the table continued with tales of college life and Paul Gatski's exploits on the gridiron. Soon Ben brought them back from the past.

"Been listening to the radio," Ben said. "Hitler is on the move."

Benny said, "You can stop worrying, Ben. John has joined the Marines. He's gonna put a stop to all that crap, aren't you, brother?" Benny gave John a friendly punch.

John laughed. "When Hitler hears there's a Gatski defending the country, he'll think twice."

"That's right," Benny said. "And back home here, Frank and me, we're gonna be supplying the coal to keep everybody warm and the factory's working."   "Hell, I know that!" Ben said. "I work with Frank so you don't have to tell me. The other day we had a water pump blow up and had to get everybody out. While the whole camp shows up to worry about what's happening, Frank is pissed off cause he's gonna set some sort of loading record."

"Well, it's the truth," Frank said. "I had ten tons – ten cars loaded - nobody had done that they tell me. Then the siren goes off..." He stopped. "Hey, maybe somebody just blew that thing to stop me..." he laughed.

Ben pulled up a chair. "Well I'll be honest. I ain't ever seen anybody work like this guy. Maybe it's cause he's young and still trying to impress someone."

"Don't surprise me," Paul said. "I know how tough my little brother is. But he still can't take me – at least not yet. He's getting better all the time…"

John confessed, "Well, he's taken me."

Benny said, "Me, too. I don't want anything to do with that animal."

Paul was surprised, "You let our little brother handle you?"

Frank interrupted, "I think I can – even if you are an all star." Frank got out of his chair.

"Look at him, brother, he ain't little anymore," John said.

"He's tall, he gets leverage and he's strong as hell," Benny chimed in. "Now he does respect his elders, so he might take it easy on you, if you want…"

"What?!" Paul exclaimed. "I'll kick his butt."

There was silence in the room. Everybody looked at each other. Finally Paul looked at Frank. "What the hell are we waiting for?" he asked. "I'll see you back home!"

Everybody stood up, chairs skidded across the floor. They headed for the door.

"I'll take Paul," Ben shouted at them as they were leaving.

"You're crazy," John shot back as the door slammed behind them.

Paul stopped for a moment, opened the door and shouted to Ben, "Thanks for the beers."

"Come back," Ben hollered.

Benny was playing the referee, "Here in this corner, the all star Paul Gatski – and here in this corner, the coal miner, Frankie boy Gatski."

In front of the Gatski home, Paul and Frank faced each other moving slowly side to side – contemplating the next move, waiting for a moment to strike. John and Benny stood on one side of them, while Richard King and Doug Kline watched on the other.

14

The screen door swung open and Eta came out on the porch. Louis and little Mary Louise followed. Eta pleaded, "Boys, please. Can't that wait till after dinner? It's going to be ready in ten minutes."

"It won't take me that long, Mom. I promise," Paul said without taking his eye off of Frank.

"Ah," she said in disgust. "Don't hurt anybody, you hear?" and then she turned to go back inside, gently pushing Mary Louise ahead of her. Louis stayed on the porch to watch.

Frank said, "You better hurry, Mom is waiting for dinner."

Paul, still in his crouch said, "I told her it wouldn't take long." He made a quick move, but Frank was quicker. He stepped to one side, grabbed Paul wrapped him in his long arms, "Hey, Jesus…" Paul screamed. "Why you bastard…"

John and Benny started laughing. Doug Kline shouted "C'mon, roommate – this is embarrassing."

Paul wrenched himself loose – for just a second. Then Frank crouched low and forward, digging his shoulder into Paul's stomach and lifting him up, before slamming him down on the grass.

By this time, everyone was laughing uncontrollably. Paul started laughing, too. He couldn't help it. His little brother was really kicking his ass and he couldn't do anything about it. He thought, "My God, how things have changed."

Frank pulled Paul to his feet. Paul brushed himself off. Eta came back out on the porch. She stepped off the porch and went to Frank, "I hope he didn't hurt you, Frank." Then she gave Paul a playful slap. "Shame on…"

Paul interrupted her, "I told you it wouldn't take long, Mom."

"That's good. Now go get cleaned up."

Paul put his arm around Frank and they stepped up on the porch. Benny and John and their guests kept laughing as they gathered around the table.

Eta was clearing the table after dinner. Frank stayed with his mother to help out. He grabbed a dishtowel and started drying the dishes his mother washed. Everybody else wandered outside on the porch.

Frank noticed his mother wasn't feeling well. "Anything wrong, Mom?"

"It's that same old pain," she looked at him and forced a smile. "It'll be okay." She changed the subject. "Paul didn't hurt you, did he?"

"Mom, I licked him."

She smiled. "I know you did. I saw you, but I didn't want Paul to know. You're the youngest, you know. You're not supposed to beat up on your older brothers."

"Ah, it was just playing. Heck, Paul's my hero - an all-conference player, that's something." Then he changed the subject. "Mom, his roommate's friend, Richard King from Marshall College, said someone as strong and quick as I am should be playing college football. What do you think?"

"That would be a very good thing, Frank. I always wanted you to go to college – but you liked the mines, working with your Daddy. That's not too bad, but college would make you a better life."

"Yeh, but I'm out of high school over a year now – could I go back to books and studying…"

"I know you could," she said.

"Well, we'll see."

"Where is this Marshall College?" she asked. "I hope not too far away."

"It's not, Mom – just four or five hours from here."

"That's not too bad. John is joining the Marines – you're staying close by, okay?" she replied. As she turned to hand Frank another dish, she winced. Frank noticed.

"Almost done," she said. "Here, the last one."

"Mom, you okay?"

"Sure, son."

Frank hung the dishtowel on the wooden rack above the kitchen sink. He looked at his mother as he followed her outside to the porch.

Richard and Doug were getting ready to leave.

"Thank you, Mrs. Gatski, everything was wonderful," Richard said.

"It sure was," Doug replied.

"Thank you for bringing Paul home," Eta said.

"My pleasure. It's good to rub shoulders with famous people. It makes me feel important!"

He laughed. Paul feinted a chase. "Get out of here," Paul said as he chased him to the car.

Doug and Richard waved a goodbye.

"Come back," Louis said.

"We will," they promised.

John, Benny and Paul followed their mother into the house. Frank turned to his father. "Mom is not feeling very good, Dad. Maybe she should see the doctor."

"She has, son."

St. Peters's, the little Catholic church on Mill Street, in Farmington, just a hundred feet from the center of town was filled.

The Gatski's knew all of No. 9 and Farmington and much of Marion County as well. Their prominence in football, basketball, baseball, and even archery, made the Gatski's a well-known name for the past decade. Eta was revered, not for just her own life, but as the mother of four highly respected sons.

Benny, Paul, John, Frank, and little sister Mary Louise, were all seated in the front pew along with their father, Louis, who knelt in prayer beside the casket.

John was in the uniform of the Marines, the other boys and Louis each wore his best suit, shirt and tie. One couldn't help but be moved by the picture of these strong, attractive, youthful people kneeling in reverence, humbly giving their mother to God.

The priest, Father Brady, was known throughout the county as a strict disciplinarian. He was pastor not only of St. Peter's but of St. Patrick's in nearby Mannington, just seven miles away. He was known for his fiery sermons. On Sundays he could raise some hell. His Irish blood would rise to turn his face red with zeal. But this was a Thursday. Today he was gentle. He respected the Gatski's for the kind of good Catholics they were. Today his sermon was personal. What he said this day resonated with young Frank.

"Your mother was one of the finest women I knew. Just look at the kind of children she raised. She made sure all of you had the values to take you far in life. She always encouraged you to be anything you want. And you can be anything you want – thanks to your mother and father. I never knew a Gatski that shied away from reaching for the very best in himself – that came from your mother and your father." He nodded to Louis. "Louis, I don't want to leave you out." His levity made the boys smile. He went on softly. "I know she is proud of you. She has guided you this far – but she will not leave you here. When you ponder decisions in your life, listen to your mother's voice. It will still direct you just as expertly as an arrow shot from a bow by one of you boys."

The reference to an arrow hit home with the boys who were well known throughout the region for their award-winning skills in archery. Father Brady could feel his sermon had a positive effect.

"God bless you and may the soul of Eta Gatski rest in peace." The congregation replied softly, "Amen."

After his mother passed away, Frank put the thoughts of college, and playing college football, aside. He didn't put them away, but just aside – since he always remembered the excitement and enthusiasm in his mother's face when they discussed the possibility of Frank attending college. But now was the time to spend time with his father, take care of him, and make sure he was as content as possible as the man faced the future without his wife and all his children living away.

Frank, still quietly and deep inside, felt an excitement himself at the possibility of at least trying to play college football, as improbable as that seemed, especially for a nineteen-year-old coal miner who had never set foot in a college classroom!

Paul's friend, Richard King, had stirred something inside Frank and now he couldn't get it out of his mind.

But time has a way of diminishing enthusiasm, and by the summer of 1939, Frank had settled back into a miner's life, with the idea of playing college football now just a foolish idea...

On a Saturday, when Frank was home with his father, the sound of a car outside caught his attention. He looked out the window to see his brother Paul getting out of the passenger's side. The driver was Richard King – the creator of Frank's dreams. The sight of Richard suddenly filled up Frank with joy. He couldn't wait to hear Richard talk to him – to encourage him. "Say the words...bring back the dream," he thought.

And that's exactly what Richard King did. This time, though, instead of just telling Frank he would make a good college football player, he got specific.

"I'll be glad to talk to Coach Henderson at Marshall College about you. I'm one of his former players. He usually takes what we say seriously." Then he laughed and nodded to Paul, "I still say the way you handled your All-Conference brother showed me all I needed to see!"

Frank Gatski climbed in the passenger side of the Jamison Coal Company dump truck. The driver, John Smith, climbed in and banged the door closed. The truck slowly climbed away from the tipple onto the hard road and headed for James Fork Elementary, just a few hundred feet away.

As the truck approached the school, Smith slowed and turned off onto a gravel lot where the school principal, Blair Wolfe, was waiting.

Blair walked in the direction where he wanted the truck to go and pointed to an area that looked like a playground, except it was not ground suitable for play – it was muddy and bumpy. There might have been grass here one day, but not since the mine opened. It was common practice for the Coal Company to supply some road fill for the grounds around the school when conditions warranted it.

The truck was loaded with "red dog," a hard, rocky residue of the mine's "gob pile" – that tall gray burning mountain of waste from cleaning the coal in the tipple. What's left after the gob pile burns up is "red dog". It makes excellent road material – and in this case, playground surface.

Frank got out of the truck, grabbed a shovel from the cab and waited for the driver to dump the load.

Mr. Wolfe made a large circling motion with his hand to indicate the area he wanted covered. The driver raised the truck bed and slowly drove around the area allowing the red dog to fall in the general area of Mr. Wolfe's circle. Frank then spread the red dog into a level surface. Just as he finished and motioned for the truck to pull away, the school doors sprang open and the kids spilled out on the "new" playground. Blair Wolfe followed and stood by the door, a watchful eye on his kids.

Ten-year-old Jim Priester, who was a fifth grader, ran in front. Several boys gave chase. No wonder. He had the football. Sam Huff caught up with Jim and tried to grab the ball from behind. Jim wrenched it away from his small hands, a little miffed that a puny second grader could think of getting the ball. Leo Coceano, Sam's best friend, was right behind him shouting in Italian, *"Io Voglio LaBalla."*

Sam said, "Speak English, nobody can understand you."

Leo shouted back, "God damn ball."

"Shut up," Sam said. "Not like that. You're gonna get us in trouble. Throw me the ball," Sam said.

Jim looked at him and rolled his eyes. "You can't catch it. You're too little."

"Yes, I can" and he clapped his hands together.

20

"God damn ball" Leo shouted again.

"Shut up," Sam said through clenched lips, as he shot a wary look at Mr. Wolfe, who was beginning to monitor the Huff and Coceano dialogue.

Jim ran with the ball, zipping past Sam and Leo and imitating the moves he saw in the Movietone News at The Farmington Theatre. He dashed to the right, then made a move past Sam with his left arm outstretched in a mock stiff arm and sped past Leo for a few feet, where he touched the ball down.

"Touchdown" for Notre Dame.

Having accomplished that feat, Jimmy now had a change of heart. "Okay, Sam, go out for a pass."

"*Anche io*," Leo said.

"Speak English," Sam said.

"Me, too," Leo said.

Jimmy cocked his arm, "Okay – first Sam. Go ahead, Sam."

Sam took off running and then turned around. Just as he did, the ball went whizzing by his head and bounced along the red dog ground.

Frank Gatski was climbing into the truck when the football came bouncing toward him.

"Ah shit," Leo shouted. "No good."

The ball ended up at Frank's feet. He picked it up and twirled it in his hands. It felt good. He hadn't touched a ball for over a year – since his senior year in high school. He twirled it again.

Jimmy ran past Sam and Leo toward Frank to retrieve the ball. "Hey, Frank, throw me a pass." He got down in a three point stance, then took off and ran past, then turned his head looking for the ball. No pass. Frank was still twirling the ball in his hands.

"I ain't no passer, Jimmy. I'm a center. So come back here and I'll center you one."

"Okay," Jimmy said as he back-tracked to about five yards away from Frank.

Sam and Leo quickly ran to get in on the action.

Frank turned around, his back to Jimmy, bent over with his arms outstretched and the ball in his hands. He looked back between his legs at Jimmy and shouted, "You ready?"

Sam and Leo moved in front of Jimmy. Jimmy pushed them aside. "Sam, step back, you're too little." Sam took a couple of steps backward pushing Leo back with him.

Jimmy got ready to receive the center snap from Frank. He clapped his hands. "Yeh. I'm ready. Let me give you signals. On three, okay?"

Frank went along. "Okay, on three."

"One, two, three," Jimmy shouted.

Whizzz.....

Jimmy never saw the ball. He did see the blur going right through his hands. Then he heard a thump... and a gasp...

He wandered what that was. "Oh my God," he thought, "who did it hit?"

When he turned around, he saw Sam on the ground, and Leo with eyes wide open, looking straight ahead. Sam was gasping for air. His face strained for a breath. Leo was walking in circles. The ball bounced wildly along the gravel lot to the feet of Mr. Wolfe, who picked it up.

He looked to see who would be coming after it. A child always follows a bouncing ball. Here came Leo, but he wasn't looking for the ball. He ran to Mr. Wolfe. He was all Italian – and completely out of control. "Sam...oh shit...Sam...oh shit..." He shouted in Italian and he took several very quick, deep breaths. He held his stomach. Mr. Wolfe wandered what in the world is wrong with this kid.

"You alright, Leo?" Mr. Wolfe shouted.

Leo spewed out Italian, "*Sammy 'e stato ucciso*"

"Speak English," Mr. Wolfe commanded.

Leo breathed, then pointed toward the other side of the playground and then ran for a few steps, turned around to make sure Mr. Wolfe was coming, and then took off. Mr. Wolfe followed. He could see Frank Gatski and Jimmy Priester leaning over a little child.

22

"Who in the hell was it?" Mr. Wolfe thought.

In a moment he was there leaning over the writhing, gasping kid. "Is he alright?" Mr. Wolfe asked. "What happened?"

"It was my fault," Jimmy said. "I should have caught it. It went right through my hands and it hit him right in the stomach."

"Boom," Leo said as he hit his clenched fist into his stomach.

Frank started to explain, "I centered the ball…"

"That's alright," Mr. Wolfe said, as he helped Sam to his feet. Mr. Wolfe handed him his handkerchief. "Here, wipe your face." Mr. Wolfe, "You're okay."

Sam wiped away the tears, took a deep breath, and was glad to be alive.

Looking for Frank

As the tall smart-looking man walked the long, dimly lit hallway of Farmington High School, the old wooden floor creaked beneath him. He removed his hat as he stopped in front of the door of Jane Gordon, who taught English, but also served as the school's counselor.

He had called ahead so Miss Gordon was expecting him. He walked in. "Miss Gordon, I'm Roy Straight. Thank you for seeing me."

"You're welcome. I understand you are an assistant coach at Marshall College – and you're here to ask about…

"Frank Gatski."

"Oh yes, Frank…"

"Yes, we thought we would invite him to try out for the football team at Marshall. I wanted to check with you to see if you thought he was college material, uh, in the classroom, I mean."

"Of course," she smiled.

She picked up a folder from the desk. "Knowing you were coming, I prepared this report." She opened the folder and continued. "Graduated in nineteen thirty-seven, two years ago. Good grades, good young man, good family."

"No character issues?" Straight asked.

"Oh, no… none."

"Why didn't he go on to college?"

"Money, probably. Working in the mines is college for most young men here."

"His brother, Paul went to Wesleyan. He was quite a football player there."

"Yes, Paul was an excellent athlete. It got him a scholarship."

"And Frank?" Straight waited for Miss Gordon's reply, hoping it

24

would be filled with athletic promise. It wasn't.

"Oh, he played." She studied the report. "Yes, it says 'football', but here Mr. Straight, almost everybody is on the team." Straight swallowed hard, hoping that his trip was not wasted and his hope for a diamond in the Farmington rough, was not a hopeless pursuit...

Miss Gordon brought him back from his despair – "But you know that business better than me. Maybe nobody noticed Frank then..." She closed the folder and handed it to him. "Anything else?"

Miss Gordon's lack of knowledge about Frank Gatski, the football player, bothered Straight. Surely she would have remembered if he had been good enough to notice.

"You think he played?" Straight asked as he nervously fingered his hat.

"As I said, just about everybody plays in a small school like this." She reached for the folder again. "May I?"

"Of course," Straight said as he handed it to her.

She opened it and pointed to the transcript. "Yes, there it is," she pointed, "football."

Straight tried to keep positive. "Do you think he can handle college studies?"

"Oh yes, he's capable... if he can get back to studying... it's been two years."

She handed Straight the folder. "Yes, I think he can. He' a determined young man."

"Thank you, Miss Gordon. I wanted to talk to the football coach about Frank. Where would he be now?"

She looked at her watch. "Probably on the football field! Practice should just be starting,"

The football field at Farmington High was crowded into a flat space between two embankments. The school was high on one hillside. Players dressed for practice in the school and walked down the embankment to the field.

The field was also used for baseball and the dirt baseball infield was also one end of football field between the end zone and the thirty yard line. The rest of the field was worn down to dirt with a few grass patches.

As Coach Straight carefully negotiated the narrow path from the school to the field, he could see the players beginning to line up for calisthenics. A small, wiry man with a whistle around his neck paced slowly in front of them. Coach Cassy Ryan had been at Farmington for eight years and was considered one of the best coaches around. He had distinguished himself as a West Virginia University halfback in 1926-28 and had even gone on to play one year of professional football with the Buffalo Bisons in 1929.

Straight, who was originally from Mannington, just seven miles away from Farmington, knew Coach Ryan. In fact, he had played against his teams a few years before.

Straight turned off of the path and headed toward the coach. Calisthenics hadn't started, so he thought it might be a good chance to talk to Coach Ryan about Frank. He was hoping he would get a little more encouragement than he got from Miss Gordon.

Cassy noticed the man walking toward him. He turned to study him for a moment. Then a smile crossed his face when he recognized him. "Roy Straight, how are you?"

"Fine, Coach," Straight replied.

"You want a uniform?" Cassy joked. "I'd rather have you on my team," acknowledging the difficulty Straight caused him when he had been an All-State player at Mannington.

"Wish I could, Coach, but now I'm on your side of the ball."

"At Marshall, aren't you?" Cassy asked.

"Right." He got right to the subject of Frank Gatski. "Coach, I don't want to take your time right before practice, but we are thinking of asking Frank Gatski to come and try out."

"Who?" Cassy asked.

Straight got that sickening feeling in his stomach. "Uh, Gatski."

"Which one?"

26

"Why, Frank"

Cassy took out a Kool cigarette, lit it and took a deep drag. "Frank Gatski – good boy, nice family."

Straight was desperate. "What about football, coach?" He held his breath.

Well, Frank was on the team, what, two…three years ago. Skinny kid played center. He was alright. Never started…

"Oh my God," Straight said underneath his breath – "never started, what the…"

Cassy continued, "I can't imagine him playing college ball. You don't see many 150-pound centers. Now I haven't seen him for two years or so. What's he doing?"

"He's working in the mines – No. 9."

Cassy shook his head. The smoke from the Kool came with the words, "I'll say this, there's no better kid. He'd give it all he's got, I know that."

Straight could see the players were assembling ready to begin practice. Even though he was dying to get a more positive opinion about his long-shot recruit, he decided his meeting with Cassy was over. Coach Ryan dropped the cigarette and churned it out with his foot – as if to extinguish any hopes for a Gatski football career. Straight watched the smoke rise from the ground and knew the conversation was ended and practice was ready to begin. Straight shook Cassy's hand. "Coach, thank you for your time."

"Good luck with Frank. I hope it works out." Cassy blew the whistle, "Okay, everybody up!"

Roy Straight had decided to go ahead with a chance on Frank Gatski – what the hell? He had already committed himself. "Go ahead," he thought. The investment by Marshall College would be minimal.

Frank was wide awake. It was 7 a.m. on a Friday morning in June. Normally he would be heading to the mine portal, but not today. Louis managed his schedule to be available to take Frank to Fairmont. He could hear his father's model T Ford running in the yard. Louis was checking out the car for the drive to Fairmont, where Frank would catch the Greyhound bus to Charleston, about 150 miles south.

In Charleston, Frank would stay overnight with his brother John and then on Sunday board the bus for the forty mile trip to Huntington, and to Marshall College and his tryout for the Marshall football team.

Frank told his Dad he would hitchhike to Fairmont, but Louis felt that he wanted to make sure Frank was there before the bus departed at 9 a.m. Hitchhiking was a good way to travel – but with a schedule to be kept, Louis insisted on driving Frank to the Fairmont bus station.

As Frank got dressed, he could smell bacon and eggs from his bedroom.

"Son, breakfast is ready," Louis said. "Come on."

Frank zipped up his duffle bag with everything for staying overnight and came into the kitchen.

Louis looked at him, "Eat now. Then we'll go."

"Thanks, Dad."

Louis shook his head at the thought of his life changing. Here was his youngest child, now suddenly making a life-altering decision.

They looked at each other, knowing the next two days could change everything. If Frank made it into Marshall, the coal mining would be over. His boy Frank, who he had seen every day of his life would now be away. Louis cleared his throat and somehow managed to resist crying, and wiped away a tear as Frank quickly ate. Frank liked the mining life and would be satisfied doing it from now on. But he was flattered that someone would think enough of him to offer the opportunity to play football, and at a school like Marshall. This was like a miracle out of nowhere. It astounded Frank, especially after barely playing in high school and settling into a miner's life for two years. And now he found himself acting out a scene that was so improbable. Was this somebody else? Could he make it? Would he actually be good enough to play college football – and be a college student?

Frank picked up the plate and took it to the sink. "Ready to go, Dad?"

"Yes, let's go," Louis said with some difficulty.

The Model T hummed on the hard road. Frank looked at the tipple and the mine portal just a few feet away. The churning of the water pumps and the slapping of the conveyor belts pulling coal up and into a rail car was drowned out by the car motor as it made its way past the No. 9 Mine and headed toward Fairmont. Normally Frank would be inside the mine, and underground dumping another Number 8 shovel of coal into the car. He smiled and shook his head again at the wild turn his life had suddenly taken.

Louis pulled the Model T up to the curb in front of the Greyhound Bus Station in downtown Fairmont.

"Thanks, Dad, for bringing me," Frank said as he leaned over and kissed Louis on the cheek. "I'll be back…"

Louis interrupted him. "I'm going to wait with you till the bus comes." "You don't have to…"

"I want to. That's alright. Go buy your ticket. You got money?"

"Yes, I got enough… I think."

Inside the station they sat on a long wooden bench in silence. The big clock high above on the wall turned slowly. Frank fingered the ticket. The sound of footsteps of the other passengers echoed in the big room. Both Louis and Frank stared out of the large front window to the place where the Greyhound Bus would appear.

Louis gently touched Frank's leg and spoke softly, "I'll meet you here on Sunday night at ten o'clock. That's when you get back, ain't it?"

Frank nodded

"And I hope you do good. It's what you want, huh?"

Frank nodded.

Louis breathed deeply through a tearful voice, "You crazy kid…you might break your leg."

Frank smiled and shook his head. "What the heck, Dad. I can't lose anything. I can always work at No. 9."

"Yeh," Louis agreed. "We'll see what…"

29

Suddenly the room went dim as the big Greyhound pulled up in front of the window shutting out the sunlight into the room. Instantly there was a scuffle of passengers moving, picking up bags – hurrying to outside where they could line up to get their preferred seat.

Frank and Louis let them go and followed behind.

"There it is," Frank said. "Guess it's time to go."

The bus door swung open and the driver stepped down onto the street to take tickets.

"Alright, son," Louis said as he took hold of Frank's hands. "Don't break your leg."

Frank smiled as he turned and disappeared into the bus. Louis looked for him and found him settled into a rear seat by the window. The driver followed Frank onto the bus and closed the door behind him. Frank smiled at Louis through the window and raised a hand of goodbye. Louis waved back and stood and watched as the bus turned the corner and disappeared behind the buildings on the edge of town.

Welcome to Marshall

West Virginia is known for its hills, but along the Ohio River it is as flat as a pancake. A long time ago Huntington's city planners laid out streets in a checkerboard fashion. The city evolved into an easy grid of very wide streets and avenues. In fact, Huntington streets are as wide as rivers.

As the bus turned down 3rd Avenue, Frank sat up with some excitement to get a view of the town, but then inevitably his thoughts turned to the task at hand – football. He felt an ache in his stomach that was both hunger and nervousness. He hadn't eaten much the night before at his brothers in Charleston – but this twinge was more about football, than food. And it was more excitement than nervousness. The bus slowed to a stop. Frank laid back while everyone else got off.

The Marshall College practice field was just a short walk from the bus terminal. Outside, players in practice uniforms were throwing the football around. Inside the College facilities building, the equipment manager was waiting for Frank. He got Frank's sizes and handed him an armful of everything he needed.

Frank sat down on the bench and dressed. He was trying to appear nonchalant, but this was the first time he had put on football equipment in three years. The Marshall equipment was definitely a step up from what he had at Farmington High School. Hip pads, shoulder pads, shoes, helmet, pants, and shirt were all brand new and fit like they should. He was ready.

The grass on Marshall's Fairfield Stadium in Huntington was the greenest grass Frank Gatski had ever seen. As he walked from the dining room out on the field, he looked around at the empty stadium that seated 17,000 – far cry from the hillside at Farmington, where a few hundred would gather for a game. The springtime sun erased the chill in the air.

Coach Straight shouted out his name and motioned for him to come over. Frank jogged over to Straight, who was in conversation with another man.

"Frank, I want you to meet Coach Cam Henderson."

"Coach Henderson," Frank said politely, as he shook his hand.

"Frank, good to meet you. We're looking forward to see how you do today."

Frank laughed. "Me, too."

"How do you feel?" Straight asked.

"Feel good," Frank said. "It's been a while, but I'll do okay."

Straight looked at Henderson encouraged by Frank's confidence – and he needed the encouragement. After all, this was a gamble if there ever was one – a shot in the dark. The kid hadn't played for three years and when he did, as Farmington High Coach Cassy Ryan noted, he certainly didn't distinguish himself. Would it be possible that he could be impressive enough in front of Cam Henderson and the coaching staff at Marshall? Or was Straight going to go hide in a hole after the workout?

Straight cleared his throat nervously as they began to walk toward the other players gathered in the center of the field

Just to break the silence, Straight said, "Frank's been working in the mines, No. 9 in Farmington."

"My father was a miner," Henderson said. "Tough life."

"This could be a way out for you, Frank."

Frank smiled and shook his head, "But I like it."

Straight and Henderson stopped, leaving Frank to walk ahead for a couple of steps. Frank turned. They resumed walking. "Yeh, I like mining. It's a good life. I like hard work and the feeling it gives you."

"Uh-huh," Straight and Henderson intoned together.

"Don't worry," Frank said. "I like football, too."

Henderson shot Straight a glance. Straight's uneasiness grew as he felt the head coach thinking why pursue this coal miner instead of more conventional and sensational high school stars. There were plenty of them out there dying for an opportunity – and they all hated mining.

32

As they walked, Henderson, Straight, and Frank approached the other four players waiting for an introduction from the coach. Two were lineman, big, burley, each weighing over 220 pounds; the other two were halfbacks.

Coach Straight introduced Frank to everybody and conducted a fifteen minute stretching and warm up session.

"First thing I want to do is a hundred yard sprint. Frank, let's go to the goal line." The group walked to the goal line and stood there. "Frank, you ready?"

"Yep," Frank snapped.

"Ready…Set…Go!"

The two halfbacks sprinted out quickly, leaving everyone in the dust. Frank got off more quickly than the two linemen and with his 6 foot 3 frame and long legs began closing the gap between him and the backs. Just when it looked like he might catch them, they burst forward to beat Frank by ten yards. Frank had run out of gas. The linemen finished twenty yards behind Frank.

Frank was disappointed, but Straight and Henderson weren't. They could see the linebacker or lineman Frank could be was fast enough. Fast enough to run down a back in a short distance of ten yards. A hundred yard dash was irrelevant in a way. Almost every football play is played within a space of ten yards or so. To be quick and agile within that space was the important measure for a linebacker or a defensive lineman or an offensive lineman.

They put Frank through some agility and speed drills, where he ran through and around barriers spaced a few feet apart. His time was excellent – especially for somebody who spent the last two years working in a mine and wasn't in football shape.

Straight's demeanor began to change and he could look Henderson in the eye. He was looking like a genius – so far.

"Let's go one-on-one," Henderson said.

Straight nodded, "Okay," "Let's go one-on-one. Who's first? Jake." The huge lineman stepped out. "Okay, Frank. Let's see how you do with Jake here."

As Frank walked over to get in position in front of Jake – almost nose to nose – like offensive lineman against defensive lineman, his thoughts raced back to his friendly confrontation with brother Paul, the "All-Star," Frank thought. "Damn it, if I can take Paul, I can take Jake." The whole five minute match with Paul went through Frank's head in two seconds, while he waited tensely for the signal. Jake was dead meat.

"Ready…Set…Go!"

There was a loud crack of helmet and pads. Frank's quickness allowed him to keep his feet and escape Jake's initial thrust toward his legs. When Jake leaned forward and out of balance, Frank got underneath him and raised him up. With the leverage of his 6 foot 3 frame, those long legs and the strength of a miner, he began driving Jake up and then down on his back.

Straight raised his eyebrow and looked at Coach Henderson, who was trying to suppress a smile.

"Let's go again," Straight said. "You okay, Jake?"

"Yeh," Jake responded with some embarrassment.

"Let's go again. Ready… Set…Go!"

This time Frank was quicker off the "go" and simply got Jake before he had time to get movement, and drove him back. Jake bounced backward and back peddled out of the play.

Straight glanced at Henderson and smiled.

"That's good," Henderson said.

"That's all." He turned to his Marshall players. "Thank you guys."

Jake came to Frank, "Good job." Then he turned and walked off with the others, leaving Frank there with Coach Straight and Coach Henderson.

Straight said, "We want you down here, if you agree. We'll give you room, board, tuition. Go back home, and think about it. Let me know."

The bus ride back to Fairmont was 200 miles of reflection for Frank. This dream he was living, he never even pursued. It was like the dream pursued him. He thought again of the improbability of a nineteen-year-old miner,

34

out of school for two years, content with his mining work, having a chance to play a game – a game he truly loved, but thought was in his past. He shook his head in disbelief and smiled at his wonderful dilemma. He couldn't lose. He still liked mining coal – and if Marshall football didn't work out, No. 9 would be waiting.

The sound of a miner's drill seemed louder today. Frank leaned on it as it bore deeper into the coal seam. The sound was silenced by the crack of helmets and pads and a grunting Jake as Frank replayed the tryout at Marshall. He pulled the drill out as Jake went down.

"Damn," he said to himself. "Pay attention."

"Damn it, Frank!" a voice sounded. The foreman was standing right behind him. "You ready to shoot this place?"

"Oh," Frank grinned. "I didn't see you.

"Yeh, I could tell."

"Yeh, I'm ready" Frank said.

The foreman stuffed the hole with dynamite and shouted "fire in the hole."

They both stood back waiting for the explosion. It came, shaking down a large section of rich, black coal.

"Good job, Frank," the foreman said as he walked away.

Frank waved the dust away from in front of him and picked up the shovel. "Let's go again, one-on-one," he thought as the shovel scraped into the bottom of the pile. "Ready…Set…Go!" His thoughts came with each shovelful. "Damn, I handled Jake…I can do that. I can't pass up the opportunity. I can always do this coal mining thing, but I might never get another chance like Marshall. If this dream is chasing me – like it seems, I'd be a damn fool to not let it catch up. This is almost a miracle… It's like my mother praying for me… could that be it?"

It was like a lightning bolt. How else could you explain it? He stopped shoveling and stood up erect. The thought of his mother pushed everything aside, for the moment. He stood there in reverence, while coal dust fell down slowly in the light of his lantern. He leaned on the shovel. He closed his eyes in silent prayer. The face of his mother came plainly into view.

"Mother would want me to go to college," he thought. "She never did push much, but was so proud of Paul's education. There was no doubt what she would tell me, especially since the chance was there for all the college expenses to be paid."

Flash! Another lightening bolt! The words of Father Brady at his mother's funeral – "When you ponder decisions in your life, listen to your mother's voice. It will direct you as sure as an arrow shot from a bow."

He shook loose of the trance and his eyes focused on a large pile of coal to be loaded. He had been lost for a few minutes – in another world, where he rarely went.

He wouldn't be setting any coal loading record today, that was for sure.

Why Chase This Dream?

Oral Huff could do anything with a car. He owned one of the few cars in No. 9.

It wasn't that he was rich enough to own one, he was just smart enough. He had saved enough money to buy a 1938 Chevrolet and was able to keep it running by scavenging parts of old junkers.

One of the other cars in the coal camp was owned by Louis Gatski, who was no slouch either when it came to fixing cars. He had a Model T Ford that provided transportation to church in Farmington and to ball games the sons were involved in.

So when Oral Huff and Louis Gatski were together, they comprised half of the car owning population of the entire No. 9 camp. The other half was the mine superintendent and foreman.

Oral Huff turned his Chevy off the hard road and up in front of the Gatski house. He had come to see if Louis had a wrench that would work on his car.

Louis was working on his Model T. Frank was off to one side practicing a center snap of a football. He had marked off a distance of ten yards and secured an old blanket to a tree and anchored it to the ground. He would snap the ball to the blanket where he would retrieve it and walk back and center it again.

When Frank saw Oral Huff pull up, he stopped and walked over, spinning the football in his hand.

Suddenly the other door of the Huff car opened and banged shut. Sam Huff, six years old and three feet tall, ran around the car to the side of his father.

"Hi, Sam," Frank said. "Didn't mean to hurt you the other day."

"I'm okay," Sam said as he clung to his dad. "I didn't catch that one, but…"

"Want to catch another one?" Frank asked.

"Yeh," Sam replied expectedly. He looked up at his dad for approval.

"Stand right here," Frank said. Then he walked about five steps away and turned. "Give me a signal."

Sam obliged, "Ready, set, one, two, three."

Frank floated an easy center back to the kid who grabbed it. He made sure it was easy – not like the missile of a center snap that whizzed through Jimmy Priester's hands and took the breath away from the kid a few days before.

"Good boy, Sam," Frank said.

"One more," Sam said, as he threw the ball back.

"One more," Frank said.

"Ready, set, one, two, three."

Sam grabbed the center, and this time ran over to his dad, where Frank caught up with him and playfully tackled him and laid him down gently on the ground.

"Are you going to play football?" Sam asked as he got up.

"Well, I'm thinking about it." Frank responded.

Louis seized the opportunity to voice his displeasure. "Oral here thinks you got a great future in the mines. He says you're the best young man down there. You could become a foreman someday."

Oral spoke up, "Yeh, Frank, why chase this football dream? What's it going to get you?"

"A broken leg," Louis answered. "That's what!"

"But, Dad, I can always come back and work here. I like the mines, but this is different. It's a chance to play a game for a couple of years and get an education – maybe be a teacher or coach. Mom would like that. You know it."

Louis shook his head. "Yes, she would. But it's too far. Marshall College – two hundred miles – would take all day for me to get there. Why can't you go to Fairmont State College. It's just ten miles!"

"I know," Frank said. "They never asked me, Pop. Anyway, if it all falls apart, I can come back and pick up that shovel."

38

Sam looked up at his dad and said something in a small shy voice. Nobody heard. "What's that, son?" Oral said.

Sam's voice was stronger this time. "I said he should play football."

I Gotta Try

Frank jumped out of the last car bringing miners out of No. 9 mine after the midnight shift. The crisp morning air of early summer was a welcome change from the air inside the dreary, dark earth a hundreds of feet below.

The morning sun and the dew, which sparkled on the hillside around the mine, showed that nature could bring its power and miracle to brighten even a desolate coal camp.

As Frank walked from the portal to make the short walk to his house, someone shouted his name. Frank looked over to see Charlie Gardner, the mine superintendent, motioning for him to come over.

Charlie leaned against one of the heavy timbers of the mine entrance. Frank quickly made his way through the miners leaving the portal and hurried over with some trepidation. Charlie spoke up, "I had to talk with you, Frank."

"Sure, Charlie, something wrong?"

"No, no, nothing like that. Your dad asked me to talk to you. Told him I would." Frank breathed a sigh of relief. Charlie continued, "I know you're thinking about quitting here to go play football!"

Frank smiled. "Not just to play football, I'll be going to school at Marshall College."

"Yes, I know, but I want you to know you have a good future here in the mines. You know that, don't you? Hell, you could be a boss someday... easy..."

"I appreciate that, I do, and I like the work. I love working here, but...I gotta give this a try. It's like something I never went after...it's like it came after me. And I couldn't help thinking it's something my mother would love... me going back to school." Frank looked down and pawed the ground with his foot as he dug deep for his feelings. "Sometime I think all this happened because my mother is making it happen for me." Then he raised his head to look at Charlie in the eye. "That's why I gotta try."

Charlie knew the conversation was over. "I understand – Now I really understand." He pushed himself away from the timber and reached out his hand. "and I wish you the best."

Frank shook his hand. "I was hoping if it doesn't work out I could come back."

"Sure," Charlie said. "Well, I'll talk to your dad about this and assure him you're doing the best thing. The job is always here for you, you know that – but then I hope I don't see you here anymore. That'll mean everything is going well at Marshall."

Frank laughed, "I guess that's right, except for the summers. Do you think I might be able to work in the summers? It would sure help..."

"I'll see what I can do... but you're right. You can't pass up this opportunity... It's too good... and your mother would want you to do it."

"I know she would," Frank said.

"Good luck," Charlie said as he slapped Frank on the back and sent him on his way.

Frank, the College Freshman

In the fall of 1940 Frank Gatski was living a dream – living in Everett Hall on the campus of Marshall College, attending classes as a nineteen-year-old freshman, and playing football – a far cry from the No. 9 routine.

Yes, the miner had become a student majoring in physical education and playing center and linebacker for the Thundering Herd freshman football team.

Marshall had an enrollment of 1,500. It was nearly 200 miles from No. 9, but it was a world away from the life he had led.

He threw himself into student life one hundred percent – like he did everything. His grades his first semester were 2.8 on a 4.0 base, not bad for someone who hadn't seen a textbook for three years.

Except for an occasional beer with his teammates, Frank did not socialize. Frank adapted to Marshall and Marshall liked him, too. He had impressed the coaching staff, playing well in games on the freshman football schedule against Xavier, Toledo, and Ohio University.

The varsity home schedule in1940 at Fairfield Stadium included Morehead State, Virginia Tech, Dayton, Toledo, Wake Forest, Scranton, Morris Harvey, Detroit Tech, Xavier and West Virginia Wesleyan. The team was one of Cam Henderson's best, going 8-2 and losing only to Toledo 7-6 and Wake Forest 31-19.

Frank went to the varsity games, but could hardly stand it. He came to Marshall to play. But freshman players could only watch and wait their turn as sophomores. Frank would be ready. He knew the varsity center, Jim Roberts, was a senior and would be graduating, leaving the job open for someone. In Frank's mind, that someone was him – the job was already his. Anybody else trying out for center in 1941 was going to be Frank's substitute. And that would be irrelevant, too, since Frank Gatski – the toughest guy in this part of West Virginia – was not going to leave the game for any reason.

During his freshman season, he had improved a great deal. He had all the natural gifts of agility and quickness. He had size, he was 6 foot 3 and 220 pounds – and he had mental toughness and courage, traits that came from home, from his brothers who always competed to win and a family that always strived against the odds to persevere and excel. And he would not take 'no' for an answer.

Football was easy. Using his God-given gifts and mental approach to competition was half the battle. The rest was to improve his technique taught by Marshall coaches.

One important thing they didn't have to teach Frank was how to center the football. He already knew. He learned that from his brother, Benny, years ago when Benny was playing center at Farmington High School and Frank was an eighth grader. The accepted method of snapping the ball to a single wing halfback about three or four yards behind the center or to a punter ten yards back was to place one hand on the side of the ball and the other beneath. The Gatski method was to have both hands on top of the ball with elbows straight. Benny and Frank believed that one hand on top and bottom created pressure that would send some snaps lower and some higher.

Marshall coaches left well enough alone, and did not try to "improve" Frank's hand positions on the ball since his snaps were always perfect.

When school was over in May of 1941, Frank headed for home to No. 9 and that summer job in the mines Charlie Gardner had promised. It felt good to be back doing work he enjoyed and making some money, but his world was different now. He had the best of everything it seemed – work in the mines now with the anticipation of playing college football in the fall. Football was fun and college had given him confidence that he could live in a world away from a coal camp.

Louis was glad to see his youngest son home. In spite of his earlier objections, he was proud that his son had become a college football player and Frank's presence in the house made life better for the old man.

Frank returned to Huntington for football practice in August determined to be the starting center on offense and linebacker on defense for the 1941 squad. And that's exactly the way it was.

When pre-season practice was completed in late August, the twenty-man roster included a number of returning lettermen, including senior backfield star, Jacki Hunt. Hunt had graduated from Huntington High School, a few blocks from Marshall and could play every position in the backfield.

The 1941 season was another great team. The 7-1 record included wins over University of Nebraska - Omaha, Illinois State, Toledo, Western Kentucky, Scranton, Wake Forest and Morehead State, with its only loss a 7- 0 defeat at Dayton. Marshall outscored its opponents 217-47.

On one Saturday afternoon when Frank was having a great day on the field – making blocks and making tackles all over the place, the Marshall radio announcer was beside himself – "Gatski, Gatski, Gatski…" Then he laughed, "Huh, say that enough and it sounds like the repeat of a gattling gun. Well, the "Gunner" is here today. It's been a Frank Gatski, a "Gunner" Gatski kind of day for sure!"

And for sure Frank Gatski had a new name…the "Gunner".

After the last game of the 1941 season, Frank looked with some satisfaction with his play and the team's sparkling 7-1 record. But still he wasn't completely satisfied. He never was. He knew he would get better for his junior season. By December he was getting ready for semester exams. On December 7, Frank took a bus to Charleston to spend the weekend with Paul and his wife.

Paul picked up Frank at the Greyhound Bus Station and drove home, where Joanie, Paul's wife, met them at the door with shocking news. Pearl Harbor had been attacked.

The world had changed.

Suddenly, the game of football seemed of little importance. Futures were in doubt. What now?

Men were enlisting to answer the call to arms; those who didn't were being drafted, even students. College football teams all across America were being torn apart by the draft. Frank waited his turn. He knew it would come.

While the draft worked its way through all physically fit males, there were ways to defer the draft – legal ways to delay service into the armed forces.

In order to field a team in 1942, the Marshall coaches asked the players to join the reserves. That would keep them stateside, while they trained weekly at the local armory. Some agreed and at least Marshall had enough players to get on the field.

The 1942 team had already lost the seniors from that outstanding 1941 team by graduation. That included their great star Jacki Hunt. The war took away other players – and what was left for the 1942 season comprised a team whose record was a complete reversal of form from the previous season, winning only one game. Then things got even worse: Cam Henderson, who also served as the Athletic Director, met with the team in November of 1942 to tell them, that because of the war, there would be no football at Marshall in 1943.

"Hell," Frank thought, "it wouldn't matter anyway. Practically the whole team would be headed overseas."

He was right. He was drafted in May of 1943 and was sent to Fort Custer, Michigan for 13 weeks and then to Camp Shanango – next to Sharon, Pennsylvania for two months.

He returned to No. 9 for one week before his assignment to Boston. His orders called for him to be shipped out to Scotland in December 1943. While at No. 9, he tried to soak in every minute of 'being home'. All of the common ordinary things became important – visiting the Leisure R Inn, archery, seeing his brother, his father, even the look of the coal tipple made him feel a sadness for leaving the life he had known.

But now it was time to go. The screen door banged behind him. The sound of it was recorded in his brain, just as his footsteps across the porch would be. "Remember this," he thought.

Frank steadied the duffle bag on his back as he walked to the car where Louis was waiting to take him to the Greyhound Bus Station in Fairmont.

A few hundred feet away in Oral Huff's house, a little kid was looking out the window. He saw this tall guy dressed in an army uniform coming out of the Gatski house. Then he stepped back. "It's Frank," he thought. He watched him come down the steps and disappear into the Gatski Model T. "Frank is going to fight the war," he said to himself.

Sam fingered the last layer of tin foil on the baseball size ball of the stuff he had made from collecting foil for the war effort. The government encouraged everyone to collect all kinds of metal scraps for recycling, even tin foil. Every kid knew it could end up being part of a bomb to blast the Japs and the Germans. Sam's tin foil ball was made of wrappers from chewing gum, candy bars, and dirty pieces from the street – a complete history of an eight-year-old kids' life was wrapped up in that shiny sphere.

The Terrors of James Fork

World War II was far away from No. 9, where Robert Lee "Sam" Huff and Leo Coceano, both now in the fourth grade, were still trying the patience of James Fork Elementary principal, Blair Wolfe.

Leo's English had improved steadily, but there were moments of high comedy, when his Italian voice would take over. Sam helped his buddy – with his English – and as protector from those who might make fun of Leo's less than perfect vocabulary. Sam wasn't any bigger than Leo, but he was willing to defend his friend.

The two were considered leaders by the other kids. Perhaps it was Leo's connection with Sam that gave him the high status, but he also earned it because of his improvement in speaking the language, his natural athletic ability, and his competitive nature.

Summer vacation of 1944 was over and the small James Fork Elementary School was filled with young kids – all hating to be there. It was one heck of a situation for principal, Blair Wolfe and three teachers. Mr. Wolfe was a small and wiry, but tough man. His sharp features and mustache gave gave him a hawkish look that led kids to believe he knew everything! He would stand guard during physical education classes where girls jumped rope and played volleyball and boys would participate in the game of the season – baseball in summer and spring, football in autumn.

He had the respect of all the children and their parents. When the word went forth from Mr. Wolfe that a student had a problem in school – inevitably, he had a bigger problem at home – without exception.

But Mr. Wolfe wasn't perfect. He had a flaw. He had only one suit. And when he wore that one brown suit, Sam and Leo figured, that was the day

Mr. Wolfe had a principal's meeting in Fairmont, ten miles away. His absence meant that the physical education period could be played by Huff-Coceano rules – tackle football, not just the sissy touch game Mr. Wolfe would supervise. Now the period would be supervised by somebody easy, like Mrs. Hornyak.

The first meeting of business for the two conspirators to check out was the attire of the principal. Since Mr. Wolfe also taught 5th and 6th grades, it was easy to determine the color of his suit. If the principal was sighted by either Sam or Leo or one of the other 4th grade boys, and the information was that Mr. Wolfe was wearing his brown suit, it was a sign of better times ahead.

On one "brown suit" day, right on schedule, Mr. Wolfe disappeared before noon. The physical education period, now supervised by Mrs. Hornyak, was actually under the control of the Huff-Coceano duo. That meant one thing! Tackle football!

Sam and Leo became self-appointed captains and they chose up sides. Leo was smaller and faster. After several plays of running just beyond the reach of his bigger, slower buddy, he was finally caught. Sam's frustration ended with a hard tackle to the ground, then he helped Leo up, brushed him off and asked if he was okay.

"Hey, buddy, that was a good tackle," Leo said in his broken English. "Don't worry, I'll get you back," he promised.

Further damage was averted when the bell sounded for the end of the physical education period.

In November, as the 1944 election neared, it was a foregone conclusion that Franklin Roosevelt would be re-elected president; just as it was a foregone conclusion that all of the Democratic candidates in Marion County would win the election.

While West Virginia was mainly Republican in the early part of the 20th century, it turned Democratic with the election of FDR and The New Deal in 1932. Since that time it remained heavily Democratic. The emerging Labor union – the "Common man" appeal – kept it that way. Democratic. So was

48

Marion County. So was No. 9. The Democratic Party had 'served the cause of the working man', and that's all there was in the coal camp. Nevertheless, Republicans did put their candidates on the ballot and went through the motions. One Republican party worker even dared to tape a sign on their car asking citizens to vote for their presidential candidate. "Vote for THOMAS DEWEY, Republican" it was just as bad as an endorsement for the KKK.

Toward the end of one school day, that Republican Party worker had parked his car near the James Fork Elementary school entrance and entered the building to discuss a matter of importance with Mr. Wolfe.

The bell rang to end the school day and the kids spilled out of the building. Sam and Leo were walking together. Sam stopped when he noticed the car parked by the entrance. He looked over to see a sign on the window. Curiosity got the best of him and he walked closer to the car to take a look. Leo followed.

"Look at that," Sam said. "Vote for THOMAS DEWEY, REPUBLICAN."

"What's that?" Leo asked.

"You know," Sam said the word slowly. "RE-PUB-LI-CAN"

"No good?" Leo asked.

"No good!" Sam replied.

"What are you going to do?" Leo asked.

""Just wait," Sam commanded quietly. Seconds went by. He knew the sign had to be removed. It was his duty. They waited for the other kids to disperse. Another look to make sure no one was watching. "Get ready to run," he whispered. Then he ripped the sign from its tape and started running. Sam had books in one hand and the prize in the other. Leo ran out of there like lightning, running past his buddy.

Then all hell broke loose.

"Sam!" "Leo!" The voice of doom had sounded from the school doorway. Mr. Wolfe's meeting with the parent had ended ten seconds too soon.

Sam and Leo stopped. The sign "Vote for THOMAS DEWEY, REPUBLICAN FOR PRESIDENT" hung limply from Sam's hand.

49

"Oh shit," Leo said, "My papa is going to kill me," he said in his broken English.

"Yeh, mine, too" Sam said.

They turned and began the long walk back to the car where Mr. Wolfe and the damned Republican were waiting.

In the spring of 1945, the game was baseball. Mr. Wolfe was fulfilling another of his duties – umpiring.

Sam and Leo, as usual, chose up sides for a game during physical education class. Mr. Wolfe removed his jacket, and rolled up his sleeves. His tie was blowing in the wind as he assumed the position behind the pitcher to call the balls and strikes. It was a preferred spot as opposed to behind the catcher, where a foul ball or a bad pitch could crush an umpire's face.

The game had become particularly intense. The score was tied and the class period was almost over. The bases were loaded and Sam was pitching to his friend – for the moment – bitter enemy Leo.

The count went to three balls and two strikes, a full count. The game hung in the balance. Sam threw the pitch. Leo didn't swing.

"Ball four," the umpire called out. Sam turned and looked up at Mr. Wolfe.

"You're cheating!" he shouted.

Suddenly, the world stopped turning!

Seventeen kids all stopped – frozen in their tracks as the words, "You're cheating" reverberated in the hills around No. 9.

Sam waited for retribution. Everybody did. It seemed like an hour went by. But it was only an instant. Mr. Wolfe grabbed the pitcher by the shirt, popping off his buttons. In the next instant, he was marching him off to the office.

Not one word was heard on that ball field from that moment on for the rest of the day. No one knew what happened in the principal's office of James Fork Elementary – but Robert Lee "Sam" Huff never forgot it.

50

Home at Last

The United States and Russian forces had Hitler's Army on the run and Der Fuher hiding in a bunker.

Frank Gatski was in London, England attached to the military police unit. He had been there for a year through Germany's last gasp blitz of the old city. His previous assignment was in France during the Allies victorious campaign there.

Like a lot of other servicemen, no one dared to look ahead too far. Just getting by day to day was the key – one day at a time, hoping and praying the day would come when they would be able to return to the states and their former lives.

With the tide turning in the war, visions of tomorrow began playing in Frank Gatski's head. He couldn't wait to get back.

But the good news of the war was tempered by bad news from home. Frank flinched when he saw the return address on the letter. It was from his brother, Benny, who wouldn't write unless there was a serious problem. Was his father ill… or worse? Did something happen to John or Paul?

After the first line, "I hope you are fine." Benny's letter got to the point… little Mary Louise, just eight years old, had died of spinal meningitis. Frank stared at the letter's harsh meaning. His sister's face came into view. He saw his mother holding her.

He slowly folded the letter and closed his eyes in silent prayer.

Frank wasn't sure of his football future. Marshall hadn't even fielded a team in 1943 and 1944. Would they in 1945? But at least Frank was opting to return to Marshall to finish his senior year of classes – then graduate. A college diploma would mean something. Then he could start coaching, if he could get a job. The high school coaches were making about two hundred dollars a month.

Hell, he could even go back in the mines. He liked it, and he could make twice as much. But in either case, he would get the college diploma. His mother would have wanted it. It was something he had started and he would finish it.

His brother, Benny was waiting at the Greyhound Bus Station in Fairmont. The bus turned down Monroe Street and pulled to a stop. Benny could see the tall soldier rise from a rear seat. He hurried outside and waited anxiously by the door. Frank followed behind several passengers. He swung his duffel bag from the bus and set it down to embrace his brother.

"Good to see you, brother," Benny said.

"Good to be home. How's Dad?"

"He's anxious to see you. Let's go."

On the way to No. 9, Frank took in the sights of home he had missed. Yes, he had taken it all for granted. Now he was seeing it through the eyes of someone longing for home.

Frank walked up the three steps of his house counting each one – he remembers going down three years before. He opened the screen door and heard it bang shut behind him – the same sound it made on his way out and into another world. He was glad to be home. Then he put the past behind him as he walked over to his dad and embraced him.

Frank felt fortunate to wind up his stint in the army in time to be home to spend time with his father, who recently had not been feeling well. His brother, Benny, was still at home – in fact, Benny didn't have to serve in the armed services because he was designated an "essential miner" – one considered important for mining coal, which was essential to the war effort at home, as well as necessary for stateside consumption.

A Return to Marshall

It seemed so long ago that Frank was at Marshall College – being a student and playing football. Two years of service in foreign lands had him wondering if this good life could ever come again. Now Frank felt the excitement of returning to it. There were times in Scotland and France that he thought it would never happen.

Returning GI's were filling colleges under the GI bill. Football players returning from service were quickly finding their college and filling up the rosters. It was not unusual to see a twenty-five or twenty-six-year-old, even thirty-year-old players returning to school and a final fling at football. And it was not unusual for a player to enroll at a school that was a bitter enemy of his former college.

Frank took a bus to Huntington to get reacquainted with his old school and inquire about admission for his senior year. He learned, with great disappointment, that Marshall would not field a football team again in 1945 as they hadn't in 1943 and 1944. Frank was out of luck – he only had one year of eligibility before graduating. He could enroll at another school that was playing football, but where, and how could that happen?

His two varsity years at Marshall, 1941 and 1942, were very satisfactory. He had gotten a reputation around the Buckeye Conference of being an excellent center and he had received "honorable mention" as an All-American linebacker by the Sporting News in 1942. He knew he had another good year of college ball in him. He wanted it. He was hoping to be playing college football in 1945 – but it just wouldn't be at Marshall.

Thinking back to the incredibly unusual circumstances that led him to Marshall in the first place made Frank believe that nothing was too far-fetched. If that could happen, then finding a place to play one more season should be easy.

At the same time college coaches were actively recruiting the football players they knew who were returning from the service. It was not a foregone conclusion that a player would return to the same school he left to enter the service. Many of the players, like Frank, found out that their schools discontinued football for the period during the war. Other players who saw their old college team roster filled chose to enroll somewhere else where they had a better opportunity.

Frank had the feeling someone would find him. Why not? His college career thus far was a dream – not something he had pursued. It had been incomprehensible. It would be much less surprising now that someone would invite him to play his senior season somewhere. He would wait for the forces to act.

Now that he had come to believe he would be playing football in the 1945 season, he knew he would have to get ready. He hadn't touched a football in three years and the center touched the ball on every play!

Frank looked out to the old No. 9 playground. The playground was a neighborhood baseball field in summer and football field in autumn. It was just a large field – barely large enough to play baseball – and bare where the infield was from which the ground rose up to a short left field and fell down to shorter right field. The backstop was chicken wire and wood and looked ready to fall down, although it stood for several seasons. But it could stop the baseball most of the time.

The field was used by the No. 9 team of young boys that played the other little coal camp teams of nearby Ida May and Carolina, as well as any "choose-up" games of softball, baseball and football.

On this day, a young boy, perhaps fifteen or sixteen years old, was out there kicking a football. Frank looked out and saw the football soar into the sky. The kid was good. Frank didn't recognize him, although there was something about him that seemed familiar.

Frank thought, here's a way I can get my hands on a football. He walked over to the field and, getting a closer look at the kid, recognized him. It was Jimmy Priester – the same boy who let Frank's missile-like snap go through his hands to darn near kill little Sam Huff.

Jimmy had grown up in three years. Frank could tell, Jimmy was ready to play high school football.

Jimmy was kicking the ball to two younger kids, who would run the ball part way back to Jimmy, before kicking it to him. Jimmy saw Frank walking over to him and recognized him.

"Hi, Frank. Bet you're glad to be home."

"Yes I am," Frank said. "You need a center, Jimmy?"

"Yeh," Jimmy laughed. "Guess I do. You want to center while I kick?"

"Who are the kids?"

"That's Sam and Leo."

Frank rose up from his center position to turn around and ask you mean "Sam Huff, Oral's boy?"

""Yeh, that's him."

When Sam heard his name being mentioned, he motioned to Leo to come with him to see who the new player was.

But by this time Frank had snapped his first center in three years into the hands of Jimmy, who sent the kick high and down into the arms of Sam who made an awkward catch that would make any ten-year-old proud. Then he ran the ball back to ten yards from Frank and threw him the ball.

"Are you Frank?" the kid asked.

"Yeh, I'm Frank!"

"I thought so," Sam asked. Then he turned and shouted to Leo. "That's Frank! He's back from the war."

Frank turned to ask Jimmy, "You ready?" Jimmy nodded. Frank snapped a center back.

Sam's eyes widened, "Did you see that center, Leo? Boy he's good."

Jimmy kicked the ball in the air.

56

"I get it," Leo said as he ran to catch up with a beautiful spiral.

Frank discovered he hadn't lost much – at least as far as snapping the ball for a punt goes.

After a few more punts, Jimmy shouted to Sam and Leo, "come here you guys. Let's go out for passes." He hurried to Frank. "Okay with you, Frank. You can center some short snaps. Like I'm a halfback, I'll throw to Sam and Leo."

"That's good," Frank said. It'll get me a chance to practice that, too."

"Are you going to play this year, Frank?"

"Don't know. Doesn't look too good now, because of the war, Marshall is not going to have a team." Frank rose up and turned around from his center position. "I'm going to play somewhere. I'm counting on it."

"I'm going to play halfback – so practicing passing will help me." He turned to his two little pass catchers.

"You guys ready, Sam?"

"Ready," he said as he lined up and got ready to go out for a pass.

Frank sent a perfect center to Jimmy's right knee just where a halfback on the single wing formation is supposed to receive it. Jimmy faded to his right and threw a perfect strike to Sam.

"Touchdown," Sam shouted.

The Forces at Work

It was a great feeling to be home and out of the army. Frank didn't want to do anything right now but relax and decide what to do about school and football.

The State Basketball Tournament in West Virginia is one of the state's most exciting sports events. In 1945 it was held in Morgantown at the West Virginia University Fieldhouse.

It was not only a place to see the states' best high school basketball, but to interact socially with a lot of other people in the West Virginia sports scene.

Frank decided to go. He hitchhiked from No. 9 to Route 250 in Farmington, then seven miles to Fairmont and another twenty miles to Morgantown. Hitchhiking on this day was easy since the tournament traffic heading to Morgantown was heavy.

Frank got there at noon. Already the old Fieldhouse was rocking with 6000 screaming fans and it would be that way all day long – one game after another.

Frank reveled in his return to civilian life and the freedom of it all. He was still troubled by the uncertainty of his football future, but still had hopes that something would turn up.

As Frank entered the gate into the main section of the Fieldhouse, he noticed a gentleman in a suit looking at him in a way to suggest they knew each other. But Frank didn't know him. He did notice the man was surveying the scene with arms crossed, giving Frank the impression that he was an "official" here at the tournament – not just a spectator, perhaps somebody connected with West Virginia University.

As Frank started to walk past him the man dropped his arms and started to walk toward Frank.

"Excuse me," the man said. Frank stopped. "You Frank Gatski?"

"Yes, I am," Frank responded politely.

"I'll be damned; I've been looking for you."

"What for?"

"Come over here where it's quiet so we can talk."

The gentleman took Frank by the arm and directed him away from the crowded stands to a corner against the wall. "I'm Johnny Brickles. I'm the assistant football coach here at West Virginia."

"Now I know you," Frank said. "You were in Huntington in 41-42, the head coach at Huntington High. I was at Marshall. I knew the name, but we never met."

Brickles continued, "But I'm leaving here to join Paul Brown's staff. You heard of him?"

"No," Frank said. "Who is he?"

"Paul Brown is the head coach at Ohio State and he is involved with a new professional football conference that's going to start next year – in 1946. We're looking for players right now. Sam Clagg, friend of yours at Marshall, recommended you."

Frank smiled. "Me?" That's great, but… I still got a year of college eligibility left. Marshall suspended football for this year. Don't know what I'm going to do this season. But I was hoping…"

Brickles continued, "This is still a year away – but we'll have tryouts next spring – then pre-season drills next August."

"Well, I'd give it a try if you want me to." Frank assured. "I can't lose anything."

"Good, I'll be in touch next year."

Frank gave him his phone number and address and said goodbye. He felt a sense of satisfaction that he would be considered for this new football league. Frank Gatski, a professional. Getting paid to play – that would be something. "Hell, I'd play for nothing," Frank thought.

But the vision as a professional football player faded in the light of trying to finish school and playing a final college year – somewhere. And he

59

thought if he ever did get the call from Brickles, then he would deal with it then.

Football seemed unimportant when Louis took a turn for the worse in July and died. All of his sons were there to comfort him in his last days. And Father Brady who celebrated the funeral mass for his beloved wife, did the same for Louis.

Walking away from the cemetery after his father's burial, Frank felt all alone for one of the few times in his life. Now both parents were gone. His brothers had other lives. But he was alone – and with an uncertain future

But somehow, he felt things would work out. After all, he had gone from high school player with no aspirations for college football to working two years in the coal mines to suddenly being asked to play at Marshall College, to getting through two years of the service. He had already felt blessed - that forces beyond him were taking him somewhere. All he had been doing was following the path layed out before him.

He thought again of his mother – was it her prayers from heaven guiding her youngest son? His life had taken such an incredible journey so that was as logical as anything else!

"So, Mother," he thought. "Now what? Will I be playing football somewhere? Who will call me? And when?"

It was getting late. It was July and nobody had contacted him. It was getting to be the time to enroll at Marshall for his senior season. And to do that – since Marshall would not have a team - would mean his football career was over. Once already, he had felt the finality of a football career – in 1942.

Still Frank took consolation in the fact that the forces could work again. For some reason, there was a glimmer of hope he would be playing football in September.

In August, Frank was in Huntington to enroll in classes. With time on his hands, he wandered over to the athletic office in the Athletic Center to see Cam Henderson, his football coach. Frank thought his coach might have some ideas for a returning football player who had eligibility left, but whose college suspended football.

The wooden floors creaked and the old halls echoed beneath his steps as he walked to the bulletin board that had a large sign shouting out his problem "No football in 1945 due to the war."

Frank stepped in to read the small print when a familiar voice interrupted him. Frank turned to see Sam Clagg, his old friend and captain of the 1942 team.

Sam shook Frank's hand. "Good to see you, Frank."

"Good to see you, Sam."

"Looking for a football team?" Sam joked.

"Yeh," Frank said. "It would be good to get one more season in. What are you doing now?"

"I'm here teaching."

They turned to walk down the hallway to Coach Henderson's office.

"The war has screwed everything up," Sam said. "Even Coach Henderson's itching to get back on the football field. Hell, he's been coaching the swim team for three years, and he can't even swim."

As they entered Coach Henderson's office, the coach warmly welcomed Frank. In answer to Frank's concerns, Henderson told him, "We're getting inquiries from other schools. They've got lists of players that have eligibility and who would normally be returning to schools who aren't having a football season this year. I'm sure you're on the list. Don't be surprised if you get contacted.

"Then what?" Frank asked.

"Then you go enroll in that school – play your final year, transfer your credits back here and continue your classes here at Marshall until you graduate.

"I'd like to graduate from Marshall," Frank said. "The school has meant a lot to me."

"Well now that can be taken care of. The next question is what will you be doing this football season."

Brachman's Tavern in Huntington was the college hangout at Marshall College. It wasn't the typical college place – nicer. A lot of the customers were guys back from the service and wives would know they could get a good sandwich there along with a good selection of beer. But better for Frank, it was a short walk from where his room was on Fourth Avenue.

Frank was preparing to enroll at Marshall for the 1945 fall semester, having decided it was his best option. He was resigned, but sad, because he knew he was through with football.

The name "Gatski" can cut through the din and conversation of any room. Its harsh consonants rise above a jukebox playing Glenn Miller's "*Tuxedo Junction*" and crowded bar noise.

Frank heard it. He turned to see the bartender pointing right at him, directing a well-dressed gentleman over to his table.

Frank straightened up as the man approached him.

"Frank Gatski?"

"Yes," Frank said, as he stood up.

The two men shook hands. "I'd like to talk with you. I'm Shott Shinn, assistant football coach at Auburn University…"

Frank stepped back. Flashes of his mother's face went through his head and made him shiver. A tear appeared uncontrollably in his eyes. "She sent this man here," he thought. Then he thought "Auburn – good football school." His mind was turning – and he wasn't listening.

The man's voice cut through, "Mind if I sit down. I'd like to talk with you,"

"Oh sure," Frank said apologetically.

Shinn pulled up a chair. Frank leaned forward. He didn't want to miss one word. This had to be an invitation to play football. Just had to be.

"Wanted to know, Frank, if you would be interested in Auburn for your final season of football?"

Frank smiled and couldn't help thinking of his mother again. The forces were at work. "Mr. Shinn, I've heard of Auburn as a good school – but I have to confess, I don't even know where it is."

Shinn laughed. "A lot of people don't know. It's in Alabama."

"Huntington's as far south as I've ever been," Frank said. "I take that back. I hitchhiked to the Kentucky Derby in 1941. But I'm just a coal miner from No. 9. Do you think they would want me in Alabama?"

"The way we think you can play football, we don't care if you're from Mars," Shinn said. "We need a center. You could start, I think."

Those were magic words "...you could start..." "Can I think about it?" Frank asked. "I'm tempted to say 'yes' right now – but I want to check on a few things."

It looked like Frank's mother was being persistent for Shott Shinn wasn't the only college coach looking for Frank Gatski. After Frank returned to No. 9, he got a call from Ray Graves, assistant coach at Tennessee. Graves traveled to Fairmont to stay at the Fairmont Hotel, hoping to meet with Frank. He called and asked Frank to come into Fairmont to meet with him.

And an ex-Marshall coach, after the suspension of Marshall College football, moved on to the staff of Minnesota – and contacted Frank about becoming a Gopher.

You would think the most likely team to get Frank back on the football field would be the West Virginia University Mountaineers located just an hour away in Morgantown. And they did come calling, after all the others. Legs Hawley contacted Frank, but he rebuffed them quickly since they had never shown any interest in him until now.

Frank was blunt with Hawley – and perhaps a little foolish turning down such a possibility close by – but he had principles. He told Hawley, "since you never showed any interest in me before – I can't play with you now."

Had Frank forgotten that there was absolutely no reason for West Virginia, or anybody else, to consider him before. He had never been seriously considered as a possible college player coming out of high school, and it was only the strangest set of circumstances that had taken him this far!

But Frank did have other options, and therefore the luxury to reject the home state team. He hadn't been a big West Virginia University fan anyway. His brother, Paul, unlike Frank, did have an excellent high school career, but West Virginia University never contacted the player from little Farmington. It angered the Gatski's and turned them against West Virginia. So Paul went to a smaller school, West Virginia Wesleyan, in Buckhannon about fifty miles south of No. 9. Frank watched West Virginia Wesleyan play West Virginia at Mountaineer Field and naturally cheered for Wesleyan. The Mountaineers easily beat the small school – there was no love lost between the Gatski's and West Virginia.

Frank's name and reputation had even been mentioned in pro circles. Now George "Greasy" Neal, the head coach of the Philadelphia Eagles was on Frank's trail, too. He sent Frank twenty-five dollars for bus fare to attend a tryout camp at Hershey, Pennsylvania. But Frank didn't respond to the Neal offer – he still was interested in his last year of college ball and getting his degree.

So it looked like Frank had a choice between Auburn, Tennessee and Minnesota. No guarantee to play, but at least the opportunity.

He figured Tennessee would be tougher. In spite of his enormous determination that he could out-work, out-hustle anyone and would be in better shape than anyone, there was some practicality in his thinking regarding the Tennessee offer.

He only had one year left and could not afford to play behind someone with the idea of being a starter the following year – 1945 was it! Tennessee, in the 1930's and 1940's had been a powerhouse. The center situation was not as promising. The Tennessee center was a regular in 1943 and, like Frank, he was returning from the service for his final year.

So he figured he would have a tougher time getting on the field. He felt he could make the squad, but he wanted to play all the time – all 60 minutes of every game – center on offense and linebacker on defense. Tennessee was out.

The other possibility was Minnesota. To Frank, Minnesota was like a foreign country – too far north, too cold, and the same problem applied with regard to playing time. The Gophers under great coach Bernie Bierman had been one of the top teams for years and great players flocked there.

Auburn, on the other hand, had struggled during the war years. Shott Shinn may have been right. Frank recalled his words "we need a center. I think you could start." For Frank, time was running out. The best choice was Auburn.

So Frank made his first trip into the Confederacy – to Montgomery, Alabama and became an Auburn Tiger. He enrolled in classes that would transfer back to Marshall – and easily made the squad. He got his wish. He was the starting center on offense and linebacker on defense – a real sixty minute man. He felt a little out of water, since he was now a twenty-five-year-old ex-soldier on a team that lost its lettermen to the war and had a lot of nineteen-year-old freshmen and sophomores. The young team didn't improve over the previous year, finishing 5-5.

One of the losses was to the Georgia Bulldogs 35 – 0, a game in which Frank had a close-up view of one of the greatest halfbacks he had ever seen – Charley Trippi. This wasn't Marshall College.

Frank sat in the locker room – longer than usual before getting dressed. Auburn had just lost its last game of the 1945 season to Miami 33-7. 'The final football game' he thought. The improbable life that came to him at his Marshall College tryout five years before had ended.

The bittersweet kept coming. "I'm going to miss it. Time to move on though – go back to Marshall – get that degree…find a coaching job somewhere…"

Frank completed the semester at Auburn in December and headed back home. He was satisfied. He had played all the college football allowed and he did it well. Damn well, in fact. And he never missed a game – not barely a minute. Hell, he never even missed a practice.

But that was all over now. And it had been good. The games were fun and he would always remember his teammates.

The bus trip from Montgomery, Alabama, to Fairmont took about 23 hours and included ten stops in small towns and 1200 miles of southern straight stretches and narrow twisting Appalachian roads. Frank arrived back in Fairmont on a Monday morning. His brother, Benny, picked him up at the Greyhound Bus Station and took him home – not to No. 9, but to Benny's home in Grant Town, about two miles away from No. 9. The Gatski's house, the family had lived in for thirty years, was taken back by the Coal Company after Louis died and someone else was living there.

Waiting on a Call

Frank hadn't forgotten there was still the slight chance he would get that call from Johnny Brickles about a tryout with that new team, the Cleveland Browns. He was at a crossroads. He was twenty-five years old and it was time to stop playing games and get serious with life. He would enroll in Marshall for the spring semester of 1946 and then complete his degree – then coach somewhere – or return to the mines at No. 9, that is unless the Brickles miracle would happen.

Everybody he knew back home twenty-five years old was married and raising a family. Shouldn't he be doing that, too? Suddenly the pressure was on. Face it. Football was over, that is unless Brickles would call.

Spring was here. Frank got back to his dorm room at Marshall. He was just finishing mid-term examinations. There was a note on his door that said, "Johnny Brickles called. Will call back."

A warm rush of excitement covered him. He snatched the note off the door. He looked at it. He stared at it. "Damn," he thought. "Damn, damn. Maybe it's not over." He glanced at the black payphone down the hall. He walked in his room and threw himself on the bed, still feeling the warmth of the small note on his hand.

"Damn," he thought again. "Man, if I ever get that chance, I'll be a pro." In Frank Gatski's mind, there was no doubt. Frank gazed at the ceiling, reflecting on his good fortune: He had played college football at two schools, served his country, was close to getting a college degree – and now maybe a chance to play...

Soon he drifted off and was awakened by a loud knock on the door. Frank jumped up.

"Frank," a voice outside called.

"Yeh."

"Telephone call."

Frank flew to the door. "Thanks," Frank said as he rushed toward the phone.

"Someone named Brickles," the friend said as he rushed by.

The warm rush came back again as Frank pick up the dangling black receiver. He felt the tension in his arm as he raised it to his ear.

Brickles wanted to meet Frank at a hotel the next day at 3 p.m to discuss the terms of tryout and the contract to play with the Browns – if he made the team.

Frank could hardly wait till tomorrow at 3 p.m. He made sure he was early. And when he walked into the Frederick Hotel on Fourth Avenue, Brickles was waiting for him in the lobby.

They shook hands. Brickles discussed the deal. It was a $500 signing bonus – now – and a contract for $2500 annually, if Frank made the team. The tryouts would be held at Bowling Green College in Bowling Green, Ohio, and 66 players were invited. The first Cleveland Browns team roster would be a total of 33 players.

All 66 players were to receive the $500 signing bonus – but who would make the team – and get the big bucks – the $2500 annual salary? Frank knew he would be one of them. The forces would see to it.

Graduation Day

On a spring day in May of 1946, the lines were long at the entrance of the Keith Albee Theatre in downtown Huntington. There was no movie or touring show playing this morning, but the story unfolding inside was as good as anything Hollywood or Broadway could dream up.

Frank Gatski – a twenty-five-year-old senior would walk across the historic stage and get his degree from Marshall College. It was the epilogue of several incredible chapters: nothing more than a substitute center in high school; two years in the coal mines; discovered and whisked off to Marshall College as a nineteen-year-old freshman; two years of war; a year at Auburn University; the improbable meeting with Johnny Brickles that led him to a tryout with the Cleveland Browns; and the final chapter, a return to Marshall College – and this day – Graduation.

The historic stage of this grand palace, called "one of America's greatest theatres" had hosted entertainers from across the country and Hollywood's finest films – and now it was presenting one of its most extraordinary events – the graduation of Frank Gatski.

His brother, Benny, was there. God, he wished his parents could have been alive to celebrate this day. Frank closed his eyes as he felt a shiver of reflection and shook his head at the improbability of the day. As he sat there with several hundred other gowned graduates, he thought of his parents. He knew they would be proud that he graduated from college. It wasn't supposed to happen. How many boys work in the mines for two years after high school and end up with a college degree? He wiped a tear from his eye. He didn't want anyone to see the tough football player cry.

Talking About a Baby

When Sam walked into the house he was surprised to see his oldest sister, Martha, there. After all, she was an "old married woman" now.

She quit school at sixteen and married Tom Martin a few months before. She had her own home, so what was she doing here. She was talking with her mother, as if something important was happening. Mickey and her mother didn't notice Sam. They were too busy talking. Then Mickey came from the kitchen with a cup of coffee and joined in the excited conversation. Mickey still had her cheerleading uniform on from school. Sam thought that was unusual. Mickey usually changed clothes immediately. But not this day. Something was up!

Mickey noticed Sam and turned to Martha and her mother. The loud conversation was turned down like a volume control on a radio into a murmuring whisper. Sam walked over to investigate.

"What's the matter?" he asked. "What are you whispering about?"

"We're not whispering," Mickey said. Martha and her mother kept talking as if no one else was around.

Then Sam heard his name.

"...Sam," Martha said. She had finished a sentence with "Sam" but Sam didn't hear the first part. He kept quiet for a moment and listened.

"Should we tell Sam?" Martha whispered in a voice loud enough for him hear.

"Tell me what?" he said with some frustration. "Tell me what?"

"Oh, go ahead," his mother said.

"Tell me what…"

Martha and Mickey spoke together, "Mom's gonna have a baby."

At first it didn't register. He was expecting to hear, "we got a new car" or "we got a puppy", but…a baby!? Heck, Sam thought, "I'm the baby." I've always been the baby brother – for twelve years! He heard a mumbling sound in his head. He looked at Mickey. She was talking to him.

"So what do you think of that? Now that you won't be the baby around here."

"Yeh," Sam thought. "That would be good. Will it be a boy or a girl?" he asked.

"Don't know," Mom replied.

"Which one does Dad want?"

Katherine reached down and patted Sam's head. "He don't know it, yet."

Now, that dumb-founded Sam. "Well ain't he supposed to…? How come he don't…?"

Sam had realized the conversation had gone far beyond his capacity to understand. So he got back to the basics. "When do you find out if it's a boy or a girl?"

"Well, Sam," Katherine said, "when it's born. Then we'll know."

Sam watched his mother's pregnancy with wonder. He would shake his head in disbelief sometimes. He had always been the little guy – youngest in the house. He was always being told what to do and he never had any say in how things were to be done. Now there was gonna be this little boy or girl to be taken care of.

Professional Football?

It seemed like the end of World War II transformed everything. It even got to the popular bar in downtown Farmington. Ben Bennett decided to make major changes to his place. He rearranged it, built a beautiful circle bar, and transformed the Leisure R Inn into Ben's Circle Bar. At night a new neon sign over the front door buzzed the change for everyone to see.

But that was nothing! The real buzz was inside where everyone was talking about Frank Gatski getting a tryout to play professional football!

Ben Bennett reached in the cooler for a beer. "I heard he got $500 just to sign for a tryout. Then if he makes the team, he'll get $2500 for the season. That's big money – and just think, for playing a game of football. Man, I'm so proud of that kid. Well, he ain't no kid…"

Ben opened the beer and sat it in front of Joe Smith, a miner who had just come from work. Joe took a drink of Iron City. "Damn right. That's a year's wages working for Jamison. But God bless him. I'm happy for him."

Joe lifted the bottle and took a long drink. "Who's he playing for?"

"Some team in Cleveland," Ben replied, "called the Browns. Now that's a hell of a name for a football team – the Cleveland Browns, ain't it?" Ben explained further, "It's a team in a new league. Lots of players returning from the war. Hope it lasts for Frank's sake."

"Yeh, me too," Joe said as he finished his beer. As he turned to leave, other miners began coming in. Just like Joe, they would stop by on their way home for a beer to quench their thirst and to bullshit with their buddies, away from the noise and dirt of their work.

"Ya heard about Frank Gatski?" Ben asked, happy to be the bearer of good news.

"What about him?" was the reply. "Something wrong?"

"No, he's getting a tryout with…" just like the best public relations man Ben repeated the information to everyone who came in.

And so in a short time, the Circle Bar was filled with miners and Frank's buddies telling stories of Frank and of Frank's brothers and dad – everyone happy to make a connection with the local guy who was going to be a professional football player – maybe.

When Ben went to work on the night shift, he carried the same story there to everyone – so by the time the shift change again, it had become the big news in the No. 9 camp and in Farmington, too.

Not everyone in No. 9 or Farmington accepted the fact that Frank would make it with football. It was still hard for some to believe that the tall skinny kid, who hardly played much high school football, could be that good. Sure, he had gone to Marshall College and Auburn – but to be good enough to be a pro.? – hard to believe. And they expected to see Frank at the mines – or drinking his $500 bonus away at the Circle Bar anytime soon.

Oral Huff took the news about Frank home with him and found a very interested listener in his son.

"You mean they are going to pay Frank to play football?" Sam asked his dad.

"If he makes the team?"

"Oh, he'll make it."

"Can't be sure, son."

Sam was sure. "You don't know Frank!"

Oral wasn't convinced. "This is just for a tryout. That means they just try out. Ain't nobody around here that good – to play in the professional leagues."

Katherine Huff came through the door with a bucket of water from the outdoor well and lifted it to the stove. The flame rose up the bucket and made it hiss and crackle at the heat. Oral began taking off his dirty clothes beside the large wooden tub – already steamy with hot water.

"Did you hear, Mom?" Sam said. "Frank Gatski's going to be a professional football player."

"Now son," Oral said curtly. "I told you he's just trying out. Most likely he won't make it! I told him he shoulda stayed in the mines. He could be a foreman someday."

"But the boy went to college," Katherine said. "I thought he was going to be a coach. At least he'd have that to go back on."

"Get that hot water, Katherine. Let's get this dirt off."

"Be patient, Oral. It ain't hot enough yet."

Sam was still trying to make his case for Frank. "When will we know how Frank did?"

Oral was getting impatient. "I don't know, Sam. If it happens, I'm sure we'll hear about it."

Sam disappeared into his room and returned with a football and headed out the door

"Where you going, Robert Lee?" Katherine asked.

Sam stopped at the door. "Going to see Leo and play some football. Leo's got to know about Frank."

Oral shouted, "Damn it, Sam, he's just trying out."

Sam didn't want to hear it. He was out the door and on his way to Leo's house with the good news!

In no time Sam was knocking at Leo's door. Leo came out on the porch and Sam gave him all the details about how Frank was going to play professional football "…and get paid for it…" and how they better start practicing so they could do the same thing someday.

Leo thought it would be a good idea, too – but then he would do whatever his buddy, Sam, wanted. They ran through the camp like pied pipers, leading kids from their homes to the No. 9 playground. Before long, the game was on and Sam was being Frank Gatski.

Bowling Green

Frank looked at the check for eighteen dollars. It was from the Cleveland Browns for the bus fare to Bowling Green, Ohio, where the tryout camp was held.

He knew he could make better use of that money. He was short on cash, and he had hitchhiked everywhere, so why not to Bowling Green. He laughed to himself about the miles he had logged on his thumb: to Louisville, Kentucky five years before, in 1941, to see the Kentucky Derby, where Eddy Arcaro rode Whirlaway to victory; to Pittsburgh, about 100 miles away, to see the Steelers play; and regularly back and forth to college at Huntington, a 200 mile trip – one way; and shorter trips all around northern West Virginia. Hell, he could make it on his thumb to Bowling Green, and sock the eighteen dollars in his pocket.

That Army duffle bag came in handy. It went with him to Huntington. It went with him to Auburn. Now it was going to football camp in Bowling Green, Ohio.

Frank pulled the strings tight and threw it over his shoulder as he walked along U.S. Route 60, just outside of Huntington. In no time he was in a farm truck heading west and watching the West Virginia farm fields go by.

Frank thought about how that duffel bag was carrying everything important he owned – everything he would need was in that bag. He would get along because he didn't need much – not now. Now he was only interested in making a football team. Looking at the duffel bag gave him a great sense of independence and freedom. He didn't have to be anywhere. He had no home now. His parents were both gone. He was strong and healthy. He could go back to the mines. He would finish school pretty soon, so he could coach. He had this great opportunity to play professional football. He had no relationship with a girl – he had dated some, but now he didn't have to answer to anyone. It was the ultimate freedom with only good things ahead. He had a chance to play a game for pay, eighteen dollars in his pocket and a duffel bag of belongings – and on top of the world.

The truck driver was impressed enough with someone trying out for a professional football team that he drove Frank directly to the Bowling Green campus.

Sixty-six players, all of who had been promised a $500 signing bonus had been invited to Bowling Green. There was to be nine weeks of camp, with exhibition games against other football teams in the new league, the Brooklyn Dodgers, New York Yankees, Buffalo Bills, Baltimore Colts, and Miami Seahawks.

While at Bowling Green, the players were housed at the Alpha Mu Sorority house, which was chosen for its proximity to the practice field. The sorority agreed to rent it to the Browns for the extra income. The house was great digs for Frank, who was now living out of his duffle bag.

At the first team meeting in the cafeteria of Bowling Green, Coach Paul Brown introduced himself and the assistant coaches and all of the players. Some didn't need an introduction. Players like Otto Graham, the All-American quarterback from Northwestern and Dippy Evans, the halfback from Notre Dame – were already well-known names. Some black players were in camp, including Bill Willis, an All-American tackle from Ohio State and Marion Motley, a big fullback from little Nevada University. Willis was well-known. Motley wasn't, except by Paul Brown, who remembered him from the fullback's days at McKinley High School in Canton when he battered Brown's Massillon line unmercifully.

Frank had never played with black players back home in West Virginia. The black students attended their own schools. In Fairmont, Dunbar, with an enrollment of a couple hundred black students participated against other black schools from around the state. The Dunbar Tigers produced outstanding athletes no doubt, but little attention was given to their teams by the general public.

The newspaper gave them token coverage of games played at East-West Stadium, where, at most, a few hundred black fans would be seated in the stadium made for six thousand.

If some players at the Bowling Green camp had a problem playing with black players, they would have to get use to it. Motley and Willis were both highly regarded by Paul Brown and were considered good bets to make the team. Brown wanted to win! The fact that Willis and Motley would be the first black players to sign a professional football contract didn't bother him.

As the camp progressed, the number of players there decreased every day. If a player came up missing, it was the one Coach Brown had called into his office and asked for his playbook. His "pro career" was over. Everyone feared his name would be called – to go see Coach Brown.

Frank wasn't going to get that call. Nobody out-worked him, out-hit him, or out-hustled him. Just as he had done every step along his improbable journey to Bowling Green, he was going to be the most determined, son-of-a-bitch out there. He would not come out second best.

As camp went on, Frank was getting more attention at defensive linebacker. Even though he wanted to play center too, a player named Mike Scary was a little ahead of Frank. Scary had distinguished himself with the NFL Champion Cleveland Rams and chose not to move to Los Angeles with the team that became the Los Angeles Rams, but to stay in Cleveland and join the Browns in the new All-American Conference.

In spite of Scary's credentials, Frank impressed Coach Brown and his quarterback, Otto Graham. Graham talked about Frank's long legs and high spread. It gave Graham the opportunity to stand up taller, taking the snap from the T-Formation. It gave him better visibility, as well as the advantage of already being in the upright position when he would retreat with the ball to either hand off or pass.

Brown and Graham also were impressed with Frank's footwork and strength. There may not have been anyone stronger in camp – and his 6 foot 3 height gave him leverage against tall, rushing lineman. However, if Frank was going to be a center with the Browns – it wasn't going to be this year.

Trying to make the best use of his thirty-three player roster, Brown felt that Scary would play center with Frank at linebacker. Scary didn't know it, but soon Frank Gatski was going to have his job.

Like Frank Gatski

The 1946 school year started – and that meant the start of a new football season.

Around No. 9, football season was a big deal. Everyone was interested in the Farmington Farmers and how they would fare against the other teams in the county. And everyone cheered for the West Virginia University Mountaineers, just 30 miles away. Their games on radio on a Saturday afternoon could be heard throughout the camp. In fact, anyone walking through the camp didn't need a radio: the game was in the air.

And now there was another team to cheer for in No. 9 - the Cleveland Browns – you know, where Frank Gatski played.

The newspaper carried a picture of the local boy who had signed with the new pro league. Twelve-year-old Sam Huff heard about the picture and he wanted it. The Huff's didn't get a paper, not many people around the camp did. But he went door-to-door until he found a neighbor who would be glad to give him their paper – after they finished reading it.

On the next day, Sam knocked on their neighbor's screen door and was given the prize, which he took home. He went into his room and shut the door and sat on the bed. He opened the newspaper quickly to the sports section and there it was – Frank Gatski in a white uniform with stripes on the sleeve bent over in the center position getting ready to snap the ball and with a menacing, maybe hateful, football look on his face under the football helmet.

Sam laid the newspaper on the bed, and scooted to the floor. He looked at the picture to try to be Frank Gatski as much as possible.

He stood up to adjust the mirror on his dresser so he could see himself. He picked up his football, got back down on the floor and checking out the picture, assumed the position of Frank Gatski, sneer and all.

The familiar sound of the screen door opening and closing broke through the daydreaming. His mother was going to the pump to fill the bucket from the outside well for Oral's bath. He would be on his way home from work.

Sam carefully folded the page of the newspaper with Frank's picture on it, and put it in his dresser drawer. Then he rolled up the rest of the paper and took it to the garbage can on the porch.

His mother was coming up the steps with one more bucket of water. Sam opened the door for her. She went by him and lifted it to the stove to be heated.

She returned to the porch and stood beside Sam. They watched as the afternoon shift at No. 9 began heading to their homes. Katherine placed her hand on Sam's shoulder. Sam stared in wonder at the huge tipple and mine portal like the giant gray monster that released it workers who then walked a dozen different paths to small homes – and then disappeared into them to stay there, eat and sleep until tomorrow morning, when they would return to it again.

"We have to know how hard these men work to provide for their families," she said.

Sam looked up, "I know it, Mom. But, I don't think I ever want to work there, Mom."

"But your dad was thinking you might be interested in doing some odd jobs at the mine – on the outside – maybe next year,"

Katherine waited to hear her son's reply. He remained silent.

"Well, what are you going to do – for work, I mean?"

"Well, I thought I'd like to be a professional football player – you know, like Frank Gatski."

His mother tried not to laugh. "Oh Robert Lee Huff, that ain't real. That won't happen. That's not work. You can't count on anything like that." She leaned down to him. "Frank was… very lucky. Nobody else will ever do that around here. You know that, don't you?" Katherine looked toward the tipple.

"Here comes your dad, don't mention anything about being a football player, ya hear?"

80

Oral, who was walking along with some fellow workers said goodbye to them and turned into his yard. He stopped at the foot of the steps. "Waiting for me?" he asked

"Just looking," Katherine replied with a smile. "Got your bath ready."

Oral walked up the steps slowly and didn't say another word.

To the Big School Building

In 1946, America was on top of the world. We had beaten the Germans and the Japs. The peacetime economy with its rebuilding and its new priorities was exciting. Everyone was working. New products were being developed. The G.I.'s had all come home, and were starting new jobs or going back to college under the G.I. bill. It made college classrooms, and even some high school classrooms a mixture of youth and hardened war veterans.

The rosters of college football teams and professional teams included guys, many of whom had been through the worst torture and hell at the hands of the Japs and Germans in foreign lands, now putting on another uniform to play a game.

One of these guys, Frank Gatski, was even playing professional football with the Cleveland Browns. Just a little more than a year before, he was in the Auburn University locker room thinking he had played football for the last time. Now he was playing again – and getting paid for it!

At the same time, in No. 9, two twelve-year-olds, Sam Huff and Leo Coceano and their friends in James Fork Elementary's sixth grade were contemplating the great change in their own lives. This was big! They were moving on to the seventh grade and Farmington Junior High School. That meant changing schools from little James Fork Elementary, a four room, one-story building – to Farmington High School, the great big red brick three-story building in Farmington, two miles away.

The Farmington High School building housed all the grades, seven through twelve, so going to the big school meant going to school with the older kids – bus rides to and from the school, changing classes every hour, and lockers with combination locks... WOW! Sam and Leo were growing up.

The High School was situated on a hill just a minute walk from the center of town. Down below, on the flat between the two embankments was the football field, where Frank Gatski played ten years before.

In late August of 1946, the Huff kids were getting ready for school – or at least three of them were. Martha Jane, the oldest, who was eighteen, had already quit school the year before. It wasn't unusual for kids who turned sixteen to stop going to school so they would start working to help out the family or get married and begin raising a family of their own.

The law required school attendance until sixteen years of age, so it was rather expected that each Huff kid would follow Martha Jane's lead and drop off the school rolls when they became sixteen.

Martha Jane did, and now Donald, who was turning sixteen soon, was prepared to quit school and follow his father into the mines. His mother objected, but she was losing the argument. Mildred, who everybody called Mickey, would soon be fifteen. She was one of the two cheerleaders at Farmington High School, but it still was a foregone conclusion that at age sixteen, she would quit also.

Her friend and the other cheerleader, Ruth Mary Conaway, kept trying to talk her out of quitting – but she, too, was losing the argument.

Sam, at this point, was only thinking of playing ball and having fun. Quitting school was the farthest thing from his mind.

The Huff family went to the big city of Fairmont about once a year.

Even though the kids wore hand-me-downs and clothes that Katherine or the girls would make, a trip to Fairmont, just nine miles away, was necessary to get shoes and articles of clothing nearly impossible to make – like coats, pants and hats.

Fairmont, with a population of 25,000, had everything! It was OZ to the Huff kids. There was Hartley's, the five-story department store that sold everything from bedroom suits to refrigerators and pots and pans and clothing for the entire family; Jones, the three-story smart store that catered to the more affluent residents with the latest fashions and cosmetics; and Golden Brothers who specialized in clothing for young and old at a Huff-like price.

83

There were dozens of stores - big stores and small shops that made Fairmont the center of retail shopping in the northern part of West Virginia. Everybody around came to shop in Fairmont.

Fairmont also had McCrory's Five and Dime and Murphy's Five and Dime – and that was as far as the Huff's got. But that was okay. It was plenty good enough for Donald, Mildred, and Sam.

Sam, though, regardless of where they went to shop, had one wish regarding clothing for school. "Please, Mom," he begged. "No bib overalls," Sam had enough. It seemed to him that he had spent his whole young life – all thirteen years of it, in bib overalls and a t-shirt.

And now – especially now that he was going to be in the seventh grade at Farmington High School, he sure didn't want to be seen in bib overalls.

Most kids who knew there was another style of pants, didn't like them either. The straps that went around your shoulders and kept the pants on and up – made going to the bathroom really difficult. You just didn't unbuckle a belt and drop your pants. No, you had to undo both straps – and there were times when Sam's timing was off enough that accidents would occur.

It wasn't just the function that bothered Sam, but the form as well. Those bib overalls were definitely old-fashioned and a source of laughter. Most young boys now were wearing blue jeans kept on with a belt around the waist. Bib overalls definitely was an outfit for comedy. In the movies, character like Pat Bultram, Gene Autry's sidekick, wore bib overalls. Gene Autry didn't. Roy Rogers didn't. What they wore was closer to blue jeans.

Gene and Roy had a swagger, you could never get in bib overalls. And these guys always got the girl. No bib overalls.

Along with bib overalls, Sam had usually worn a white t-shirt. His mother gave him his wish and returned from the shopping trip in Fairmont with two pairs of blue jeans, a belt, some new t-shirts, and a new pair of brown shoes.

Sam gave his mother a big hug for releasing him from the bib overalls. And in one quick moment he had blue jeans with his first belt, which he quickly looped around himself. He put on the brown shoes and stood up.

84

The blue jeans were too long and a little big around the waist – but that was planned. They would last a couple of years, while Sam grew into them. Sam sat down to roll up the legs just so they would touch the top of his shoes. That was the way everyone wore them.

Sam went to the mirror. He liked what he saw – new t-shirt, blue jeans, and shoes. Now he was ready. He was leaving James Fork Elementary and heading for the seventh grade at Farmington High.

In the haze of a September morning, Sam and Leo stood together as the big yellow bus turned the bend and slowed to a stop. Sam's heart beat faster. He had never been on a bus before.

Katherine Huff and Maria Coceano stood behind their boys ready to relinquish them to the seventh grade of Farmington High School. The boys both turned to their mothers for a last look

The big door swung open, Sam looked up at the bus driver who shouted, "Step up, boys. My name is George."

It was a big step, both literally and figuratively. They both made it and quickly found a seat together. Young strangers gave them a quick look and some young friends spoke their names, glad to share in this exciting and scary experience of the first day of seventh grade.

As the bus pulled away, Sam and Leo looked out the window to wave goodbye to their moms, who now seemed small in the distance. As the bus continued out of sight of home, Sam and Leo turned to face the road ahead, two miles to Farmington.

The first day of school at Farmington High School was an experience for Sam and Leo.

While being the big deals at James Fork Elementary, suddenly they seemed liked minnows in this big pool. Four hundred kids were here for grades seven through twelve.

Sam and Leo were puny seventh graders on the first floor of the three-story building. All the excitement was happening upstairs. And even on this first day – everyone talked about the first football game. That was happening now! The Farmington Farmers were going to open the season on Friday against East Fairmont High School.

An announcement was made in all of the classrooms that the thuse for the big game would be held in the auditorium at 2 p.m. Everyone would attend.

At 2 p.m, as the seventh grade paraded to the auditorium, Sam could hear the noise from the inside growing louder as his group approached the door. The teacher opened the door and the loud band music jolted them. They quickly got to their seats and sat down. It was Sam's first visit to the auditorium at Farmington High, which served dual purposes for plays and band concerts, and assemblies; as well as a basketball court for the Farmers Junior High and High School basketball games.

As Sam took his seat, he looked up to see the cheerleaders and behind them Coach Kelly and the players in their red jerseys.

After the cheerleaders and the school spelled out FARMERS, and after the band played the school song – to the tune of the West Virginia University fight song – Coach Ray Kelly stepped forward to introduce players and the starting eleven who would carry the good name of Farmington High School into battle against the East Fairmont Bees.

Coach Kelly also took the occasion to announce that the 1946 football season would be the first for a new conference the Farmers would play in – the Mason-Dixon Conference. It would include the county's five Class B schools, Farmington, Fairview, Monongah, Rivesville, and Barrackville, along with Clay-Battelle, in adjacent Monongalia County.

He closed his remarks with a promise, "We plan to be Mason-Dixon Conference Champs!"

On the bus ride home, Sam felt a sense of pride – he was finally in the high school. Okay, so it was only the seventh grade – but he had already experienced the big stuff, a football thuse in the auditorium with seniors – in the

86

same place with his brother, Donald, who was in the tenth grade and his sister, Mickey, who was one of the cheerleaders.

Not too long after school started Donald turned sixteen. Early in the morning, Sam was awakened by loud noises. It was voices shouting in the kitchen. He got out of bed and opened the door just wide enough to see. There were his father and mother and Donald arguing.

"The boy is sixteen," Oral shouted. "He can do what he wants."

"I want him to stay in school," Katherine said.

"I don't like school," Donald said. "Never did."

Katherine ignored him. "Are we going to raise a bunch of children who don't get an education?"

Oral didn't budge. "Don't matter. He can make more money in the mines than all the 'so called' educated kids make."

"And maybe get killed!"

"Aw, nothings going to happen…" Donald shot back. "And besides, I can help out with paying for things…"

The argument went on. Sam closed the door to his room quietly. In a few minutes he heard the outside door open and close and muffled voices outside. Oral Huff and his oldest son were going to work.

Sam opened the door to see his mother sitting in the kitchen chair alone. He went to her. She embraced him.

"I like school," he said.

Brown's First Game

Two days before the season started on September 6, 1946, the Cleveland Browns first football team was finalized with a thirty-three player roster that include linebacker Frank Gatski.

Municipal Stadium, home of the Browns, was built in 1931, and was one of the largest stadiums in America, seating 74,000. For the Cleveland Browns first games the ticket prices were $3; bleacher seats would sell for 25 cents.

The year before, in 1945, the Cleveland Rams of the NFL, filled the place and won the NFL title before their move to Los Angeles to become the Los Angeles Rams.

Frank sat on the bench in the locker room staring at the ceiling with his head rested against the wall. He and the rest of the Browns waited mostly in silence for Paul Brown to enter the room and send them out for the first game ever – an exhibition game against the Miami Seahawks.

Frank tried to keep his mind on the game. He went over his assignment as linebacker.

Since it was the first game in this brand new American Football Conference, nobody knew what to expect from the opponent. Neither the Browns nor the Seahawks had ever existed before, so there were no scouting reports; however, teams were familiar with the personnel of the teams.

While the Browns were a team of excellent players – a mix of All-American college players, hand-picked by an acknowledged coaching genius, the Seahawks were a ragtag group of mostly journeymen at the end of their careers. Typical was Albert Wuktis, a guard, center and linebacker, who played with the "Steagles"; the temporary war-time merger of the Pittsburgh Steelers and Philadelphia Eagles and also "Card-Pitt," the temporary merger of the

Chicago Cardinals and the Pittsburgh Steelers. Another was Harry Hoop, a fullback with the Detroit Lions 1941-43, and Buffalo Bisons 1946.

The Seahawks roster was filled with such players. One of the reasons for the deficiency was money – or the lack of it. Seahawks owner, Harvey Hester, was substantially less wealthy than the other owners and the only one who was not a millionaire. Paul Brown commented that Hester was out of his league among the other owners to the point that he wasn't comfortable playing poker with them.

It was about fifteen minutes before kickoff. The noise of the crowd outside the stadium grew louder as the fans continued to file in. Frank struggled to keep from getting emotional. Here he was sitting with Otto Graham, Lou Groza, Bob Willis...and others. His journey to this moment was unlike any of the others. The war had carved an indirect path for almost every player there, but nevertheless, the Gatski story – from No. 9 to Municipal Stadium was the most rare and most compelling.

Assistant coaches, Johnny Brickles and Blanton Collier walked around giving words of encouragement and smiling, trying to lighten the load of players who they were counting on to make the team – and make the conference a success.

Brickles approached Frank and slapped him on the shoulder pads. That didn't do anything to help Frank maintain his concentration on the game. Immediately Frank thought of the time he met Brickles at the State basketball tournament at the West Virginia University fieldhouse a year before – when Brickles told him how the new team called the Cleveland Browns was looking for players.

"Forget all that shit," Frank thought. "Think about the game and the Miami Seahawks." His mind was on overdrive. "What if Mike Scary gets hurt? I'm the substitute center...Keep your head up...Protect Otto on the screen pass...Play number 48...I've got to pull and lead interference...They don't ask centers to do that...But Paul Brown does...I'll be starting linebacker...Watch for the opportunity to fill the gap...Key on the halfback – that's my responsibility..."

Suddenly there was the scraping of cleats on concrete – players shifted their attention to the hawkish, angular face coming through the door. It was Coach Paul Brown, slender and agile ... the hat, the trench coat always in motion over a smart sport coat and pressed pants. His presence demanded attention and respect. He looked like a businessman, not a coach. He was both.

The players stood and encircled him. Brown, confident, but calm, paced slowly with his right hand on his hip and spoke slowly, "Men, this is the beginning. We've assembled thirty-three of the best football players around to make up this team. You have to be proud of that. You're making history today as you play the first game of this franchise. Let's make sure we feel this same pride after the game. Let's go."

Frank picked up his helmet and began walking with his teammates to the tunnel leading to the playing field. The sound of the crowd appeared to grow louder as the players neared the entrance to the field. Louder. Louder. Frank was in a place where he had never been before. He never heard a crowd like this – the sound of 70,000 fans even in the confines of the tunnel pressed down on him. Now he could see the field up ahead at the entrance. The noise grew louder as the players stepped from the tunnel and in view of the crowd. Louder. Then the noise became a roar. Players in front started running out on the field. Frank's head was spinning. He kept thinking, "How in the hell did I get here?" The noise became deafening. Suddenly, he was on the field, running beneath the goal posts and crossing the chalk lines with thirty-two other players, all clad in white with brown trim.

The Movietone News

The word went forth – throughout No. 9 – that the Farmington Theatre had a Movietone news segment showing football.

"How long was it?" Sam asked.

"Maybe a minute."

"Who was playing?"

"I don't know – Notre Dame and somebody, I think."

But it didn't matter. To see football on a big movie screen - well, for a minute, it was like being there. Nobody got a chance to <u>see</u> football, but everyone <u>heard</u> it on the radio on Saturday, when the West Virginia University Mountaineers played and on Sunday when the Pittsburgh Steelers played.

Morgantown, home of the Mountaineers, was just thirty miles away from No. 9 and Pittsburgh was just ninety miles away. These were the teams everyone followed. Of course there was Notre Dame.

In No. 9 and Farmington, the Catholic School had a strong following among the immigrant and Catholic population in the coal camp.

More often than not, the football team featured in the Movietone News was Notre Dame because of their strong national following. It seems they were always playing a big game – and of course, they always won. Young football players and Notre Dame fans made sure they were at the movies when the Fighting Irish were on the big screen.

A new invention, television, hadn't made it to Farmington, yet – but Mannington, about ten miles away, had one. Pete Hoffman, who owned an appliance store, had a small set. The picture was usually snowy, but people watched anyway. And there was a tavern in Metz, about twenty miles from No. 9, that had a set. And because of its location at a high elevation, the tavern owner was able to install an antennae that brought in good reception. When Notre Dame played, the tavern was usually full.

The game of the century, Notre Dame versus Army was set for November 9 in Yankee Stadium. Every football fan in the country was interested in this one.

Notre Dame had all those returning war veterans – Johnny Lujack, George Conners, Jim Martin and so many more. Some were calling it the greatest team ever. Notre Dame was undefeated and had beaten Illinois, Pitt, Purdue, Iowa and Navy.

Army had Doc Blanchard, and Glenn Davis – the touchdown twins, and a record of 7-0 with wins over Villanova, Oklahoma, Cornell, Michigan, Columbia, Duke and West Virginia.

Army had beaten Notre Dame the two previous seasons 48-0 in 1944 and 59-0 in 1945. That was when Notre Dame's best players were in the service. Now they were back on the football field and wanted revenge.

In No. 9, everybody tuned in. Every kid had a football board game of some kind with a cardboard football field. So it allowed anyone who was listening to the radio to actually position the location of the ball with each play and follow the action up and down the field.

Leo Coceano and his Catholic and immigrant family lived and died with Notre Dame.

Sam Huff was a Mountaineer through and through – and didn't care who won the Army-Notre Dame game. No one did. The final score was 0-0. On that day, West Virginia beat Fordham 39-0.

92

Seventh Grade Figures

The 1946-47 school year at Farmington had begun – and the contest was on!

Mrs. Smith, the math teacher, stood at the blackboard writing down a series of two digit numbers. She positioned her body carefully in front of the numbers so that the class couldn't see them.

Three members of her seventh grade were poised with pencils and paper ready. The contest for "rapid addition" had eliminated all of the class, but three.

"Three boys!" Mrs. Smith said. "Now that is unusual. You girls are going to have to try harder." Murvyn McDowell, the class brain, was one; Leo Coceano and his buddy, Sam were the other two.

As Mrs. Smith continued writing the numbers down, the chalk made a tapping and then a screeching sound on the blackboard. It made Sam shiver and even more nervous.

Murvyn, Leo and Sam all had their eyes on the blackboard and their fingers ready to pull the trigger on their pencils.

"Are you ready?" Mrs. Smith challenged.

Sam could feel his finger press hard into his pencil.

"Ready… Set… Go!"

Mrs. Smith stood aside quickly. There were the numbers!

Leo pointed his pencil at them and whispered the answers as he rapidly moved down the column. The whole class could hear him.

"Five, thirteen, twenty-seven…"

Murvyn squinted through his glasses as he sucked in the answers to his brain. Sam fidgeted with both hands as he tried to catch up.

He noticed out of the corner of his eye, Leo writing down the result of one column. Then Murvyn did, too. "Oh shit," he thought. "I'm behind." He finally got the first column. Now he started on the second one.

"One hundred fifty-eight," shouted Murvyn.

"Correct!" Mrs. Smith said…

"One hundred fifty-eight," shouted Leo. He looked up to see the contest was over. "Who won?" he asked.

"Murvyn won, Leo." Then she turned to Sam. "Is that what you got, Sam?"

"Yes, ma'am, but I got it too late, didn't I?"

The class laughed and Mrs. Smith smiled. "Yes, a little too late, but it was still a good contest. Better luck next time."

"There would be a next time," Sam said to himself. He had to be the best – or die trying. There was just no way Sam was willing to accept to fact that Leo or Murvyn could beat him at anything.

Where did this come from? Nobody in his family was that competitive – at least as far as school was concerned. Was it growing up in No. 9 in a leadership role with his young peers? On the playground, Sam was the best player there was – whatever ball was being used. He was the one that kept reminding Leo to speak English – and helping him with it. Now, was he going to let Leo pull ahead of him in math? No way!

Murvyn was another matter. He was smart! But he was no great ballplayer either – so that was alright.

Whether it was football or baseball on the No. 9 hillside playground, Sam was one of the boys choosing sides. The other was usually Leo, who, in spite of the language barrier, was respected for his tenacity and his innate athletic ability … and for being Sam's buddy.

Sam had assumed the leadership role in No. 9. But Farmington Junior High School, just two miles down the road, was a different world.

The Farmington seventh grade had kids from all around - within a radius of ten miles – from in and around the town of Farmington and outside in coal camps and towns like Rachel, Ida May, Carolina, and No. 9. The kids

94

from the coal camps were pretty much like Sam and Leo – whose parents were coal miners.

The town of Farmington with a population of several hundred included children of coal miners, but also grocery store owners, pharmacists, and other merchants, as well. These kids dressed much better, and had advantages of schooling that could suddenly make a No. 9 kid feel inferior, but at the same time, fanned the flame that was a burning desire to be as good, if not better, than their friends. Some would flame out – and just quit. That's what the Huff kids did. Others would tend the flame; once in a while someone would kindle the flame into a roaring fire.

The girls were on one side of the gym. The boys were on the other side. That was the usual line-up for a dance at the gym for junior high kids at Farmington.

Crepe paper streamers hung from the baskets in a futile attempt to turn the gym-auditorium combination into a festive dance hall. But that was no use. Teachers and parent chaperones were seated along the back wall chatting with each other, waiting for the mingling to begin and the ice to break. The record player was turned up to full volume. Eddie Fisher singing *"Tell Me Why"* was echoing through the place, but no one was dancing.

Still there was an excitement – or was it fear – in the air. Sam Huff, Leo Coceano, Murvyn McDonald, Jimmy Wolfe, or any other boy there, had never danced with a girl. They had joked and talked and thought and dreamed about the things they would do with a girl, if they had a chance. But this was hands-on now – and just plain awful.

Some kids who wanted to be there, but did not want any part of dancing, had taken a seat in the auditorium, just off of the gym floor. They didn't have the courage to be up there, but they were happy to snicker and laugh at those who were. Teachers would come down into the auditorium seats to ask the kids to come up on the gym floor to be with the other kids, but they wanted no part of it.

A small stand where refreshments were served was set up along the wall near the center of the gym floor. Thank God for the refreshment stand. It offered a way to "do something" – to participate in a way – yet not have to face the opposite gender across the gym floor.

The loud hiss of the phonograph needle on the record told everyone that a new song was coming. Everyone quieted down to hear…"*The Old Lamplighter*."

"That's a good song," Sam thought. He liked Frank Sinatra. His sister played the radio a lot and "Frankie boy" seemed to be the most popular singer of the day and there was the Hit Parade every Saturday night, for which everyone gathered around the radio to hear the top 10 songs.

Sam could even remember the words of the song, "*He makes the night a little brighter…*"

A high pitch sound of giggling across the floor caught Sam's attention. He looked over to see a girl looking at him. At least he thought she was. He turned away. Then back around. She was still looking at him, or that's what it felt like. Then he recognized her. It was a girl he saw in school, but he didn't know her. He turned around to find the comfort of his buddies, Leo, Murvyn, and Jimmy, but when he looked across the floor again, she was still looking at him – or let's say she was looking in his direction. The others around her were talking but she didn't pay attention to them. Sam suddenly felt a little warmer – and nervous. Should he go ask her to dance.

The song played on – " …*the old lamplighter of long, long ago.*"

Sam fiddled with the few pennies in his pocket. He jumped as a voice interrupted his thinking. It was that broken English voice of his best friend. "What do you think we should do?" Leo asked.

Sam swallowed hard. "I don't know. There's that girl, Sally…looking over here. Maybe I should go ask her to dance."

"Yeh, what do you think?" Leo asked again.

"I don't know!" Sam was irritated at Leo asking a question for which he had no answer. The song was almost over… "*the old lamplighter of long, long ago.*" Sam took a deep breath. "Oh shit. I guess we'll have to wait

96

for the next song." He didn't have to wait long. "*I'd love to get you on a Slow Boat to China…*" He turned to Leo, but he wasn't there, Murvyn was standing there instead – not looking at Sam, but across the floor. Sam turned to look. He saw a familiar walk heading for the girls. "Oh hell," Sam thought. "It's Leo!"

"That damn Leo. He's got guts," Murvyn said.

"Yeh," Sam replied meekly. "Yeh, he sure does and he can't even ask in good English."

Sam and Murvyn watched as Leo made it to the giggling girls. Sam was hoping he wouldn't ask the girl he had his eye on. He waited. He looked at Murvyn, who just stared across the floor.

Finally a girl emerged from the group followed by Leo. It was Patty Rankin. Sam and Leo knew her from their bus rides back and forth to No. 9.

"Oh shoot," Sam thought.

Leo and Patty walked out to the foul circle painted on the floor. Leo clumsily took her hand and then the other hand… and the song ended, "*I'd love to get you on a Slow Boat to China, all to myself alone.*"

Sam and Murvyn and Jimmy Wolfe retreated to the darkness with relief that there would be a little more time before the challenge awaiting them when the next record started.

Leo felt foolish that he had finally progressed to a position with a girl on the gym floor – and now he had to wait. He looked down and twisted his foot on the floor.

Patty was ahead of most girls. She took advantage of the silence to take Leo's hands and teach him the basic box step. "One, two, three, four…one, two, three, four…"

Leo picked up the count with Patty as he followed in her footsteps. "One, two, three, four…one, two, three, four…"

The hiss and scratch of a record meant a song was coming. "This was it," Leo thought.

"*You must remember this, a kiss is just a kiss…*"

"Oh good," Patty said. "a slow song. Just follow me, Leo."

"One, two, three, four…" she said over the lyrics.

"One, two, three, four…" Leo repeated as the song played on.

"…*As time goes by..*"

Across the floor, Sam, Murvyn and Jimmy stared at their friend.

"Look," Sam said. "He's dancing."

"Yeh," Murvyn and Jimmy said in unison.

The three looked at each other, knowing that the next move was theirs. They had to follow Leo's lead now. He was definitely getting out of control and getting ahead.

Murvyn took out a handkerchief and wiped his glasses, stuffed the handkerchief in his back pocket, steadied his glasses on his face, and headed across the floor.

Sam looked at Jimmy knowing that it was their time. Before Sam could say a word, Jimmy hitched up his blue jeans, checked to see if his zipper was up and was gone – just a few steps behind Murvyn.

Sam felt the sweat in his hands. He wiped them on his blue jeans. He looked across the floor as Murvyn and Jimmy disappeared into the group of girls. He was hoping that neither one of them would ask the girl he had been looking at. If he had to dance, he thought it would be best if it were with her.

Sam, saw "his girl" step back as if to avoid the approach of Murvyn and Jimmy. "That's good," he thought. "She's waiting for me to ask her." Sure enough, there came Murvyn out on the floor with Jane Morgan. Jane wore glasses, too. Maybe that's why Murvyn asked her. And Jimmy came walking out with Ann Summers.

Leo had advanced past the counting out loud stage to doing the box step. It even looked like their bodies were touching. Murvyn and Jimmy were struggling as they looked down at their feet while moving more shoulders and arms than anything else.

Sam took a deep breath and… the song ended… "*the world will always welcome lovers … as time goes by.*"

"Oh shit," Sam said. "I waited too long." But that disappointment was mixed with the relief of a minute reprise before the next song came up. Leo,

Murvyn and Jimmy stayed on the floor waiting for the next song, too… and for Sam. Leo looked back at Sam and nodded a 'come ahead'. Sam shook his head in response. Yes, he was definitely on his way.

The record hissed and the Jo Stafford began singing …"*See the pyramids along the Nile.*"

The song filled the gym and got inside Sam. It was one of his favorite songs, so maybe that was a good luck sign. The girl he had his eye on was still there. He looked across the ninety feet of dance floor. It seemed so far, as he headed out. The steel taps on the heels of his shoes echoed with each footstep and made the music go silent. He could feel the eyes of the chaperones and teachers following his lonely walk. As he reached center court, there was Leo and Patty. Leo looked at him and nodded his approval. Four more steps and he passed Murvyn and Jane, and finally Jimmy and Ann.

Suddenly Sam felt good about himself. He had finally taken the big step – or more like about a hundred steps – across the gym floor to ask a girl to dance. He looked back at Leo. Leo was waiting for his buddy to join him on the dance floor…. "*I'll be so alone and lonely. Maybe you'll be lonely, too and blue...*"

"Better hurry," Sam thought. "The song is half over!" The Sally "somebody' Sam had his eye on was talking to another girl. They saw Sam coming closer. They stopped talking.

Finally Sam had made it, and now there was no turning back. He cleared his throat. He felt it hurt, like it always did. But he forgot about it immediately. He looked at her right in the chest and spoke, "would you like to dance?" Sam's eyes focused on the squares in her dress.

He waited.

She replied, "No!"

Then she giggled and turned toward her girlfriend.

Sam felt his face getting hot. He wanted to disappear. His embarrassment was mixed in with some relief that he wouldn't actually have to dance. But now he would have to get back on the boys side of the gym – and without a girl.

The song ended… *"Just remember when a dream appears you belong to me."*

Sam had turned around and was on his way back – that ninety feet looked like a mile. He could hear the steel tap of his shoes on the floor – every step seemed louder than the one before. And without a song playing, each step sounded like a hammer hitting steel. He tried to keep his taps from sounding out by walking on his toes, but he realized that looked stupid, and too much like how a girl would walk.

"Keep walking," he said to himself. His buddies were on the floor with their girls waiting for the next song. He passed Murvyn and Jane, then Jimmy and Ann and finally Leo and Patty.

Sam was at half court. He knew everyone in the building was looking at him as he returned from his failed mission. Clack, clack, clack. He was almost there. The gym floor foul line was a welcome sight. It meant he was almost off of the floor. Just a few more loud steps and he was there.

Finally…at last to the welcome darkness off of the basketball court.

He took a deep breath and said he would never do that again, no matter what. "I will never ask a girl to dance."

"Hey, what happened?" It was Murvyn, who had followed Sam
Jimmy had followed close behind, "Yeh, what's wrong?"
Sam didn't turn around. "Nothing… She don't want to dance, that's all."

"She's stupid," Murvyn declared.

"Real dumb," Jimmy agreed.

"I didn't want to dance anyway."

"It's dumb anyway, ain't it?"

"Hey, where's Leo?"

"He's still dancing," Murvyn said.

Sam looked, "He sure is!"

It was bound to happen. "The Cleveland Browns was on at the movies!'

100

"In the previews?"

"Yeh."

"How long?"

"About a minute."

"Could you see Frank Gatski?"

"I don't know, they didn't say his name. They showed the quarterback."

"What's his name?"

"Otto something. That's what I remember."

Sam couldn't wait to get home, beg his mom for a quarter, go get Leo and get back down to Farmington, somehow, to go to the movies.

How do two boys, twelve years old, get from No. 9 to Farmington, two miles away? You walk or hitch a ride.

The Farmington Theatre wasn't built as a theatre. It was a retail store converted into a theatre. Take a big room, add two hundred seats, a screen, a projector, turn the lights out – and it's a theatre!

It wasn't a fancy movie house in this golden age of movie palaces – just four walls – but when the lights went down, you could go any place and be anyone.

Sam's 25 cents got him in and a bag of popcorn. When the lights went down, Sam's eyes opened up because right away was the Movietone News – and here it came. First, there was the World Events – a hurricane in Florida, thirty seconds; the new country of Israel, twenty seconds; and the monkeys at the San Diego Zoo, twenty seconds. Then the music changed. The voice boomed out. The "Cleveland Browns Continue Their Winning Ways." The Cleveland Browns of the new American Football Conference prove they're the best of the league beating the Brooklyn Dodgers 35-10.

Otto Graham led the way with passes like this one to Dante Lavelli for a touchdown."

There was that familiar Movietone News music and –

The End.

That was it.

Sam took another bite of popcorn and leaned near to Leo.

"Did you see Frank?"

"No… but I betcha he was there."

"Yeh. I think I saw him."

The Three Stooges lit up the screen and everybody cheered.

Browns Win Championship!

The Cleveland Browns first year was a tremendous success. They breezed through the season, obviously the best team in the conference. They had won 12 games and lost 2 and defeated the New York Yankees 14-9 for the league championship title. Most games weren't even close: the Browns outscored opponents 423-137.

Toward the end of the 1946 season, with two games to go and a championship on the horizon, Frank Gatski made a big decision. He bought a car. It was a brand new 1946 Chevy – two doors. Frank's first car cost $800, about one third of his Cleveland Brown's salary for the entire 1946 season. The rest was spent renting an apartment and the usual living expenses. It didn't leave much room for extravagant living, but extravagance wasn't one of Frank's traits. No problem there. He had acclimated himself to a life without money. He never had it, so he never missed it. But the car was all he needed – and with it was a sense of pride and a symbol of achievement. He had wanted one for a long time – but there was no way he could afford it.

He thought back to when he arrived at the Brown's training camp to a nearly empty parking lot. Coach Brown and the assistants each had a car. So did the trainer and a couple of other members of the staff. But not one of the players owned a car. Not one. The car Otto Graham was driving belonged to his father.

Now thirty-three new automobiles were in the parking lot. Just like Frank, every player went out and bought a new car with his first check.

When the season was over, Frank headed home. This time he didn't have to take a bus or hitchhike. He was driving. But there wasn't any real home in No. 9 to go to. The only home he had ever known had been taken back by Jamison Coal and rented to another mining family. So the professional football player on top of the world, who didn't have a home, made one with his brother,

103

Benny and his family in Grant Town, another mining community just a couple of miles from No. 9.

Benny welcomed his brother. He was thrilled for his success. Frank became a local celebrity. There hadn't been a professional football player from the area for years. The last was Joe Stydahar, the outstanding tackle who played his college ball at West Virginia University and was a tremendous tackle for the Chicago Bears from 1936-1942, and after a three year hitch in the Army returned to the Bears for the 1945 and 1946 seasons. Joe grew up in Shinston, about ten miles from Farmington. Now Joe was a coach in the NFL with the Los Angeles Rams.

Frank could draw attention to himself without trying. The tall, muscular, ruggedly handsome guy would show up in Farmington at Manchins Store or the Circle Bar or a high school basketball game and everyone looked his way. In winter, when he wore the jacket with his team's name B-R-O-W-N-S across the back, the word spread quickly that Gatski was here.

Frank was flattered at the attention, but certainly not content with himself. Just one year of professional football wasn't enough. Now there was next year and that starting center position.

And there was life outside of football. After all, every professional football player had to supplement his football season income with an off-season job. The average pay of a couple thousand dollars wasn't good enough to keep even an unmarried guy for the entire year.

But Frank was feeling some satisfaction in knowing he had earned his bachelors degree in physical education at Marshall. Frank's desire was to coach high school football, but of course, that would be impossible, while playing professional football, since the seasons overlap. But the degree would be an advantage for an off-season job in public relations or as a salesman. Completing the degree was necessary for another reason – his mother would have wanted it.

Frank smiled at the thought of his mother. What would she say to him now if she were living. Something like, "Frank, you are twenty-five. Ain't it time to get married and raise a family, get a home, settle down. You ain't getting any younger. Please, Frank."

His mother was right in a way. Everybody Frank knew, who was twenty-five, was married and most had children, and had already established a home. He appreciated the generosity of his brother, Benny, to allow him to have an off-season home there, but he knew it had to be temporary. While at Marshall, he lived in the dorm - but that part of his life was over.

It was Christmas, 1946. The snow came down hard as Frank came through the door with a Christmas tree he had cut down in the nearby woods.

Blanche Gatski, Benny's wife, handed him the handmade wooden Christmas tree stand. Frank chipped away at the tree trunk and forced it into the stand and stood it in the corner. He stepped back and looked at it.

"Looks good," Blanche said. "Now you're not through. Here are the icicles. Held me put them on, one by one. They look better that way."

Frank took the icicles from her and began to decorate the tree... carefully – one by one, just as she had instructed.

He was glad he had some money left from his first year pay of $2500 and the $500 bonus check for the championship game. It would allow him to buy some pretty decent presents for Benny, Blanche, and their kids.

As he reflected on this time, he thought of his parents – both gone now – and how he wished they could be here to experience his successful year as a professional football player.

Through the icicles, he caught a glimpse of his Browns jacket over the chair. It still didn't seem real. Yeh. That jacket belonged to him – just one of only thirty-three players to have one. He felt so grateful, humble, acknowledging silently that it appeared he was guided throughout his life by some force – that had brought him to this point.

He picked up another handful of icicles and continued with the lower branches. Blanche came from the kitchen to check on Frank's progress with the tree. "Frank, that's a great job. Just like everything else you do."

""Oh sure," Frank said. "You didn't see the Miami game where I made a bad snap from center and we lost."

The Shingleton's Move In

Sam Huff couldn't have been happier - school was out for Christmas holidays. He hopped off the school bus, with Leo Coceano right behind him. They said goodbye and Sam turned to take the short walk to his house. Then he stopped. He felt the lunch box and books in a tight grip. What was this? Who were these kids sitting on the steps of his house?

He walked to the foot of the steps and stopped. "Who are <u>you</u>?"

The little girl, about seven years old, giggled and took a bite of her jelly sandwich.

The boy, an older brother, said "We're living here. Who are you?"

Sam blinked his eyes. He walked up the steps forcing the boy to step aside. He opened the door and... What the... there were...two more kids, about his same age. "What the heck was going on?" Then he heard voices in the next room. His mother came through the door with another woman, who looked a little like her.

"Sam, this is my sister, Myrtle, your aunt. Her kids are coming to stay with us for a while. They are your cousins, you know."

One question, 'who' was answered. But why were they here and most importantly..."where in the heck were they going to sleep?!"

The four room home was already overcrowded with three kids. Fortunately the fourth Huff kid, Martha, was married and gone; still add four more kids – that sounded impossible.

But they were there. Blame Okey Shingleton. Myrtle Hartsell married Okey Shingleton twelve years before. Okey was a talented cabinet maker and he could do anything with wood. He was a likable person, who loved to play the guitar and sing. But he also loved whiskey. Sooner or later it got the best of him – and he couldn't hold on to jobs. His work suffered and so did his income. In order to feed his family, he attempted to steal chickens from his neighbor.

Unfair as it seems, the theft of chickens landed him in the state penitentiary in Moundsville. Although Okey's support of the family was shakey, it had been better than nothing. But with no support at all, Myrtle turned, in desperation, to her sister, Katherine.

"It won't be a problem. We'll manage," Katherine assured her sister. The Huff children, Sam Mickey, and Donald all helped make the Shingletons welcome and doubled up in beds.

If the Shingleton's were dirt poor – and they were, the Huff's were rich in comparison. They had an income from both the father, Oral, and the son, Donald, who quit school in September, to start work. Their steady incomes kept the family – now families – going, food on the table and the lights burning!

Katherine and Oral and the Huff children were willing to share their "fortune" with the Shingletons, but it was obvious, the dual family of eight children strained the Huff financial pot.

But they managed. Christmas of 1946 came and went, with no great fanfare. Santa Claus did not come to No. 9, or if he did, he missed the Huff house. They celebrated the holiday and the birth of Jesus and wished each other a Merry Christmas, but didn't complicate the day with gifts. And there wasn't any money to do it anyway. And besides, where was the toy store?

108

Frank Gets the Girl

When 1947 came in, Frank headed for Huntington to enroll at Marshall in order to complete his Masters's Degree.

The local new football hero was big news. Even going back to Marshall for his Master's merited a feature on the sports page of the <u>Fairmont Times</u> on January 21: The story shouted a headline: "Gatski Returns To Marshall For Degree." The story began "Frank Gatski, substitute center of the Championship Cleveland Browns of the All-America Pro Football Conference last season, leaves this morning for Huntington and Marshall College, where next week he will resume his studies in order to gain his Master's Degree…"

The story went on to briefly chronicle the last few years of Frank's life – from playing football at Farmington High to Marshall to the armed services to Auburn to the Cleveland Browns and back home… his new home was with his brother in Grant Town.

This trip to Marshall was different, though. For the first time, he was driving there in the new 1946 Chevy, the spoils of his first professional football season.

What happens after a guy gets a car – he gets a girl. Frank went back to Marshall to get his Master's Degree, but he was going to end up with a lot more than a diploma.

Frank had always been – not shy exactly – reserved, and certainly respectful, of women. That came from a background of moral values of his home life, and his Catholic upbringing.

A girl had to be a virgin when she was married. Everyone knew that. And it was considered important. So a young boy who was going to be the first man a girl made love to had to be prepared to make a serious commitment. Getting pregnant, and not being married was absolutely the worst thing that could happen to a girl. When it did happen, the girl generally dropped out of sight. Getting rid of the baby by some medical method was not acceptable. All the consequences of pregnancy kept couples from going all the way.

In No. 9 and in Farmington, everyone knew each other, so there was considerable pressure to behave properly. So dates became a movie and a walk home, and if a guy was lucky, a kiss at the front door. More involved couples would spend time alone on the girls couch petting and kissing until one of the parents would call the girl to come to bed and the boy went home to a cold shower.

Frank had been the boy in that picture a couple of times. No serious involvements. Like nearly everyone else his age, he lacked "auto mobility" – he didn't have a car. So where could a guy go with a girl. Occasionally he would borrow his brother's car or his dad's and take a girl to a movie at the Farmington Theatre or to a dance at one of the nearby clubs or taverns.

He became one of the best dancers around – a talent honed at polka dances his family would attend at the Paw Paw Inn in Rivesville or the Monongah Union Hall. The quick and nimble footwork necessary for the polkas became a slight variation of the jitterbug – the dance of the day. It was a sight. This 6 foot 3 tall Tarzan making all the right moves to Glenn Miller's "*Jumpin' at Savoy*" the with a 5 foot 2, 110-pound Jane – moving her around anywhere he wanted on the dance floor.

When Frank pulled his Chevy into the Marshall College parking lot, he headed for the Student Union. Wearing his BROWNS jacket, the tall, handsome blonde was a billboard for "who is that guy?!"

One girl, Ida LaFon, just a seventeen-year-old freshman from Gassaway, West Virginia, asked that question and got the answer from a fellow Marshall student named Jim Brown, who was a friend of Franks. He introduced them. Frank put a nickel in the juke box, pushed A-3 for Glenn Miller's "*String of Pearls*" – and it was all over for Frank. The 110-pound Ida ran over him like Bronco Nagurski. Frank felt comfortable with Ida. Maybe it was her small town roots. She was from Gassaway, just about the same size town as Farmington. Before meeting Ida, Frank was preoccupied with getting a degree from Marshall and with making the Cleveland Browns football team. He wasn't ready for

110

serious dating. That would take time or attention away from both of these pursuits. Now he had the degree – he was even working on his master's degree – and he was a member of the Cleveland Browns. Yes, it sure was different! And besides, now he had a car. He was ready for Ida LaFon.

Frequently, he took Ida to a drive-in movie, or drove forty miles to Charleston to see his brother. When big bands, like Kay Kyser or Oron Tucker came to town, Frank and Ida made a night of it, dancing and a late night or early morning breakfast at the College Corner, the popular Huntington twenty-four hour meeting place, located on 16th Street across from Old Main.

On campus, Ida and Frank were a steady. They met at the student union between classes and danced to the music from the jukebox. Frank wore out the Andrews Sisters recordings. Their version of *"I Don't Know Why"* became a love song for the couple. Ginny Simms, *"Deep Purple"*, was a close second. Ida stayed at Laidley Hall on the campus. The lady in charge of the dorm, called the dorm mother, kept everyone on their best behavior. The college rules for a girls' dormitory included a curfew of 10 p.m. When a girl left for the evening, she would 'sign out', which meant she had to 'sign in'. The blank space under 'sign in' was a ticket to probation for future evenings. Habitual offenders could even get expelled.

Sometimes Frank broke the speed record down Third Avenue and across 16th Street to make the deadline, but he always did.

The door was locked after that. And any girl coming in after 10 p.m. had to gain entrance by knocking on the door and talking to the dorm mother – a humiliating experience.

On weekends when Ida would go home to Gassaway, Frank would take the opportunity to go back to Grant Town to visit his brother, Benny. They had so much in common – football, archery, hunting. Being here was being home. Their other home – where they grew up in No. 9, just a couple of miles away – was occupied by another family. Both parents were gone and the boys felt closer than ever, even though most of their lives were spent miles apart.

111

Frank knew that he would eventually move back home to Grant Town, near his brother, if he could. Someday.

On a spring Saturday in 1947, the power of the morning sun shot through the tall oaks as Frank and Benny tramped the hills around Grant Town.

That evening Frank and Benny headed for the Circle Bar in Farmington. Frank looked forward to saying hello to old friends. He enjoyed the night having a few beers and talking about professional football. The BROWNS jacket Frank wore left no doubt who the man was and when the word got around that Frank was in town, the bar was full of old friends happy to get close to the guy they had worked with. Even the ones who said he would never make it with the pros were there. Ben Bennett smiled at Frank and placed another Carling Black Label in front of him.

When Frank reached for his money, Ben said, "It's on me. Hell, Frank, you're good for business."

The Sweetest Sound

By March, the basketball season was over, which meant one thing to any kid at No. 9. It was baseball season.

Everyone played all of the sports and in Farmington, just like every other small town around, football, basketball, and baseball were as certain as autumn, winter, and spring. Most kids in these small schools went from one sport to the other. And there was a great chance to earn a letter in all three sports.

But there was no baseball for seventh and eighth graders. You had to be a freshman to participate in high school sports. Underclassmen waited their turn.

As Sam and Leo and the rest of the No. 9 kids boarded the bus for home, they could see the high school baseball players warming up on the field below. The crack of the baseball bat, the sweetest sound of spring faded into the sound of the bus engine at it pulled away and headed toward No. 9.

By mid-March, the high school season was underway. Teams from Marion County – Barrackville, Fairview, Rivesville, Monongah, Mannington, and others in nearby towns – came to Farmington to play the Farmers. On those game days, Sam could see his team team dressed in their gray uniforms with the red FARMERS spelled across the chest.

In spring, baseball took over the small towns in the area. Nearly everyone cheered for the "home team," Pittsburgh Pirates, who played just ninety miles up U.S. Rt. 19. And if you were lucky, your dad might take you to Forbes Field to see the great teams of the National League, like the Brooklyn Dodgers with stars Jackie Robinson, Duke Snider, and PeeWee Reese or the St. Louis Cardinals with their stars Stan Musial, Marty Marion, and Red Schoendist.

But if you couldn't go to the game, you could tune in on the radio to hear Rosie Rosewell describe the action. His call on a Pirate home run was "open the window, Aunt Minnie, here she comes!" which was followed by ten seconds of toy whistle nonsense.

The Pirates radio sponsorship must have been bare bones, because when the team played an away game, Rosie wasn't there; instead he stayed in Pittsburgh and described the game by reading the play-by-play off of a ticker tape. The radio listener heard the "ticky-ticky" sound of the tape and Rosewell's bland reading – bland, except for positive Pirate plays, which would cause his voice to rise excitably – but against a silent crowd noise – and complete silence, except for the "ticky, ticky, ticky…"

When the school bus returned kids from school back to No. 9, it didn't take ten minutes for a crowd of boys to gather at the field across from the mines. The field was absent of grass, except for a patch here and there. The backstop, made of posts and chicken wire didn't look like much, but it did manage to keep the ball from disappearing over the hillside. That was crucial, since losing the ball, the only ball, would have stopped the game.

Sam and Leo would usually choose up sides. One would toss the bat while the other one would catch it with one hand. The two would then alternate placing hands toward the knob of the bat, until one could hold the bat by the end. That kid would then have the first choice of a teammate.

Every day after school, weather permitting, the game went on, as long as there was a ball and a bat – usually someone had a ball and someone had a bat. If the ball would lose its thread, the cover would come loose, in which case it became necessary to tape up the ball. The tape most available in a coal camp was black –black electrician's tape that seemed to "show up" in miners' lunch buckets. Unfortunately, the black tape made the ball harder to see, especially as night began to fall. But still the game went on. When the ball tape began to unravel and the inner strings of the ball would start to show, it became apparent that a new ball would have to be obtained. Sooner or later another ball would appear, courtesy of a parent or the high school coach or from someone who committed a minor theft at the Ace Hardware in Mannington – and so the game went on.

One of the parents who became most interested in the No. 9 games was Robert Dudash. Everyone called him "Duck", a nickname he picked up at a young age. But that child-like name attachment didn't fool anyone who knew him. He was one tough man!

The short, stocky, barrel-chested "Polack" had worked in the mines for several years – and had earned his respect by winning all of his fights at the local bars and generally gaining the reputation as one "hell-raising son-of-a-bitch" when he wanted to be. He owned a Harley-Davidson, probably the only one in the county, and he could be seen frequently tearing through No. 9 and along U.S. 250 – bare chest and bare feet. Occasionally, he did wear a shirt, which would be open and flying in the wind.

One of Duck's sons, Steve Dudash, was one of the regular players of the games, so naturally the father would show up to see how the son was doing, observing the action from his Harley-Davidson seat.

Duck had heard that Manchin's Store in Farmington, just two miles away, was going to have a team of young kids. A. James Manchin, one of Papa Joe Manchin's sons, had watched the kids playing in Farmington just like they did at Number 9, and decided to make them an "official" team. He even talked Papa Joe into buying red jerseys with white sleeves and the name MANCHINS spelled across the chest.

The next day, when the choose-up game was on at No. 9, Duck Dudash arrived on his Harley, hauling his old army duffel bag completely filled with something. This time he parked the Harley, got off and lifted up the duffel bag and set it on the ground. Duck Dudash, dismounting from his machine, got the attention of the players.

In his gruff voice, he shouted, "Hey boys. Come here."

The game stopped and the kids hustled over to Duck and gathered around him.

"We're gonna have a team," he announced.

After a moment of stunned silence, the kids responded joyously, "Wow!

Great! I'm ready..." They slapped each other playfully, then waited for Duck to continue.

"Look, Manchins in Farmington has a team. They want to play somebody, so we'll play 'em. What do think?"

"Yeh, we'll play 'em," Sam said. "And we'll beat 'em, too."

Duck started to open his bag. He felt like Santa Claus. "I figured we need some equipment, and balls and bats." He reached in the bag and pulled out a catcher's mitt and mask

"Who's the catcher here? I think it's you, ain't it Sam?"

Sam shook his head, "Yes, it's me." His eyes widened as he took the mask and glove from Duck.

"Geez, I never saw a new glove," Sam said as he slipped it on his left hand and pounded his fist into it. He picked up the new mask and slipped it over his head. It felt tight against his face, muffling the sound of his speech.

"Man, that feels good," Sam said in a voice garbled from the compression of the elastic band holding the mask on.

"You sound like you're in a hole," Steve said. Everyone laughed.

Duck was just getting started. "Here's a first baseman's mitt. Who's first base?"

Steve Priester held up his hand. "It's me."

"Here," Duck said. "First base." Steve took it and slipped it on. "Damn, that feels good," he said with a big smile.

"Who needs a fielder's glove? I got two."

"I don't have one," Jimmy Wolfe said. "I play third base."

"Ya do now," Duck said as he tossed it to him, "I got one more."

Sam spoke up, "Leo don't have one."

"Okay, here catch."

Then Duck turned the duffle bag over and three brand new Louisville Slugger baseball bats and a dozen Spalding baseballs fell out and rolled on the ground. Nine kids moved all at once to pick one up.

116

There was instant mayhem – new balls, gloves, bats, everyone wanted to throw a new ball, catch with a new glove, swing a new bat...

"Hold on! Hold on!" Duck shouted. "If we're gonna have a team, we got to start practicing. Let's put the balls and bats away and get started. How about infield practice."

He picked up a new bat and ball. "Sam is catching. Steve's on first..." He named the infield. And there was the crack of a new Louisville Slugger bat against a new Spalding baseball – the sound never heard in No. 9.

"Over to first," Duck shouted as he hit a hard grounder to Jimmy Wolfe, the third baseman.

That summer of 1947 was the first summer of "organized" baseball in No. 9 – thanks to Duck Dudash. The No. 9 team played the team from Farmington – the elitist team, with their own red jerseys and the word MANCHINS on the chest, and the teams from the other nearby coal camps, Carolina and Ida May.

Coach Cassy Ryan, the football, basketball and baseball coach at Mannington High School had a summer job provided by Jamison Coal Company to supervise the playground at those two coal communities. Ryan, who was coach at Farmington High, when Marshall coach Roy Straight was discovering Frank Gatski, moved to Mannington High in 1944. Now, in this summer, he was getting considerable interest from the kids to have a baseball team. So Coach Ryan organized one in each camp. The baseball fields were the coal camps playground – large areas of dirt and hard packed sand, no grass and no fence. So if a batter hit one to the right spot between outfielders, the ball would roll forever on the rockhard surface.

No. 9, Manchins, Ida May, and Carolina became an informal league. A game would be scheduled and the visiting team would walk the two or three miles to the playground - ballfield. It was not uncommon to see a dozen kids and a couple of adult coaches walking the hard road from home to the visitor's coal camp to play the game.

Sam loved catching. It was the only position he wanted to play. You had to be tough – that was Sam. You had to control the game – that was Sam. You were in the middle of the action – and that was Sam.

Baseball and softball were very important types of recreation for each of the towns or small communities in the county – Farmington, Carolina, Worthington, Grant Town, Watson and Mannington organized adult baseball teams. They were comprised of high school and college players, and workers and businessmen in their thirties and forties and sometimes older, some of these were ex-professional players: Rusty Pearl, the Watson outfielder, had played with the Brooklyn Dodgers minor league team; Tony Pizatelli, the Watson shortstop, previously played with the Charleston Senators, a farm team of the Washington Senators; Tom Alkire played AAA ball on the West Coast; Hack Retton, the Grant Town pitcher, was a former Pittsburgh Pirate minor league player. These guys and others stood out for their rare experience as a "professional" and became heroes to young boys like Sam and Leo. Outstanding players and the closeness of the towns made for formidable teams, fierce competition, and entertaining baseball.

Every Sunday, through the summer, there were games somewhere. There was never any admission charge. After all, there was no gate or fence to keep someone from watching. But someone would pass the hat to get enough donations to pay an umpire and help buy a few baseballs.

The team of Farmington players, just like the kids team, was sponsored and supported by Manchin's and, therefore, wore that name on their uniforms.

When the game was on at Farmington, Sam Huff would often walk the hard road to the Farmington field for the game. On his way he would try to hitch a ride and often times got picked up.

Uncle Leroy

For Sam Huff, July 4 of 1947 was a special day. Not only was there a baseball game at Farmington, but all of the relatives were coming to the house for a picnic.

And the picnic meant Uncle Leroy from Akron, Ohio, would be there playing his guitar and singing songs all evening long. Sam loved to hear his uncle play and sing. It was better than anything he heard on the radio. Throw in all the fresh corn, baked beans, and watermelon a kid could eat and Sam's day was perfect.

By noon, Sam and Leo were walking toward Farmington, trying to hitch a ride as they walked along. Very soon they were picked up and delivered to the Farmington ball field. People were beginning to gather for the game. Some, who had picnic baskets, found a spot down the left field line to spread out and enjoy the game.

The visiting team was the Grant Town Cubs, one of the best teams in the region. The crack of the bat and the chatter of the ballplayers mingled with the noise of a hundred fans, who came to watch.

The baseball field was the same field used by Farmington High School for football, as well as baseball.

Unfortunately, the use of a football field for baseball offers some problems.

It was a long rectangular field set between two banks, wide enough and long enough for football, but insufficient for baseball. The long length and narrow width resulted in a very long left field, but a very short right field.

The short right field ended abruptly at the bank, which made the right fielder, who played at the base of the bank, climb the hill to catch a "deep" fly ball. A ball hit down the line that might otherwise be a routine fly ball would often end up in the hard road for a home run. On the other hand, left field went on forever and into the playground, a distance probably longer than the deepest point in the New York Giants Polo Grounds. A hard drive in that direction would have to be chased down by the left fielder, who might disappear from view into the playground.

Down on the field, the hometown Manchin's team was taking infield practice. Manchin's was an excellent team of college players and local ex-high school players who never went to college, but went off to war and returned to play the game they loved.

On one sideline, the Grant Town Cubs were warming up. They looked sharp in their white uniforms. Year after year, it seemed they were the best ball club. Not only were their players outstanding, but their home field, with a manicured grass infield and the appropriate dimensions and an outfield fence, had the look of a field that belonged to a minor league professional ball club. Their "baseball park" showed the amount of support they received from local businesses and the coal company. It was a stark contrast to the football field turned baseball field they were playing on this day.

Grant Town was led by the Retton clan – Dick, the pitcher and former Pittsburgh Pirate hopeful; Joe, a young pitcher who was still in high school; and Hack, an outfielder and catcher.

And there was a young kid, Ronnie Retton, warming up with them, the son of Sam "Tally" Retton. Ronnie served as the bat boy. The ten-year-old had an obvious baseball talent that belied his youth. So at times, the bat boy, a four foot five kid would go in to play an infield position. This was no joke. He was a "phenom" – who, aside from the limitations of the size of a ten-year-old, could hold his own in the field – and at bat.

Sam and Leo found a place on the bank near third base to watch the game. Hundreds of conversations underscored the crack of the baseball bat and the shouts of the Manchin manager hitting infield practice.

Leo nudged Sam. "Hey, look over there," he said as he pointed to Sam's right. About twenty feet away was a gang of guys gathered around someone, laughing and joking – and listening intently, too.

Leo stood up to get a better look. "Hey, it's Frank Gatski."

120

Sam stood up quickly. He could see the blonde hair and Frank's face in the middle of the crowd. "It's Frank!"

Frank often came to the local games when he was in town. In about three weeks –he would be reporting to Bowling Green for pre-season football camp. But now was a time to spend with old friends – reveling in being part of the Cleveland Browns 1946 championship season. Now for sure, he had become a local hero.

Guys he worked with in the mines a few years before could hardly believe their co-worker, the nineteen-year-old grimy face kid they dug coal with was playing professional football and part of a championship team. But Frank's modest and casual attitude didn't set him apart from his old friends. He was the same old Frank. It was an attitude stemming from the improbability of his fame – even Frank didn't understand it.

In a few minutes, when the word got around that "Gatski was here," the crowd around him grew, everyone eager to hear about his experiences first hand.

Leo nudged Sam, "Hey, let's go over."

Sam thought about it for a second. Then decided it wasn't a good idea. "We'd never get through those guys."

They sat back down to watch the game. Every few moments, Sam would look over to catch a glimpse of his hero. The baseball game had begun, but Sam was more interested in Frank and looking for an opening where he might go over to him.

Suddenly, Sam's attention was drawn back to the field when the crowd erupted in a loud cheer. A long drive had taken the Grant Town left fielder into the playground. Two runs scored on the play and Manchin's took the early lead.

Through nine innings, Sam continued to monitor Frank, who moved around to watch the game, drawing a small crowd wherever he went.

When Sam looked again for Frank, he was gone, but he looked away from the field and saw the tall muscular form with that mane of blonde hair walking away in the distance.

He was sorry to see Frank leave without getting a chance to say hello to him – but even that disappointment faded when Sam felt one gnawing hunger pain in his stomach.

"Let's go," he said to Leo. "My relatives are coming in and there's a picnic at my house."

Sam and Leo jumped out of the truck. "Thanks for the ride, Jake," Sam said.

"Yes, thank you," Leo echoed.

"You're welcome, boys. Don't eat too much watermelon," Jake shouted back.

As Sam and Leo started walking toward the Huff house, they could hear the sound of a guitar and a strong voice singing a country song.

"It's Uncle Leroy," Sam said. "C'mon – man I love to hear him sing."

Leo chased after Sam as they ran toward the house. The lawn was crowded with not one family – but two, all of the Huffs and Uncle Leroy's, too.

The Fourth of July get-together had become a tradition. It started years ago. Leroy planned his vacation to make sure he could be in No. 9 every July 4th.

Everyone greeted Sam as he ran onto the crowded small front lawn. Sam acknowledged his friend. "This is my buddy, Leo." He turned to Leo. "C'mon, let's eat."

They piled corn and beans on their plates and sat down on the porch steps. Uncle Leroy was singing "*Anytime*," the number one country song by Eddy Arnold. Sam liked the song, and he especially liked the way Leroy sang it. Leroy ended the song…"*anytime you say you want me back again, … I'll be coming right back home to you.*"

Everyone applauded. "Sing another one," Katherine said.

"Gotta eat," Leroy shot back. "I'm missing out on the good part of this July fourth." He leaned the guitar against the porch and filled his plate and sat down on the porch step beside Sam.

122

Sam felt proud that Leroy would sit beside him. "This is my buddy, Leo," Sam said.

"Hi ya, Leo"

"Hi ya, too," Leo replied as he chewed on an ear of corn.

Sam looked up to Leroy. "I like to hear you sing, Uncle Leroy."

"Thank you, Sam. Do you like to sing?"

"I sing by myself. I don't play no guitar or anything – except when I sing, my throat is sore sometimes."

Leo corrected Sam, "His throat is sore everytime!"

"What do you mean everytime?"Leroy asked.

"Ah, he means a lot," Sam explained.

"If it is sore a lot, you may need to get your tonsils out."

"Oh no, I …"

Larry shouted to his brother, "Oral, does Sam still have his tonsils?"

"Yeh, sure does."

"He says his throat is sore."

"Doc says he'll outgrow it."

"Oh yeh – but when. He's how old now?"

"Twelve. Ah, he'll be okay. Sing another song, Leroy."

"Let me finish these beans first."

Oral got up from his chair and walked over to Leroy and Sam. "Your throat sore now, Sam?"

"No, pa, not now – but it's sore a lot!"

Oral rubbed Sam's head, "You'll be okay."

Leroy still wanted to talk tonsils. "Some people say bad tonsils can keep a kid from growing. Sam ain't that big for twelve."

"Well, Leroy, dang it, look at me and look at you. I ain't big, so don't expect Sam to be big. Don't blame it on tonsils –blame it on me. I don't think it's his tonsils that is keeping him from growing."

"Okay," Leroy finally conceded. He picked up his guitar and strummed a C chord. "What do you want to hear? – How about "*On Top of Old Smokey*"

"Yeh, that's a good one," Oral said.

Leroy picked up his guitar and the conversation died down as everyone turned their attention to Leroy who played a three chord intro.

Black Water

The summer of 1947 – what a year it had been for Sam Huff. The twelve-year-old had finished the seventh grade; his hero, Frank Gatski started playing football and was getting paid for it; his mother was going to have a baby; his brother, Donald, quit school and went to work in the mines.

Boy life was changing. Soon he would be going to the eighth grade at Farmington High School. He would be thirteen soon. Thirteen! Donald was only sixteen when he quit school and started working with his dad. Sam did the math. Sixteen minus thirteen was only three years. His dad had already started talking to him about a job in the mines

But Sam wasn't like his brother – or his dad. He was afraid to work in the mines. He wanted nothing to do with it. And he liked school. He liked learning. He liked being with his buddy, Leo, and his other friends. He couldn't imagine leaving them. He liked school and competing with Leo in class on arithmetic problems, and for grades.

Sebastian Coceano, Leo's dad, and Maria, his mom, were different than Katherine and Oral Huff. The Coceano's talked about school and how important it was. Leo and his brother were expected to do their homework and make good grades. Not so in the Huff household. Instead, the idea there was to get through school till you were sixteen, the age at which a kid could drop out. Katherine would offer some encouragement to stay in school, especially for Donald and Sam, but the lure of a paycheck from Jamison was too strong to keep a kid going to classes. But the Huff's didn't count on the Coceano factor.

Sam was influenced by Leo. And Sam was determined not to let his buddy get the best of him. So if Leo was going to graduate, Sam sure was, too. One thing was for certain, Sam wasn't going to work in the mines and he was going to stay one step ahead of Leo Coceano.

Leo's older brother, Dominick, had become one of Farmington High School's best students, in spite of dealing with the language barrier. Dominick even was talking about going to college and becoming an engineer. Now from time to time, even Leo would talk about himself in the same way. Sam couldn't stand it. Leo was getting out of hand. Didn't he know he was living in No. 9?

The steam from a large bucket of boiling water rose to the ceiling – Katherine Huff, wiped her brow with apron. She lifted the bucket from the stove and carefully turned to dump the water into the larger low barrel. She looked out the window for her son.

"Robert Lee Huff," she shouted. "Robert Lee."

Sam knew when he heard his full name, there was work to be done. He came in from outside.

"Get more water for your father's bath. He'll be coming home soon."

"Yes, ma'am."

Sam went outside to the pump and began filling the bucket. He heard the sounds of men coming from the mine – familiar sounds of a shift change. His dad worked the morning shift – eight to five – and the clanging of his metal lunch bucket against his belt, along with the rhythmic sound of heavy boots on the gravel roadway was the sound of his dad coming home.

Oral would want his bath. Sam knew the barrel was only half full. He pumped harder and faster, filled the bucket and carried it into the kitchen, where he dumped it into the barrel.

"Check that water out, Sam. Is it okay?"

Sam put his hand into the barrel. "Yeh, it's good."

"Do you see your dad yet?"

Sam went to the door. "Yeh, he's coming."

Then Sam went to his mother to pop the question. "Do you think Dad will let me go to the fair?"

"You'll have to ask him."

The Plum Run Fair was the last celebration of summer before the kids went back to school. Plum Run was just a mile from No. 9. There were rides, games, cotton candy - and classmates. Everyone would be there.

Oral Huff came through the door and to a corner of the small room off of the kitchen, where he took off his clothes. He tried to keep the coal dust away from the main area of the kitchen, but that was impossible – but he did the best he could.

Oral felt the water. "One more bucket of water, Sam."

Sam hurried outside with the bucket and quickly filled it. He returned to dumped it into the barrel. "How's that, dad?"

"That's fine, son." Oral said as he stepped into the steaming hot bath. The clear water quickly turned gray as it took on the coal dust from Oral's body. "What are you looking at, son?"

"Nothing," Sam said as he took the bucket to the porch. He came back in anxious to bring up the subject of the Plum Run Fair.

He stood there watching the water turn from gray to black as his father rubbed soap on his arms. "Here," Oral said to Sam. "Do my back."

Sam took the soap and rubbed it across his fathers back. "Boy that water is getting black," Sam said.

"Black as coal."

Oral turned to look at Sam. He noticed he didn't take to the joke.

"And so what about it."

Sam stood up straight. "I don't ever want to do that, pa."

"You'll get use to it."

"No I won't. Look at your face... You look like..."

At that moment Oral had his grimy hands on Sam's face. "Now yours is like mine, son."

Sam turned to grab a towel. Oral laughed. Sam wiped his face and spit out the bitter taste.

"This is how we make a living, damn it! You like to eat and sleep under a roof. This is how I make sure all you kids are kept."

Oral wanted to make his point. "Sam, I'm taking this bath and when I'm finished, I'll deal with you. Go clean your face off, "Sambo."

Sam backed off and felt the comfort of his mother's arms that embraced him. She turned him around and took a wet towel and wiped off Sam's face.

Sam changed his mind about asking whether he could go to the Plum Run Fair that night. But the fair did run for a whole week.

It was late summer, which meant that football practice would be starting soon. Sam would be in the eighth grade in 1947 – and students didn't go out for football until they were in the ninth grade. But Coach Kelly allowed interested boys in the eighth grade to practice with the team if they wanted.

Sam opened his dresser drawer and took out the newspaper picture of Frank he had saved from last year. He was getting ready.

Frank was pictured in his Brown's uniform in his center position ready to snap the ball – a fierce look of determination in his face and his huge hands wrapped around the football.

Sam laid the picture on the floor on front of him, got down to mimic Frank's stance and screwed up his face. It was perfect! He was just like Gatski.

His mother's voice brought him back to No. 9. "Sam, come here."

Sam got up, took another look at Frank's mean demeanor – matched it – then put the picture away in his dresser drawer.

"I see your dad coming home soon. Get his bath ready, will you?"

"Yes, ma'am." He grabbed the bucket and went outside to the pump and filled it. He saw his dad in the distance coming his way and he pumped quickly to beat him inside. The water had to be heated over the stove – and his father wasn't willing to wait long once he got home. Sam took the bucket to his mother and set it down. Katherine Huff was eight months pregnant, but that didn't hinder her in her housework. She took the heavy bucket and lifted it to the stove.

Sam was thinking of football. "Practice starts tomorrow, Mom."

128

"Practice for what?"

"Football."

"You going to play football, son?"

"Sure am – Leo is too – and Murvyn… Everyone around here is"

"That's good son – hope you don't get hurt."

"Huh, I won't."

Oral Huff swung the door open. "You won't what?"

Katherine answered, "He won't get hurt."

"Football starts tomorrow," Sam said.

"Football? Didn't think you was old enough."

"Eighth grade, uh, I mean junior high school football."

"You wear uniforms?"

"Yeh, we wear the old ones - the ones the high school players wore last year, and the year before, too."

"Ain't they big for you?"

"Yeh, some of them are."

"Well they'll be big for you, that's for sure."

Oral had taken off his work clothes and stepped into the tub. Katherine lifted the steaming bucket from the stove and dumped it in. The steam rose up around him as he settled down into the tub.

"Well, like your mother says, don't get hurt."

Oral lathered up a washcloth and handed it to Sam. "Here, Sam, wash my back for me." Sam took the cloth and quickly ran it across his dad's back and handed it back to him.

"You need to get use to this, son. This will be you sitting in this tub someday."

Katherine overheard Oral and fought back for Sam. "Not so, Oral. Sam may not want to be a miner."

"What else is there, Mother?"

"Playing football," Sam said.

"Oh not that again," Oral replied. "You ain't gonna be Frank Gatski – get that out of your mind."

129

Katherine argued back, "Oh hush, Oral. You don't know."

"Anyway, you got to make a high school team first, ain't you?"

All of a sudden, that seemed to be a lofty goal – Maybe it was his father's discouragement - or Sam's realization that he wasn't very big. He swallowed hard and his throat hurt. Suddenly, for one of these rare times, he felt incapable of competing against his friends. But tomorrow would change that.

First Stringer

On the campus of Bowling Green, the Cleveland Browns were getting ready for the 1947 season. The August days were hot. The hotter the better for Frank Gatski, who was determined more than ever to be a first string player. He had started two games in 1946 as a linebacker. Now he was working at center, too. The regular center, Mike Scary, was an all-pro in 1945 with the Cleveland Rams. The Rams beat the Washington Redskins for the World Championship that year; however in 1946 when the Cleveland Rams moved to Los Angeles to become the Los Angeles Rams, a number of players chose to stay with the new Cleveland team, the Cleveland Browns, of the new All-American Conference. Scary was one of those players. His commitment to the new team and his all-pro status in 1945 made dislodging him at center difficult for the rookie. But Scary was small for a center, about 6 foot and 200 pounds. He was getting beaten up by opposing defensive linemen. He was also feeling the competition for the center job from Frank Gatski. The relentless newcomer was supremely determined – and much bigger at 6 foot 3 and 225 pounds – and much stronger. The writing was on the wall. Frank Gatski was going to take over.

Paul Brown was impressed! Frank never missed a practice – just as he had never missed a practice in high school and in college – both at Marshall and Auburn. Never. And Brown admired the fact that Frank never complained, always cooperated, was always prepared, and besides was "the toughest son-of-a-bitch I've ever seen." And Otto Graham, the Brown quarterback really liked playing behind Frank. Frank's height and "high split," the long legs and the wingspan of his long arms – allowed the quarterback a comfort zone he never had with Scary. In practice and in games, Frank proved to offer outstanding protection for passing plays. Scary had mentioned that the 1947 season might be his last. Quietly Frank Gatski knew it would be. He wasn't content being a substitute- not even for an all-pro.

But Coach Brown felt some obligation to Scary. As long as the Browns were winning, it would be hard to justify changing the team that won the 1946 Championship.

"Mail call."

After a team dinner at the college cafeteria, the mail received at the training camp was distributed. Just like the army. Frank was happy to receive a letter from Ida. He stuck it in his back pocket, where he would read it later that evening. He was anxious to read it to see how she was getting along. She was spending the summer working for an awning company in Charleston and staying with her sister. Frank had returned to Grant Town in May and stayed with brother Benny while working the B&O Railroad driving spikes. It was damn hard work, but he was happy doing it, since it hardened him for the football season.

The letter was like a lot of the others – and it wasn't the content of the letter as much as the act of writing it and receiving it. She missed him. She thought about him all the time. She wrote that "work was fine." She wished him good luck at practice, and she couldn't wait for the season to be over – only because that is when they would be married.

Frank smiled as he stared at the word "married." It was a big step for him. But it was a good feeling to have someone in his life who loved him. His mother and father and were both gone now and it was time for him to think of a home and family. He went along agreeably with Ida's strong initiative to get married.

As he folded up the letter and gently put it back in the envelope, he dismissed all thoughts of that future December date and picked up his Cleveland Browns playbook. Right now he was married to Paul Brown.

Coach Ray Kelly

Coach Ray Kelly, the big burley, sunny-faced, Irishman was well liked by everyone. He was in his second year at Farmington. He graduated from Farmington High in 1938 and played with Frank Gatski on the 1936 team when Frank was a senior and played a substitute center.

Kelly succeeded Clarence "Cassy" Ryan, who had been his coach in 1936 and 1937. Cassy coached at Farmington through 1943, then moved on to Mannington High School, just seven miles up Route 250. The proximity of the schools made for a tremendous rivalry; and the pupil-coach confrontation of Kelly vs Ryan added to the games interest.

Kelly was stern, but friendly – even gentle. He always seemed to be smiling. It was that glint in the eye of the Irishman – along with a constant sunny disposition that belied that tough determined man inside.

There wasn't a day Kelly walked on the Farmington High field that he didn't think back to his junior and senior seasons of 1936 and 1937 when he played on the teams coached by Cassy Ryan.

Coming back to Farmington after the war was Kelly's fondest wish – to coach at his high school was a dream come true! He kept in touch with his old teammates, many of who worked in the mines at No. 9, Rachel, Ida May and Carolina or at one of the factories in Fairmont.

From time to time he would meet up with his most famous teammate during the Browns off-season, and they would reminisce about their Farmington High days.

Ray confessed that he used Frank as an example to his players. Why not? Here was a guy from this school now playing pro football, that just a few years before was walking in their shoes. Yes. You can play at Farmington High School and become great!

It was the first day of practice of the Farmington High School Farmers 1947 season.

Sam and his buddy, Leo, along with Murvyn McDowell and a few other eighth graders stood against the wall of the equipment room watching the upperclassmen get their equipment – pants, shoulder pads, hip pads, and helmet.

Sam grew nervous, wondering if he could put everything on correctly. For sure there would be nothing that would fit just right. Eighth graders got what was left over and made do – regardless of the size.

Sam tried not to be too obvious as he studied the players putting their equipment on. He focused on Rudy Banick, who was a freshman, but thought to be a future star. Rudy stepped into his jockey strap, pulled it up to his waist, and then strapped on his hip pads. He lifted his arms up through his shoulder pads, then stuck his head into his shoulder pads. He threw the jersey over his head and stuck his neck through, then turned to the player beside him, who pulled the jersey down over his shoulder pads.

"Can I do that?" Sam wondered. Suddenly Sam's attention was drawn away from Rudy by a loud voice yelling his name.

"Sam, you ready?" It was Coach Kelly.

"Yeh, sure," Sam said with confidence.

"Leo, you and Murvyn, too," Kelly said. "Here, let's see what we got left."

"Shoes. Sam, what size?"

"Eight, I think."

"How about these, they're nines?"

"Okay," Sam said.

"Now here's pants, probably too big! Hip pads, shoulder pads, socks, jock strap. Is that it?" He paused – reviewed that it was all there. "Yeh, that's it." Okay, Murvyn and Leo, you'll get about the same stuff."

He gathered it together in a pile for each of them. "Here you go."

The three took their equipment to a bench, dumped it on the floor and began to put on a football uniform for the first time. The first thing to go on was the athletic supporter. There it was lying on top of his pile of equipment.

Sam tried to remember what Rudy Banick did. The jock strap wasn't like a pair of shorts; the straps were getting in the way. And on Sam's first attempt to put it on, he got the strap in front.

Coach Kelly walked by and noticed Sam studying the essential piece of football equipment.

Suddenly Sam was confused. It didn't look like anything he had ever worn, that was for sure. "Shit," Sam thought, "Where do you put your leg through?" He could find the front – that was easy – but then what?

He tried to be calm and not look stupid. Then he noticed Murvyn had figured it out. The straps had to go behind! He watched Murvyn, who suddenly looked like an expert.

Sam grasped the front of the supporter in his left hand and the strap in his right hand and stuck his foot through. That was right. He quickly shot a glance at Murvyn to check for accuracy. Then the left foot. Now he stood up and pulled the supporter up to his waist. Then he took a deep breath. He had his athletic supporter on!

By this time, Murvyn and Leo, too, had gotten to the hip pads, which were no problem. Of course neither were the pants.

The shoulder pads went on without a hitch. And finally when they put their jerseys on, each turned around to the other two to get help pulling the back of the jersey over the shoulder pads. It was the final act – a ritual almost – that said "Look at me, I'm a football player."

Coach Kelly smiled at the sight of the eighth graders who were "out" for football. Allowing them to participate in this manner, even though they couldn't be on the team, was a way of encouraging them. He was amused at the sight of these youngsters whose "ill-fitting, much too large" uniforms were a hindrance to any normal football movement.

The Manchin Way

After football practice one day in late August, Sam walked from the school to town to get some ice cream at Parrish's Drug Store.

After getting a double dip cone of chocolate, a noise outside caught his attention. Across the street on the steps of Manchins Grocery Store, was a small, but boisterous crowd of people. In the center of the crowd was a tall black haired man wearing a white shirt and tie, smiling broadly. He was obviously the center of attention.

Mr. Thomas came to the window, too. "That's John Manchin. He just had a baby boy last night. I guess everybody's congratulating him. First boy, I think!"

When Sam went outside the crowd had grown – as customers entered and left Manchin's store. Many stopped to join in the conversation that included words of other worlds. Mama Kay and Papa Joe, the proud grandparents, also joined the group to carefully detail the birth of their first grandson, the one who would carry on their work and name in the new country. A daughter Janet was born in 1944 - but the birth of a son was something special to the smiling father.

The conversation was a melange of sounds of different tongues. "Congratulations!" was heard in Polish, Lebanese, Russian, Italian… and English.

Mama Kay was proud. "Bella figla… bella figla… what a beautiful child," she gushed. "His name is Joseph…after Papa Joe!"

Papa Joe didn't say much, but smiled. After all this was to be expected. No big deal. He would have even more grandchildren, too. A granddaughter and a grandson so far. This was just the beginning!

Sam was thinking back to when his brother, John, was born last year.

Heck, no one was there and now his mother was pregnant again. He

136

noticed a big difference in the way the Manchin's welcomed a newborn. He had never seen anything quite like this. But it was just another example of the Manchin's way of doing things. It seemed like the Manchin's were always doing something special: they sponsored baseball teams; gave banquets for the football team; gave money to the fire department; heck even having a baby was not just like anyone else having a baby.

American Dream

Sam Huff was pretty mixed up. On an afternoon of a late summer day, he sat on the porch eating a peanut butter and jelly sandwich looking down at the coal tipple in the distance.

The sound of coal mining – the rhythmic pulse of the water pumps and the conveyor belt lifting coal up the tipple and out to coal trucks played underneath the sounds in his coal camp home. He heard his baby brother, John, cry and his mother consoling him with baby talk. Yes, John Huff made it into this world and was, of course, the object of his mother's attention.

Outside, he heard the shouts of kids playing in the gravel street cowboys and Indians, "bang, bang, you're dead."

He looked back at the tipple. He thought of his dad and brother underground, getting that coal out. He knew that in two years, when he would be sixteen, he might be there, too. His dad was counting on it – and counting the days.

Sam shook his head. He said to himself, "I'll never do that! I'll never do that!" It seemed he could sing that to the beat of the coal mine pumps, "I'll never do that… I'll never do that…"

He noticed how quiet it was around the house now. The Shingleton's were gone – those four kids, along with their mother Myrtle, who moved in several months back when the mother was running away from an abusive alcoholic husband, had filled up the little house. Even though they made eight kids in the house, and an infant, it didn't matter. It was fun. They would play hide and seek and tag and wrestled and just messed around. The Huff's always believed there was room for one more.

Oral and Donald kept the money coming in by working in the mine, so everyone had enough to eat. Katherine didn't mind, after all, it was her sister, Myrtle – and she would do anything for her. When Myrtle's husband, Okey failed her, Katherine stepped in to help out.

The months the Shingleton's were here had gone by fast. Myrtle had recovered from the relationship with Okey. She kept her kids together, finally gained the confidence and resolved to get a job at the Westinghouse plant in Fairmont. Now, she and her kids had moved out and moved on with the rest of their lives.

It might have been the birth of John that finally pushed Myrtle to take her step. After all, she had intruded on the Huff's for almost a year. A new baby in the house signaled the need to move out and allow Oral and Katherine and the family to get back to normal.

The screen door screeched open and banged closed. Suddenly in front of him Sam saw his sister, Mickey, in a cheerleader pose shouting, "Gimme an F."

Sam swallowed the last bit of his sandwich and through a mouthful of white bread and jelly on his mouth shouted back, "F."

Mickey raised her arms into an A shape. "Gimme an A."

"A," shouted Sam.

"Gimme an R."

Sam didn't. Instead he stopped her. "Are you going to be a cheerleader?"

"I'm gonna try. Tryouts are next week when school starts."

"Will you be cheering for the first game?"

"Yes, silly. If I make it."

"Gimme an R," she shouted.

"R," Sam shouted. "You're going to spell out FARMERS, ain't you?"

"Yes, what do ya think, silly?" Then she finished the cheer – "That's the way you spell it, here's the way you yell it. FARMERS, FARMERS, FARMERS!"

"I'll be playing football next year when I'm in the ninth grade and you'll be a cheerleader then, too, won't you?"

Mickey kept running through cheering poses while she answered. "Don't know! I'm going to be sixteen this year. I may quit and get married."

"You and Billy? Why do you want to quit? Ain't you gonna graduate?"

"No, I'm gonna be a housewife. Don't need to graduate," she stopped cheering nodded her head for emphasis. "Mrs. Maxwell!"

The screen door banged again. It was Martha, Sam's oldest sister. "Like Martha," Mickey said. "She is Mrs. Tom Martin!"

Martha quit school two years earlier after she was a sophomore to marry Tom, who also worked at No. 9. She and Tom moved into a coal camp home a few doors away. Martha came to visit her mother - as she did regularly and to see the baby.

"Shoot, I don't want to quit school," Sam blurted out. "You're crazy."

"You don't want to work in the mines either," Martha said, "but you probably will."

"Huh-uh," Sam argued. "Leo and, me talked about it. We're going to college someday, maybe West Virginia."

Mickey and Martha looked at each other and laughed. Mickey rolled her eyes. "Oh, Sam, West Virginia University?"

"Well, yeh, maybe – Leo's brother, Dominick, is going there now!"

"That's the Coceano's, that ain't us."

Sam fought back. "Well I know one thing for sure. I ain't working down there!"

Just then the clank of a metal bucket against a belt buckle – the walking sound of miners coming home – sounded in the distance.

The Huff kids looked away to see their brother and father coming up the hill away from the portal, leading the charge it seemed, of dozens of others who were leaving their work for another day.

"But I am thinking of getting a job," Sam continued..."just a part-time one."

140

Mickey stopped posing. "Where is that?"

"Triangle Market that Neal Thomas owns. He said I could stock shelves and carry groceries to cars and stuff like that. I get forty cents an hour. Pretty good, huh?"

"Yeh, that's good, Sam," Mickey replied.

Oral and Donald were walking along the path toward the house along with Sebastian Coceano, Leo's father. The kids turned their attention to their elders, as they approached. It was obvious that their conversation was about their kids.

"Yes, we gotta get ready for school," Sebastian was saying in his Italian accent. "School is everything." Then he finished the sentence looking at Sam. "ain't that right, Sammy?"

"Yes, sir," Sam said. "Is Leo ready, too?"

Sebastian stopped. "He better be." He turned to Oral and Donald, who had stopped on the porch. "We gotta go shop in Fairmont for new clothes – Always something for the kids... and school. That's important, but what else is there, huh? We don't want them to work in the mines, too?"

Oral shook his head 'yes' and answered courteously, "uh-huh."

Sam liked what he heard from Mr. Coceano. He moved a little closer to Sebastian, an unconscious action, to echo the man's, point of view.

As Sebastian Coceano walked up the hill toward his home, Sam took a deep breath – a deep breath of Coceano wisdom and watched him go. He had taken in an earful of what he was beginning to feel, that there was something else out there besides the environment of his Huff house and working for Jamison Coal.

Oral and Donald had already disappeared into the house – quickly dismissing the Italian's wisdom. Mickey and Martha followed their father inside where the attention had turned to the youngest Huff, the two month old brother.

Sam, still outside, stood there till Mr. Coceano disappeared into his house.

Sam had experienced a little about the Coceano's family life through Leo, but didn't think much about it. Now he was beginning to. It was sure different than his own.

Sam took the words of Mr. Coceano to heart. He felt pushed to go ahead. He wished his father would push, too. But no one in his family was "going ahead." They were "giving up." Giving up to the way of life that was there in No. 9. Mr. Coceano was pushing his son out of No. 9. "Push me, too," Sam silently pleaded.

"Sammy, come into dinner." It was his mother's voice shaking him loose from his Coceano's "going ahead" dream. His shoulders sagged. He glanced at the coal tipple below and went into the house.

Come to the Fair!

The Mannington District Fair was THE event of the year in Marion County. For some older folks and alumni of all the local schools, it was homecoming. For younger pre-teen kids, it was a magic place – a carnival with rides and cotton candy and hot dogs and popcorn... For junior high and high school kids it was "coming out" – a way to meet other young kids – yeh, a way for boys and girls of different schools to meet -and to "meet-up".

The largest fair in the state, next to the West Virginia State Fair, the Mannington District Fair, drew 50,000 over five days, pretty impressive for a town of 3,000.

And it was always held in early September, right at the end of the high school teams' football practices, before the season began and at the beginning of school – a perfect time for that "coming out." At the same time, the local newspapers the Fairmont Times and the Times-West Virginian were in the process of previewing the high school football teams, so by "fair time" the interest was building for the football season.

The Mannington District Fair – the final fling of summer, transformed the Mannington High School football field into the fairgrounds – with the usual fair rides like the Ferris wheel, tilt-a-whirl, the carousel, and all of the others, with food booths and exhibits tents around the football field and midway.

The lights to illuminate the Mannington High football field for night games had just been installed. Now they were being used to great advantage for the fair providing terrific lighting for the midway - the center of the football field, from goal line to goal line – and making it easy to identify faces in the crowd. It was an enormous improvement over all the previous years when the fairgrounds were illuminated, but poorly, by strings of lights. Now the lights bright enough to catch a bullet pass in a football game could easily light up the smile from a pass being made for more romantic reasons.

With the football season beginning in just a few days, high school players had already been given their jerseys. It was "cool" to wear them to the fair – a ritual of showing your colors – and to show off. A kid wearing a green jersey was from Mannington; red and black identified a Monongah High School player; blue and gold was Barrackville; a darker blue and gold was East Fairmont; red and white, Rivesville; Fairview, red and black; blue and white, West Fairmont; and scarlet and gray, Farmington.

The football field, now the fair midway, would be filled with hundreds, and sometimes thousands, of people walking from one end to the other – back and forth, stopping to say hello to old friends. School kids would cluster with their friends, looking for new friends. Football players would stop and talk with players from other schools, friends they had known through competing against them last season.

"I'll meet you at the fair," was a good way to arrange a date without having to ask parents permission. After all, "running into someone" at the fair was not exactly a date, was it?

The county was only thirty miles from one end to the other – and from Fairmont to Mannington, just fourteen miles, there were ten high schools – so it was easy to understand how everyone, even students from different schools, would get to know each other. Parents of students often worked at the same coal mine or at one of the factories in Fairmont, like Owens Illinois or Westinghouse. Students were drawn together by religion. Farmington and Mannington each had a Catholic church, but shared the same priest. The annual church picnic – a large social event at Hough Park drew together Catholic kids from both high schools who became friends – but enemies on the football field, basketball court and baseball diamond.

The fair crowds that tramped up and down the Mannington High School football field always turned it into a grassless surface that was as hard as any asphalt parking lot.

The first game on the field only a few days after the fair did not allow any time for the ground to renew itself. The other high school fields in the county were not much better, since they were worn from everyday practices, but the Mannington High Field was known throughout the county as a combat zone because of the fair-hardened surface.

The major solution was to plow up the hardened areas, which would provide a granular dirt surface – better than asphalt – except when it rained. Then it would turn into a muddy quagmire.

But when the fair was on, nobody gave a damn about the grass. Anyway, the first game wasn't for two weeks or so. But now the most fun a kid could ever have all year was to be had now.

Members of high school bands – hundreds of kids – who had marched in the parade an hour before, were now let loose to enjoy the fair for a couple of hours before the buses would take them back home. Dozens of majorettes in their thigh high skirts were an eyeful for young boys – and older guys, too. This time of year when the chill of autumn was in the evening air, bare skin above the knee made young boys think of summer.

The majorettes and band members joined the crowd parading up and down the fair midway while their buses waited in the adjacent parking lot. Like the football players, band members and majorettes were school identified by their colors. They clung together, most often sticking with their classmates, but here and there one might see the shocking sight of a student from one school talking to someone from another, their colors clashing while crossing barriers. Shocking! A Farmington majorette talking to a West Fairmont football player in broad nightlight in the middle of the fairgrounds was brave, brazen conduct – and one hell of an ego trip, for both of them.

Everyone was talking about the 11th Annual Mannington District Fair set to open September 9. It was promised to be "bigger and better", so you knew half the county would be there.

And then considering that the fair would feature a dozen bands – all the county high school bands plus some from outside the county, you knew that definitely everybody would come to the fair!

The traffic into this small community made parking impossible. So if you were going to drive to the fair, you had to beat the crowd. Be there within walking distance of the fairgrounds by four o'clock, or suffer the consequences: stuck in traffic in Sunshine on Route 250, two miles outside of Mannington, going nowhere! The parade traveled the main road - and only road – from downtown Mannington to the fairgrounds. Once the parade started, you stopped wherever you were. If you were in Sunshine, you stayed there, waited until the parade was over and the traffic started moving again.

Mannington residents knew the plan, and so did those who regularly attended the fair; they didn't get stuck out there, but made it into town before the traffic and parked their car somewhere.

The parade started on Water Street just a block from the middle of downtown and would proceed through downtown across a concrete bridge and for about a mile through neighborhoods and to Hough Park and the fairgrounds-football field. All along the path, the route was lined with people sitting on stone walls and on porches of houses whose owners were favored with choice seating.

The bands and clowns and fire trucks all continued their procession to the fairgrounds, past the admission gate and to the Community Building. Consequently, band members were on the fairgrounds free of charge, which was for many students, at least, a chance to enjoy the fair – free.

Lots of kids tried to sneak in – and they did. The fair had hundreds of yards of unfenced area and any kid so dedicated to the proposition of free admission could find a way in.

Admission to the fair wasn't cheap; it cost a quarter just to get in. But at least that would allow you the privilege of walking up and down the midway. Then if you wanted to take a ride or eat, you would need at least another dollar or two.

The parade was over – and the crowds moved slowly along the narrow sidewalks. Young kids, "on their own tonight," would jump off the curb, out onto the street, and run past the older slower walkers. A young mother pushed her baby carriage with baby safely inside. A young couple walked briskly, the husband carrying a two-year-old on his shoulders, while a four-year-old hurried alongside. Everyone was going to the fair!

There was an extra excitement tonight for Sam Huff. It wasn't just the fair. It was Mary, too!

Mary!

Yes, Sam now had a girlfriend. Mary Helen Fletcher of the eighth grade – good student and French horn player - had flirted with him and made him think of something besides football.

Mary's parents were also going to the fair and had okayed the "rendevouz". The "fair date" would last as long as Mr. and Mrs. Fletcher would. Mary was going home with them.

Sam Huff felt the two quarters in his pocket. Those quarters were the whole night. He kept his hands in his pocket, just so he could feel them and make sure they wouldn't fly away! One quarter would get him through the main gate and on to the fairgrounds, and the other quarter would buy something for him and Mary, maybe a candy apple or cotton candy. He would have to count on Mary for financing the rest of the night. Sam was sure her parents gave her some money to spend at the fair. Mary didn't mind. It had become part of their dating routine. Mary knew Sam's poor financial situation, so if she and Sam would plan a movie date at the Farmington Theatre, Mary would buy her ticket and meet Sam inside. Mary got extra money for popcorn and candy, which she would share with Sam during the movie.

They got lucky tonight. Since Mary was a member of the Farmington High School band and marched in the parade and onto the fairgrounds, she didn't have to have an admission. Sam figured there's an extra twenty-five cents to spend once he got inside.

Sam waited anxiously in the long line of people buying tickets. Twenty-five cents would take half of his net worth. He could hear the carnival organ music of the midway and see the flashing lights and hear the buzz of the crowd already filling the field. He grew excited – Mary and the Mannington Fair! Wow. Heck it didn't matter if he didn't have any money. He was happy!

"Next."

Sam quickly put a quarter on the ticket booth counter. The clerk snapped off a ticket and handed it to Sam.

The fairs' joyful noise grew louder as Sam turned to run past the gate, stopped to hand his ticket to the gatekeeper and stepped into fairy land. Now, the music from all the rides fell on top of one another in a cacophony of sound, while the lights flashed and danced in big ferris wheel and carousel circles and rapid back and forth of the cars of the tilt-a-whirls. The smell of popcorn and sweet cotton candy filled his senses. He looked at the sign. "Ten cents for cotton candy" and "ten cents for candy apple." Sam felt for the quarter in his pocket. It was there.

Mary told him she would be at the community building waiting for him. Sam headed there, still fingering the quarter in his pocket. Mary saw him coming and went to meet him.

"We only have till 9 o'clock, Sam. My mom said we would be leaving then. What do you want to do?"

Sam's reply was based on his quarter. "Let's go get some cotton candy. I guess we don't have time to do much else."

Sam didn't want Mary to know exactly how low his funds were. But if they didn't have much time to spend, there was no need to make an issue about the lack of money.

They made their way to the cotton candy and candy apple booth. "Or would you want a candy apple instead?"

"Cotton candy is fine."

Sam placed his quarter on the counter. "Two cotton candies, please."

"Yes, sir." The candy man replied.

148

Sam's face lit up as he watched swirls of pink sugar and air wrap around the cardboard cone as the candy man built a football size glaze of the sweet stuff blown from the candy machine.

He handed them to Sam, who handed one to Mary.

"Twenty cents," he said as he took the quarter and quickly handed Sam back a nickel – all of the money he had to his name. He took a deep breath and hoped the cotton candy would last at least a half hour – and although he wanted to stay with Mary longer, he didn't have money to do anything with. He quietly thought that it was getting important to make some money since now, that he was dating Mary, he couldn't depend on her to furnish the fun. He heard Mary's voice, but was lost in the thought about money.

"Sam, did you hear me?"

"Oh yeh – what was it?"

"I said 'Let's walk around some," Mary said excitedly.

"Oh sure," Sam said.

They turned to join the crowds and walked slowly side by side, tilting their heads back and forth biting off the cotton candy as they went.

Sam was still thinking about his money life. "My dad thinks it's time I started working and earn some money." They resumed walking. "My dad thinks the coal company would give me a job this summer. I ain't sixteen yet, so I can't quit school - but I could quit in just two more years."

"But you wouldn't want to quit, would you?"

"Everybody in my family – all my sisters and my brother did."

"Everyone?"

"Yeh, so heck I'm almost fourteen…"

"Please Sam, you gotta stay in school so we can do some things together…" Suddenly Mary caught a glimpse of red and gray clad young boys in Farmington red and gray football jerseys, "That's Rudy and some of the football boys. Let's go over."

Rudy Banick was a year ahead of Sam and Mary. He was just a freshman who had already started making a name for himself around Farmington.

All the local football fans – the guys who went to the Circle Bar, the local pool halls and beer joints to talk about the upcoming football season, were talking about little Rudy Banick – and how he was going to be a great player someday.

The dark, wiry, small handsome kid was expected to play a lot this 1947 season, even if he were just a freshman. In practice he was running a lot of plays with the first team.

The first game with East Fairmont High School was coming up in just ten days – on September 11 at East-West Stadium.

A game at East-West Stadium was special. The big imposing structure built by the WPA in the 1930's seated 6,000, had an outstanding lighting system for night football and was considered one of the best high school stadiums in the state.

Playing here could be a shock for many of the high school kids who were use to playing on their home fields, most of which had wooden bleachers to seat a few hundred.

The Farmington High School field had no bleachers – just a bank of ground on both sides where people could sit and watch. Most chose to stand. And Farmington's field had no lights either, so most of the games were played either in the daytime, after school on Friday or on the fields of other schools. A game between Farmington and one of its small enrollment Class B opponents usually drew a few hundred fans. Monongah, Rivesville, Fairview and Barrackville fields were no better – maybe worse. No lights – therefore no night games, and afternoon games were sparsely attended.

A game of importance might be rescheduled to East-West Stadium to handle the demand in attendance. And whenever East Fairmont and West Fairmont played their games at the stadium, the games always attracted large numbers. The games were well covered by the local newspapers – The Fairmont Times and the West-Virginian.

Now Farmington High School and freshman Rudy Banick were going to face both Fairmont schools to open the 1947 season: the East Fairmont Bees on September 11; followed by the West Fairmont Polar Bears the following Friday night, September 18.

How could little Farmington compete against these two Class A giants? Both East Fairmont and West Fairmont had great reputations – and had produced great players over the years.

Mary took a piece of cotton candy. "Are you ready for the first game, Rudy?"

"Yeh," Rudy said with a nervous laugh. "Are you coming?"

"Oh yeh – we'll be there," Mary said. "My Mom and Dad always go!"

"I'm coming, too," Sam said. "Me and Leo are going to hitchhike down. I hope you beat 'em."

"Me, too," Rudy said. Another nervous laugh.

Mary finished her cotton candy and turned to Sam, "We better go. Mom will be waiting for me."

"Bye, Rudy – See you in school," Sam said.

"Yeh bye," Mary added. She turned to shout back at Rudy. "Beat those Bees."

The Kid on the Floor

Ray Kelly, the second year football coach at Farmington High School, was shopping for groceries in Triangle Market.

"Coach Kelly."

The voice was familiar. Ray Kelly turned away from the vegetable bin. Frank Gatski was looking at him. Kelly had to smile. His eyes widened to see his old high school buddy - and now famous professional football player.

Ray couldn't help but be embarrassed by the greeting coming from the Cleveland Browns center. "Coach Kelly! That sounds pretty damn good coming from you." He shook Frank's hand. "How are you? I'm so glad you're doing so well. We read about you…"

Frank interrupted him. He wasn't good at hearing praise, especially this up-close and from an old friend who had played alongside him on the same Farmington High team in 1936. Frank knew how lucky he had been to be with the Browns – and he was doing what was expected of him. There was no need for praise.

They reminisced about 1936. Then, Ray was a junior playing first string guard. Frank was a senior who was the substitute center. Ray smiled – "The substitute center? – I guess I've improved some," Frank quipped. "It shows you can't underestimate what a man can do."

Frank was home visiting Benny for a couple of days after the 1947 opening game victory over Buffalo on September 5, 30 – 14.

The two men talked about the "old days" together while Ray filled his basket with vegetables for dinner at home. Finally the talk turned to the high school game this weekend.

"We have our first game with East Fairmont this Friday," Kelly noted.

"Yes, I know. We'd like to beat those Fairmont teams, if we can, but we never did when I was in high school, but you did - that next year in '37."

"Yes," Ray said. We had a hell of a game."

"I saw it," Frank said. "I was working in the mines then with some guys from Fairmont. Boy, did you make it nice for me. Just think, I was able to brag to those big city boys."

Kelly laughed. "Yeh, we had a good team in my senior year."

"Yeh," Frank acknowledged, "and beat both Fairmont teams!"

As Kelly headed toward the meat section, Frank walked alongside. "You're supposed to be in Cleveland, Frank, so why are...?"

"We just had an opening game – beat Buffalo 30 – 14. We play the Brooklyn Dodgers next. Coach Brown gave us a couple of days off. He's good that way. I go back tomorrow. I came in to see my brother Benny in Grant Town. I'm staying with him. And sometimes I stop and see my buddies here in Farmington. I plan to stop at the Circle Bar for a beer before I go back to Benny's. Benny needed bread. I'm glad I stopped here to get it 'cause I had a chance to see you – and wish you good luck on the season. I still think a lot about the old Farmington school days."

Kelly laughed. "Yeh, me, too. Except I got to think about the new Farmington school days, too.

They both laughed.

"Let's get some bread," Ray said.

As they turned the corner around shelves near the bread rack, Frank nearly stumbled – over a kid kneeling on the floor. Frank's knee bumped him in the back and sent the boy face down toward the floor. Frank and Ray bent down to help the kid up.

"I'm sorry boy. You okay?" Frank asked.

"Yeh, sure, I'm okay..." the boy replied. "Didn't mean to be in your way."

Kelly took him by the arm to help him to his feet. "It's Sam Huff. Frank, you remember him. He's No. 9."

"Sure I do. Oral's boy. How you doing, Sam?"

Sam's face turned red. "Geesh, I didn't expect to see you here, Coach – or you, Frank. Geesh…" He shook his hand. "Geesh…"

There he was standing like a fool in front of the two most important men in his life – Frank Gatski, the guy he had come to idolize and Coach Kelly, who had Sam's eighth grade success and the future of his high school playing days in his hands. Sam looked up at both of them and they seemed ten feet tall. Sam wanted to run and hide.

He tried to explain, "I was looking for a can of beans… Geesh, I almost knocked you down, Frank."

Kelly nudged Frank, "That's better than most of the pros can do, Sam."

Frank placed a hand on Sam's head, "Is he going to be a player, Coach?"

"Yeh, I think so. If he can grow a little. I think he's tough enough. That's that Number 9 stuff you all have, I guess."

Suddenly there was a small, sweet voice of a young girl from the next shelves.

"Sammy, I found the beans… are you ready to go?"

Sam turned his face to the floor. "Oh shoot…" He was hoping the voice would go away. Instead, the young pretty face of Mary Fletcher was looking right at him and then up at Frank and Coach Kelly.

"Oops… I'm sorry." She turned quickly and ran around the shelves and out of sight.

Sam could feel the heat in his face as he watched her go. This was not the time for any girl to be around. She had done enough damage to Sam's intention to become a star football player someday.

The Mary Fletcher charms had stolen something away. She had kissed him – and put her arms around him – and her young body against him – and now football was not the only thing Sam was thinking about. Yes, Mary Fletcher had kissed him and Sam Huff was hers.

Sam struggled to explain his presence in the store to his coach and idol. "Mary's mom sent her for groceries… I was helping…"

154

Frank helped Sam out of his embarrassment by getting back to the important business of football. "What position do you play, Sam?"

"I play on the line. I'd like to play center someday – maybe next year when I'm in the ninth grade."

Coach Kelly explained, "The eighth graders are just learning the basics. At least they're out there learning how to play."

Frank and Coach Kelly walked toward the check-out counter. Sam followed, then he saw Mary at the cash register. He breathed a sigh of relief. He didn't want to be anywhere near her as long as Frank and Coach Kelly were in the building. He stopped and walked to the back of the store and watched Mary as the clerk rang up the bill.

Fight for Farmington High!

"Gimme an F!"

"F" the auditorium shouted.

"Gimme an A"

"A" was given.

Mickey Huff made it as a cheerleader. Now she and Ruth Mary Conaway and the Farmington High student body, were spelling out FARMERS - all three hundred and twenty students, from seventh through twelfth grade, jammed into the auditorium to raise their voices in support of their team. Up on the stage were the boys in their red football jerseys. The crowd roared.

"That's the way you spell it! Here's the way you yell it! FARMERS! FARMERS! FARMERS!"

Sam Huff and Leo Coceano sat in the back in the eighth grade section and waited for Coach Kelly to step up to the microphone.

"This will be our first game. East Fairmont is a good team. We hope you can come to East-West Stadium in Fairmont to cheer these young men on. We're going to do our best and I hope that will be enough to beat East Fairmont."

Coach Kelly introduced all the players, each of whom stepped forward to loud cheers. Finally he said, "One of our seniors, Mitch Napalo, will speak to you."

The big tackle spoke nervously, "You know, we've got a tough game tomorrow – but, you know, if you'll be there to, you know, support us, you know, we'll come away …(he cleared his throat) with a victory!"

The crowd yelled! East Fairmont was dead meat!

The headlines in the Fairmont Times shouted back louder than the Farmington student body. East Fairmont 34, Farmington 6

The Class A school was too much for the Class B Farmers. The game was no contest. And in fact, East Fairmont physically humiliated Farmington by getting rid of their main backfield threat, Neil Doll, in the first quarter, and in addition, knocking three other first stringers out of the game. Little Rudy Banick, the freshman, who in practice, showed considerable promise for a fourteen-year-old, got a chance to play and performed well for his first action.

The game bore out the general consensus that the Fairmont teams, both East and West, used the early games against Class B opponents of the Mason-Dixon Conference as "warm-up" games for their "regular" season against the states' bigger schools.

Sam Huff and Leo Coceano watched the game in despair. They had hitch- hiked the nine miles from No. 9 to East-West Stadium. Getting a ride was easy in the caravan that flowed down No. 9 Road and Route 250 to Fairmont. John Butcher, a No. 9 neighbor, spotted the pair on the road, got them to Fairmont, and waited for them after the game for the ride back.

Butcher reviewed the game for his passengers in a loud voice over the loud noisy rush of the motor in his '42 Chevy.

"Those boys from Fairmont are just too good for us," Butcher said. "Don't know the last time we beat 'em. They got too many boys in that school for us. Next week we play West Fairmont and the same thing is going to happen."

Sam and Leo didn't say anything but "uh" and "yeh" – inaudible to Mr. Butcher who continued his insight on the high school game for nine miles.

"Yes, sir," he concluded, "Next week when we play West Fairmont, it's gonna be the same thing."

Mr. Butcher was wrong. It was worse!

West Fairmont Polar Bears 48, Farmington 0

West Fairmont, one of the best high school programs in the state did "warm-up" on the Farmers. The Bears were good. Yes, some said 'big time'!

Bill Leskavor, the big star of the 1946 Polar Bears, was regarded as one of the best players to ever play in West Virginia. His exploits at West Fairmont made him a local legend and prompted the states sports writers to award him the trophy given to the "best football player in the state". After considering several scholarship offers, Leskavor chose the University of Kentucky and Coach Bear Bryant, who was counting on him to play a major role.

The West Fairmont coach, Paul "Biz" Dawson, was determined to contend for the state championship every year. He was not content with what most considered outstanding material. He even "recruited" – persuading some of the county's best player's to come to school there. Jimmy Priester, the kid from No. 9, who grew up with the Huff's and Coceano's, went to Farmington High until 1946 when Dawson persuaded him, he would do better ten miles up the road at his big school. Jimmy got the message and became a Polar Bear. "Biz" was right. Jimmy was good enough to make All-County in 1946 and received a football scholarship to West Virginia University, where he became a member of the 1947 squad.

Now, in 1947, the rumor was going around about a boy named George Calich, a 6' 2", 165 pound, three sport star at little Rivesville, just a couple of miles from Fairmont. Calich was just in his sophomore year and showing tremendous promise – and was being coveted by Coach Dawson. The boy's parents were already considering a move two miles to Fairmont, at which time the Rivesville Ram would become a Polar Bear for his junior season.

Sam and Leo followed the routine of the week before and caught a ride with Mr. Butcher to East-West Stadium for the West Fairmont game. Of course they had to listen to his dire analysis on the way back to No. 9. "It's what I told you last week," Butcher sounded high and loud. "We can't play with those Fairmont teams. They're just too good…too many players."

"Uh-huh," both boys replied.

"I'll say one thing," he shouted, "that Rudy Banick is going to be a good player someday. The boy's only a freshman, but he's so small, I thought they'd kill him."

The Chevy screeched to a halt. Sam and Leo got out. Sam slammed the door shut. "Thank you, Mr. Butcher, for the ride. Maybe we can win next week."

"We're playing Clay-Battelle. That little school is more our speed. Bye boys."

Sam and Leo were discouraged by the two straight losses 34 - 6 and 48 – 0.

Leo shook his head, "We got skunked."

Sam agreed, "It makes me mad as hell. I mean to lose by that much. No, it makes me mad as hell to lose. Period."

"One good thing. Rudy got in the game."

"Why is that good?"

"I mean he got to play."

"Rudy is a good player – and he's only in the ninth grade."

"We'll play with him next year."

"Yeh, we will. I like Rudy. Coach Kelly said some of us eighth grade players were going to scrimmage the second string. Does that mean Rudy- he's a second stringer."

"I don't know. Guess we'll find out."

Two days later on Monday, the eighth grade versus ninth grade scrimmage was on. Rudy took the short pass snap from center, spun around, faked the ball to a halfback, spun back and headed up field. Sam Huff was in the hole and ready for the tackle – Rudy stiff-armed Sam and shoved him to the ground. As Rudy dashed to the right, Leo came from his end position. He would nail him. Rudy went in, then out, and Leo caught air and fell on his face. Touchdown!

Coach Kelly smiled. That beaming narrow-eyed glint. He could see a future star in the slick little freshman. "OK, boys, ball on the forty yard line – eighth grade's ball."

This was a fun time for Coach Kelly. He would call the plays for each team – so that he could involve all the players that he wanted. There were no kick-offs, but instead, the ball was placed on the forty yard line for each team. If there weren't enough eighth graders or ninth graders for their respective

159

teams, the coach would pick an upperclassman who was a second or third string player to fill in.

Kelly barked, "Ball on the forty, first down." Now it was the eighth graders ball. Sam was playing center, just like his No. 9 hero, and Leo was the left end. Harry Sopuch, a talented kid, was the left halfback.

"Huddle up," Kelly shouted.

In the huddle, Kelly whispered, "Pass two seventy." He repeated, "Pass two seventy." Everyone understood that!

Eyes looked up at him in acknowledgment. "Okay, break."

They came to the line. Eleven players, all in uniforms too big, make a loud, rattling sound of leather against leather as they come to the line of scrimmage. Kelly couldn't help but smile.

The snap went to Sopuch. He rolled left, turned and threw back to Leo, who was wide open. The pass on first down had come as a surprise. Leo gathered it in and ran toward the goal line. Twenty yards later Rudy would make the tackle.

"First down," shouted Kelly.

The players hustled to the line of scrimmage. In the huddle Kelly whispered, "One forty-eight." It was a running play to the right. "On two."

Sam led the team to the line of scrimmage.

Sopuch barked the signals, "Set, one, two…"

Sam centered the ball, but behind Sopuch, who was moving to the right, the ball went past Sopuch, who turned quickly to fall on it for a ten yard loss!

"Sam," Kelly shouted, "you got to lead him with that center."

"I know it," Sam replied. "That was my fault. I forgot."

"Well you can't forget," Kelly shouted back.

Leo slapped Sam on the butt, "Dat's okay."

As the scrimmage continued, Rudy Banick showed why he was going to earn a letter in his freshman year. Sam and Leo were feeling a little more grown up after having "played against" the older boys. The eighth grade never did score, but Leo and Sam had a lot to talk about after. They showered and began to hitch- hike back home to No. 9.

Just like John Butcher had predicted, the Farmington Farmers did get their first win of the 1947 season by beating Clay-Battelle 28 – 0. The smaller school did match up much better than the Fairmont schools. The Farmers won their next two games against Fairview 14 – 13 and Mannington 21 – 20, before a 33 – 0 loss to Barrackville and a scoreless tie with Rivesville.

Sam stayed out for football the entire season. He was smaller than most kids his age, 5 foot 5 and 120 pounds, but he was a tough kid, nevertheless. Coach Kelly tried to make sure Sam and boys his size were kept out of harms way. Sam liked the idea of being a football player. It made him feel grown up and admired by girls, especially Mary. But Sam knew he would have to grow to be a good player. On the field against bigger boys, he was getting pushed around, and even if he tried his best, he was still the one ending up on the bottom.

Mary knew he would be on the team next year, and wouldn't that be neat. She would be in the band and Sam on the football team.

Sam felt he would be on the team, but that wouldn't be enough, he wanted to be good, he wanted to be the leader like he was in James Fork Elementary, when he and Leo would choose up sides - but it wasn't that way yet at Farmington High School.

Welcome to Mountaineer Field

"Welcome, ladies and gentlemen. It's September 27th and we're across the airwaves from Mountaineer Field in Morgantown on a gorgeous autumn day along the banks of the Monongahela River. Today the West Virginia University Mountaineers play the Otterbein College Cardinals in the 1947 season opener."

Talk about excitement! It was the voice of Jack Fleming coming through loud and clear and West Virginia University football was on the radio. Sam rubbed his hands together. Jack Fleming got into the head of Sam then, and never left. It was the sweetest sound he ever heard outside of Uncle Leroy's harmonica. West Virginia was his team!

Morgantown was only about thirty miles from No. 9, but for young Sam Huff, it might as well have been a thousand miles away. It didn't matter – Fleming was bringing the game home to Sam. It was an autumn Saturday ritual – not just for Sam, but all of No. 9. You didn't have to stick by a radio. If you went outside, you could hear the broadcast from a neighbor. Everywhere you went, the voice of Jack Fleming was in the air. "The punt sails high to Jimmy Priester…"

"Jimmy Priester!" Sam shouted out loud. Sam ran to his mom. "Hey, Mom, did you hear that? The punt went to … Jimmy…"

Katherine looked up from the table, where she was folding clothes. "Jimmy who, son?"

"Jimmy Priester. He's playing for West Virginia. Listen."

It was Fleming again. "… and Jimmy Priester made a beautiful return of the punt to the Otterbein Cardinals 45 yard line."

Katherine became interested for a moment. "Is that the same Jimmy Priester that lived here?"

"Yeh, it's him!"

Sam turned away from his mom and layed down on the floor beside the radio – and Jack Fleming – to be transported to Mountaineer Field.

Mickey walked in the room. "Who's winning?"

"We are... West Virginia is. I'd like to play for West Virginia someday..."

Mickey smiled. "Sam, you gotta get through Farmington High School first – and none of us got through yet." And she was gone.

All at once Fleming was gone, too. Sam began to think of the truth in Mickey's statement and wondered what would make him different than his brother and sisters. Would he quit at sixteen, just like they did? It seemed the Huff way of doing things. He couldn't imagine it. He liked being with his buddies, Leo and Murvyn and the other guys. For sure they weren't going to quit. Leo's parents were even talking about college for his older brother, Dominick. And Murvyn, the smartest kid in school, was sure as heck going to college.

"Damn it," Sam thought. I can't quit school. I just can't quit. I got to keep up."

The 1947 high school football season was coming to a close. Farmington had one game left with Monongah to decide second place in the Mason-Dixon Conference. The Farmers had three losses, but two were to the Class A Fairmont teams.

The game played on a muddy Farmington field ended in a 14-7 loss and enabled Monongah to finish ahead of Farmington in the final conference standings.

Rudy Banick continued to impress everyone – coaches, fans, writers. The small, wiry freshman scored the lone touchdown against Monongah. Because of his elusiveness he acquired the nickname "slick".

First Check

Sam Aloi was looking for someone. He needed help.

The big man was a "do everything" man for the Manchin family that had begun to dominate the business community of Farmington.

Papa Joe Manchin and his wife, Kay, who established a grocery store in Farmington, were a part of the American Dream wave of the early twentieth century. The young couple had come to Farmington where Papa Joe began business with a tavern on Mill Street.

Papa Joe Manchin's grocery store was the biggest and the busiest place in town. There were other stores, too, the Neal Thomas' market across the street, Philip Gango's store, on the corner – but Manchin's was the place with the best selection. You would have to go the A&P Stores in Fairmont or Mannington – both seven miles away, to find more to choose from.

Like all good American dreamers, Joe and Kay had children – three boys, John, Joe, James and twin daughters, Rose and Francis.

Of course all of the family contributed at the store, and in the early forties, they decided to expand. Papa Joe bought the building next door and John opened a new venture, Manchin's Carpets. Before long, furniture was added, and shortly thereafter, you could buy every appliance you would need

The business was growing – why shouldn't it. The mines, at least six large operations within five miles of Farmington, were all working. Hundreds of miners reached a production of 200,000 tons per day. The associated businesses like machine shops and trucking companies were all busy, too. Unemployment was unheard of. The groceries went flying out of Manchin's – especially on payday.

Sam Aloi was one of the more faithful employees who the Manchin family could count on and trust without question – and besides he had

164

become family by marrying Francis. Like almost all grocery stores, Manchin's delivered groceries. Not everyone had a car, so if a customer came in with a list of groceries they wanted, the items were selected, boxed, and then either paid for or charged, and marked for delivery. That's where Sam Aloi came in. And that's why he needed help.

Sam was walking down the steps of Manchin's when he saw Mary and Sam leave Neal Thomas' market. They crossed the street toward him.

Big Sam's voice boomed out, "Sammy, you working at Neal's place?"

"No," Sam replied.

Aloi got to the point. "Why don't you help me? We gotta stock a da shelves and deliver the groceries…"

"I ain't old enough to drive."

"Don't matter. How old are you?"

"Fourteen!"

"That's okay. I drive, you take in the groceries. You get groceries in the boxes."

Mary smiled proudly that her boyfriend was being offered a job. Her smile was a nod for Sam to say 'yes'.

Aloi continued, "You ask your mom and dad. You think about it. You come after school. I'll tell John Manchin about you."

"Okay, I'll think about it." Sam promised. But his mind was made up. He was excited. He was seeing dollar signs.

Big Sam Aloi opened the door of the Manchin's delivery truck and slid in behind the steering wheel. He banged the door shut. "I see you… maybe tomorrow, ok?"

"Yeh, I'll see you," Sam promised. As the truck disappeared around the corner, Mary held Sam's arm close to her as they turned to walk toward the school.

As they walked and talked, money wasn't mentioned, but Sam was seeing dollar signs again, and for the first time in his young life, the chance to take care of his girl. He could pay for them both to go to the movies, instead of meeting her inside. And he could buy the popcorn, pop and caramels. This was pretty heady stuff. Instantly, the offer of a job made Sam feel more grown up. He wondered if the Manchin's gave him a check – a check with his name on it. "I never cashed a check before. How do you do it?"

"You sign the back, silly."

"You do?"

"Do you think they would give me a check?"

By the time they arrived at the school, Sam was ready to go tell Mr. Aloi 'yes', he would work at Manchin's. What he didn't realize was how much his life was about to change. He was about to experience some Manchin magic.

Sam looked at the check in his hands from Manchin's. It was dated December 20, 1947 and made "pay to the order of Robert Lee Huff". The memo stated "23 hours at 50 cents per hour," his first check – for $11.50. His fingers were growing numb from holding it tight.

Mary gave him a playful nudge, "Pretty good."

Sam smiled, "Now we can go to the movies and I can pay... for everything."

And with Christmas coming, Sam was already thinking ahead. "And I can buy Mom and Dad something for Christmas."

The first check was the beginning of a relationship with the Manchin family that benefited Sam in more ways than earning minimum wage. The young boy was beginning to see how business worked – that you could make money outside of working in a deep coal mine.

Now every day when he worked, he was associating with others who counted on him to stock shelves or deliver groceries with courtesy – and be helpful when necessary.

By getting to know the Manchin's, he was seeing life as never before. Hell, the Manchin's could do anything. Just decide what it was, and then do it! Sam didn't know the word "optimism," but that's what he was feeling.

Education was important. He saw everyone in the Manchin family going to school. And quitting school was unthinkable. College was necessary. He felt the kindness and respect for God and man in their religious faith. He watched the informal celebration outside the store of the birth of Joseph Manchin II, the first son of John Manchin, who was the first-born of Papa Joe.

Now, Robert Lee "Sam" Huff, who had the capacity to be something special, was seeing the world in a whole different light and being tapped and fed a good dose of American Dream.

At Manchin's, work didn't end at the whistle sound of shift change. You did what you had to do to get the job done…done right!

Manchin's store, while being one of the largest stores in town, and the one with the biggest business, gave back in many ways. John Manchin annually held a banquet for the football team and coaches. Whenever the town needed something, you could count on a generous contribution from the Manchin's.

The Farmington Volunteer Fire Department was especially blessed by the Manchin's. The local pick-up baseball team of young teenagers coached by Bob Pasko, also came under the Manchin umbrella. A. James, youngest son of Papa Joe, took the team in and made it his own. "We'll call the team Manchins," he ordered. He paid for the "rights" with red and white jerseys with MANCHINS printed across the front and supplied all the balls and bats they needed. When "Manchins" would "tour" two miles to No. 9, and three miles to Ida May and Carolina to play other coal camp teams, they often went in a Manchin's truck.

Manchins, other team – the older guys, semi-pro caliber, baseball team of high school, college players and older veteran ballplayers also got the Manchin's treatment with full uniforms, equipment and everything necessary to compete in the Marion County Sandlot League.

The number of charitable activities supported by the Manchin's was endless. Pretty soon Sam was wondering why they just didn't name the town "Manchins."

Now with a little money in his pocket, even though it was minimum wage, part-time money, Sam had more to think about than just the fun and games. It was December, and football was over. Several of the eighth

167

graders thought about junior high basketball, and he thought about going out. But that would mean practicing after school, which would mean less hours at Manchin's. Less money. He wondered what his buddy Leo was going to do? And he wondered if Leo could get a job at Manchin's? That'd be great, the two of them working together. Heck, they could hitch hike home to No. 9 together, too.

Sam couldn't wait to get back home so he could see Leo and talk about his new life plan.

He knocked on the door, and waited. He heard a voice inside shout. "It's Sammy."

In a few seconds Leo came to the door holding a book from school, a math book and a pencil.

Sam opened the screen door and Leo stepped out on the porch.

"I got an idea?"

"Yeh."

"I'm working now, ya know, at Manchin's and…" Then he stopped. He now paid attention to the book in Leo's hand. "You studying?"

"Yes, I got to. My mama and papa…"

"Yeh, yeh. I know. You're gonna make straight A's, ain't you?" Sam leaned over to look at the book cover. "That's math, ain't it?"

Leo set the book on the banister. "What's your big plan?"

"Oh, shit, it's nothin'. You would say 'no' anyway. I was gonna see if you wanted to work at Manchin's with me. We could make some money…"

Leo interrupted him. "We already talked here. Nobody works. I mean – my dad he says, "My work is school. So that's it!"

"That's what I thought."

"Hey, I'm sorry…"

"Yeh, me, too." Sam changed the subject. "You going out for basketball – junior high. But, well are you going out? I wouldn't mind, if you are…"

Sam often tested Leo for his opinion, in spite of having taking the leadership from their second grade days at James Fork Elementary. Sam

168

knew Leo was smart and was growing more independent every day. Oh hell, he hated to admit it, but Leo was smarter than he was – and yes, Sam the leader wanted to follow him sometimes.

"So what do you think… about basketball?"

Leo picked up his math book. "We're only in the eighth grade – junior high. Maybe next year, when we're in the ninth… I could ask my mom…"

"If you go out, I will, too," Sam finally declared.

"What about the work at Manchin's?" Leo asked.

"I'll work when I can, if I'm on the team. It's like being in school."

Leo did not go out for basketball – and neither did Sam.

Browns Repeat!

By December 7, 1947, Frank Gatski was on top of the world. He was the starting center of the Cleveland Browns, who had just won their second consecutive Western Division Championship of the All American Conference.

They completed the regular season by whipping the Baltimore Colts 42 - 0. Their record of 12 - 1 - 1 included a win over the New York Yankees in Cleveland in October, 26 - 17 before 80,067 fans, the largest crowd in professional football history; and in late November, a 28-28 tie with the same Yankees in Yankee Stadium before 70,060 fans, the largest to ever watch a game in New York City. The 28 - 28 tie was a classic. The press called it "magnificent, an almost unbelievable comeback", as the Browns, behind 28 - 0 midway in the second period, came back, behind the passing of Otto Graham to tie the game and protect their lead in the Western Division.

The Yankees, in spite of a loss and a tie with the Browns, won the Eastern Division Championship and would challenge the Browns again on December 14 for the Conference Crown.

The All-American Conference, now in its second year was still shaky, and pessimists knew it wouldn't survive. Sportswriter, Franklin Lewis, of the Cleveland Press, said the conference would "fold up unless a complete and dramatic reorganization is effected." After only the first year in 1946, the Miami Seahawk franchise folded and was replaced by the Baltimore Colts beginning in 1947. The attendance bore out the Seahawks demise: only 9,000 fans showed up for a home game with the Browns. Attendance all around the League was sporadic. While the Browns drew record crowds, the Brooklyn Dodgers, the Chicago Rockets, and others struggled to make payroll.

To make matters worse, the "other" league, the established National Football League, was proposing something that would further diminish the All-American Conference.

On December 10, 1947, just four days before the All-American Conference Championship game at Yankee Stadium, the National Football League Commissioner, Bert Bell told the press about the establishment of a football hall of fame to be built in Latrobe, Pennsylvania. The memorial "to be controlled and operated by the NFL or it's designate will be built on a sixty acre tract, and will include a large stadium, recreation area, a community center and a national shrine for professional football."

Was this announcement intended to minimize the importance of the American Conference, while elevating the NFL to heights justifying a "shrine"?

If the All-American Conference was having second-year growing pains, you couldn't tell it by the championship game between the Cleveland Browns and the New York Yankees at Yankee Stadium on December 14.

It was the third game the two teams played in 1947, and it drew 61,879 fans and headline attention around the country – enough to rival the older, National Football League.

Writer Leo R. Petersen started his Monday column with a summary of the win.

> "The Cleveland Browns won the All-American
> Football Conference Championship for the
> second consecutive year today when the passing
> of Otto Graham and the pile-driving of Marion
> Motley carried them to a 14 to 3 victory over
> the New York Yankees."

The article closed with the financial spoils of victory and defeat.

> "The gate receipts totaled $200,820.50, which,
> along with the attendance, created new All-
> American Conference records. Each member of the

winning Cleveland team received $1,191.99, while a losing share was worth $794.66 to each Yankee."

Oscar Fraley, another writer, reported on the mood of each team after the game, which was played on a frozen and slippery field.

"Massive Marion Motley, 230 pound fullback from Nevada, was the Browns standout and for the Yanks it was Buddy (Black Lightning) Young. They must have spent the week working out with The Ice Follies because they were the only two who were able to go for any distance on the slippery turf! In the dressing quarters of the winning Browns there was little excitement. Only a few cheers, mostly from scrubs, with nice clean suits marked the occasion. The Browns have mostly young players, but already this is old stuff. They won the first championship last year and now had repeated."

Coach Paul Brown climbed onto a trunk and shouted, "Congratulations! And listen, just as a special memento, keep your jackets."

Gatski was making a good living – for him. He didn't need much. But he was getting paid $2000 for the season which was fine with him. But still just about anyone playing professional football had to be concerned about job security. And even though the money was good, Frank, like most players, had to supplement their income with an off-season job. For Frank, he would be back to hard labor – driving spikes on the railroad tracks in West Virginia.

The Great Gatski at Midnight Mass

On Christmas Eve, Sam was putting the finishing touches on his present for Mary. He had heard "good things come in small packages." So he was feeling pretty good about his.

The bracelet, $2.95 at Parish's Drug Store in Farmington, ended up being smaller than he had imagined when it was boxed up. He was sitting on the floor watching Mickey wrap a present for her boyfriend Billy Maxwell. He tried to follow her folding method. It was the Scotch tape that was giving him problems. So Mickey jumped in.

"Here, let me help you, Sam."

"I can do it," he demanded.

"Oh sure," she replied as she yanked it from him. "Just a minute."

Sam sat back on his rear and watched Mickey's magic fingers fly from the Scotch tape to the little package. A small bow instantly appeared on top.

"How did you do that?"

"It's being a woman, Sam. Here." She handed it to him and returned to Billy's present.

Sam stood up. "Listen, I hear Leo's car."

Mickey stopped for a moment. "Yep," she looked at the clock. "Midnight Mass. They always go to church."

Outside, the car door closed shut, then another, and another. Sam could imagine the whole Coceano family – Leo, Dominick, Tranquilla, Maria, and Sebastian – getting in the car.

Sam looked outside. He could see the lights of their car as it pulled out onto the main hard road for the two mile trip to St. Peter's in Farmington. Leo was an altar boy and they got an early start so he could get ready for Mass. But it was also necessary to go early for Christmas Eve because the little church

173

was always crowded. If you didn't, you ended up standing in the line-up along the walls or in a jammed vestibule in the back of the church.

As Sam stood at the window looking out into the darkness, another pair of headlights approached, and then another. In no time nearly a dozen cars lit up the streets and alleys around No. 9. It reminded Sam of a scene from a war movie he saw at the Farmington Theatre when airplanes were taking off on a midnight bombing mission. The cars, one after the other, entered the hard road like planes approaching a runway, to take off for their destination, St. Peters. Soon they were gone and stillness fell on the shadowed dwellings.

At church, the altar boys, eight in all, were dressing, putting on their cassocks and surplices. The choir was singing "Silent Night" as Father Gleeson put on his vestments.

Mike Arcure, one of the altar boys, brought out the water and towel used for the consecration and placed it on a table. He looked out into the crowded congregation. His eyes immediately fell on the pew in the middle of the church where his family sat. Everyone's family, it seemed, always occupied the same pew every Sunday and holy day. He nodded to his father, Nick, who, with arms folded, acknowledged him with the slightest nod. The front row of the church, the entire front row – both sides of the center aisle were occupied by the Manchin clan: Papa Joe and Mama Kay and their boys, John, Joe, Jimmy and daughters Francis and Rose and Mary Gouzd Manchin, the young wife of John, who was holding a small baby, their first boy. They named him Joseph, after Papa Joe. Their first born, a daughter, Janet, was two years old now. But a boy… the first boy…

As Mike turned back toward the sacristy his thoughts took flight… "the small Manchin baby is wrapped in swaddling clothes and lying in a manger… just like Baby Jesus…"

Inside the sacristy Mike joined the other altar boys, who stood in silence awaiting further orders from Father Gleeson. Nobody dared to speak.

But Mike had a burning question for Leo. So he whispered.

174

"You going out for basketball?"

"I don't think so," whispered back Leo. "Got homework. Mom says next year maybe."

"Sam asked me if you were going out."

"I know, he asked me, too."

The altar boys were all dressed. Church was filling up. Leo lit the candles. Father Gleeson poured the wine and carefully put the hosts in the chalice for communion.

As Leo left the altar to return to the sacristy, he turned around to take one last look to make sure all the candles had remained lit. His eyes set on the gigantic man standing in the back of the church.

"Holy Sh_ _ ," Leo thought. "It's Frank... Frank Gatski..."

Leo quickly entered the sacristy, and before you knew it all the altar boys knew that the Browns center was in the congregation.

Father Gleeson looked over his spectacles at the altar boys whose whispering was beginning to annoy him. After all it was approaching the sacred moment of Christmas at midnight. The altar boys should be contemplating more heavenly images in their preparation to serve mass. Finally Father had to speak up. He turned to the boys and spoke in a soft hushed, deliberate voice.

"Boys, I know who's out there. It's Frank...what's his name... the famous soccer player."

"No, Father, football!" the chorus of altar boys shot back in unison and in a voice loud enough to break the silent night in the sanctuary.

"Shh" Father admonished.

"Yes, football!" Father conceded. He was embarrassed to think he could not forget his Irish roots – and the other football game of soccer. He cleared his throat. "All right, boys. Merry Christmas to you all. Let's begin now."

Father and his eight altar boys went out to celebrate midnight mass.

Leo couldn't wait to get back home to tell Sam that Frank was at church, but it would have to wait till after all the presents were opened on Christmas morning.

By ten o'clock, Leo asked his mom if he could go see Sam and was off and running with his message. He knocked on the door and Sam answered.

The door banged closed as Leo came in.

"I got something to tell ya."

"What's that?"

"I saw Frank last night."

"Frank Gatski?"

"Yeh, he was at church, at midnight mass."

"Oh, man, wish I was there."

"Yeh, well, he was there."

"Wonder where he'll be. Do you think he'd be coming to town? I saw him at Neal Thomas' grocery store a while back. Maybe we could see him some there."

In the Huff's small house, a conversation is bound to be overheard. Oral and Katherine came to the door to wish Leo a "Merry Christmas" and he responded.

"Merry Christmas to you, too. I came to tell Sam I saw Frank Gatski at church last night."

Oral spoke up, "Yeh, I saw him a day before at Circle Bar. Guess he comes in there regularly. They won the big game the other day. Saw where he got twelve hundred dollars for that one game."

"My goodness," Katherine said. "Twelve hundred dollars for playing one football game."

Leo had delivered his message to Sam, but thought it was best to get back to his own home to celebrate Christmas with his family. Sam and Leo were thinking the same thing: the possibility of meeting up with the great Gatski was as simple as the Circle Bar.

Photos

"Hail to Farmington High School Hail"

Early family picture (about 1924) of Louis and Eta Gatski and their children,
Benny, Frank, John and Paul. *(Courtesy of Joan Gatski Kingery)*

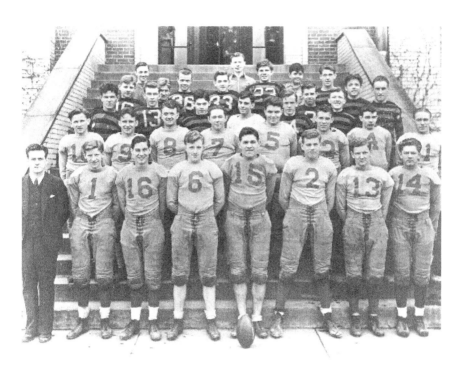

Farmington High School football team of 1934 coached by Clarence "Cassy" Ryan. Frank Gatski is far left, row four. His brothers Paul Gatski, No. 15 and John Gatski, No. 2 are front row, center. *(Courtesy of Joan Gatski Kingery)*

Paul Gatski, West Virginia Wesleyan football, 1938 *(Courtesy of West Virginia Wesleyan College Archives, Brett Miller, Archivist)*

Farmington Junior High School basketball, 1949. Front row Sam Huff No.53 and Leo Coceano No. 50. *(Courtesy of Murvyn McDowell)*

Farmington High School Coach Ray Kelly.

Farmington High School cheerleaders for 1947-1948. Mickey Huff, Sam's sister, and Mary Ruth Conoway. Mary is the mother of Nick Saban, who has coached LSU and Alabama to National Championships. Nick played quarterback at Monongah High School, Farmington's chief rival, before attending Kent State and establishing himself as one of college football's great coaches. *(Courtesy of Rick Maxwell)*

Rudy Banick, Farmington High School halfback 1947-1950,
one of the best to ever play in Marion County.

Sam Huff and Leo Coceano, co-captains of the 1951 Farmington High School football team. *(Courtesy of Murvyn McDowell)*

Senior yearbook pictures: Sam Huff, Leo Coceano, and Murvyn McDowell.

(Courtesy of Murvyn McDowell)

Sam Huff and Leo Coceano receiving the 1951 Mason-Dixon championship trophy from Larney Gump, President of the Mason-Dixon Conference.

The legendary Marshall College Coach Cam Henderson and Assistant Roy Straight. *(Courtesy of Special Collection Department, Marshall University, Nat DeBruin, University Archivist and Manuscripts Librarian)*

Frank was the center for the Marshall College Thundering Herd in 1941 and
1942. *(Courtesy of Eli Camden "Cam" Henderson collection accession No. 391,
Special Collection Department, Marshall University, Nat DeBruin, University
Archivist and Manuscripts Librarian)*

Frank and Ida dancing the night away at Marshall College.

(Courtesy Steve Gatski)

Key players from the 1946 champion Cleveland Browns stayed together for years. Here are some of them in a 1955 photograph: from left, Dante Lavelli, Otto Graham, Frank Gatski and Lou Groza.

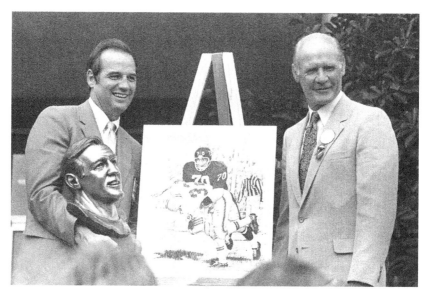

August 7, 1982 – Sam Huff and his presenter Tom Landry at the NFL Hall of Fame ceremony in Canton, Ohio. Landry, an assistant coach with the New York Giants from 1954-1959, later became a head coach of the Dallas Cowboys for 29 seasons. *(Photo Credit Pro Football Hall of Fame via Associated Press)*

August 3, 1985 – Frank Gatski with his presenter Abe Gibron, Frank's
Cleveland Browns teammate for seven season. Gibron later served several years
as a coach in the NFL including three seasons as the Chicago Bears head coach.
(Photo Credit Pro Football Hall of Fame via Associated Press)

The Jacket

The boys at the Circle Bar were reading about the Browns victory. The whole town of Farmington was buzzing about the center who snapped the ball to the great Otto Graham, now beginning to make everyone wonder if he wasn't the best quarterback in all of pro football – even better than Sid Luckman and Sammy Baugh. Gatski not only snapped the ball to Graham, but he was his first line of defense. Nobody got to Graham through Gatski – Frank made damn sure of that!

Outside of Manchin's store, the employees were filing out in the late December night. The small town was dark, except for the street lights on the two corners, and the lights in the bars and pool room. They would stay on for sometime.

As Sam Huff left Manchin's Store, he started walking to the hard road of No. 9 to hitchhike home, but the neon glow of the Circle Bar sign caught his attention. He stopped and looked at it from half a block a way. He remembered what his dad said.

"Frank could be up there right now," he thought. "What the heck, it won't hurt to go up and look in." He remembered that the windows were large and you could see the whole place and everyone in it.

The excitement filled him up, and his steps grew quicker – until he was a few steps away from the bar. Not wanting to seem so obvious, he went across the street, where he could be in the shadows and away from the lights inside the bar. He retreated as far back as he could to the wall of the old hardware store. Then he looked in. There was the owner behind the bar pouring a draft beer. There were just two men at the bar and a couple of guys playing pool. No Frank Gatski.

His mission fulfilled, he felt satisfied and left quickly, back to the corner of Manchin's Store, where he started walking the two miles toward No. 9

with his thumb out for every car or truck going that way. But he would go back to the Circle Bar. He knew sooner or later, Frank would show up there.

Sam repeated his spying the next two nights, with the same result. No Frank Gatski. He was beginning to feel stupid. So what if Frank was there – then what would he do? He figured he'd cross that bridge then.

But the next night, December 30, the night before New Year's Eve, as Sam leaned back against the wall of the hardware store and looked, he saw the back of a man near the window and the letters on a jacket. He spelled it out. B-R-O-W-N-S.

"Oh, shit" he said out loud. "Browns! That's Frank. It's got to be!" His eyes scanned the room and the place was filled. No wonder, Gatski was there. Ben Bennett was behind the bar with a helper, taking care of the customers; most were gathered around the man in the Browns jacket.

"Oh man, I wish I could be there," he thought.

Sam's constant stare must have unconsciously got the attention of someone in the bar, someone who was talking to Frank and facing the window began to turn his attention to the mysterious figure outside looking in. When he did that, another customer turned to look; then Frank turned around, and before you knew it, everyone in the whole bar, at least twenty men, were staring at the person in the shadows outside.

Ben Bennett tore around the bar and was out the door to investigate the sudden intrusion. Sam wanted to run, but it was too late.

"Sam! What the hell are you doing standing back here looking in? You scared us to death. You can't stand out here alone in the dark and look into a place. You might get hurt and besides you might run off all my customers. You best get home anyway."

Sam was embarrassed. He was caught red handed, "But I was just looking at…" He didn't want to say it, but he had to "…uh Frank… I saw that jacket with BROWNS…"

Bennett understood the hero worshipper. Hell, everyone in the bar was just as bad. But he still admonished Sam, "Well don't stand out here all alone looking in…"

178

By this time Sam was backtracking out of trouble… he turned and started to run. His mind was giving directions – "turn right… get out of town…away from the lights…to the darkness." He made it to the corner at the edge of town still talking to himself, "damn that was Frank in that Browns jacket!"

There in the sanctuary of dark he stuck out his thumb at the approaching light.

In spite of the order to stay away from the bar, Sam was prepared to return to get a glimpse of his hero, but the next time he would be prepared.

On an evening in early January when Frank was still staying in Grant Town with Benny, Sam retraced his steps from Manchin's to the bar and then across the streets, but now he had company. Leo and Murvyn and Rudy Banick went with him. Now a larger shadow fell on the hardware store. When Sam looked in, sure enough, there was the BROWNS jacket on the tall strapping blonde giant, and a lot of guys asking questions and talking about the good old days at No. 9 mine, as well as the good new days of the Cleveland Browns football. Sam scanned the room. It was filled, but where was the owner. Ben wasn't behind the bar – because now he was standing right beside him!

Sam jumped ten feet in the air. "Jesus Christ… You scared me." Leo, Rudy and Murvyn started to run.

"You boys come back," Bennett hollered.

They stopped. They wouldn't leave Sam standing there all alone.

Suddenly the bar door swung open. The customers had heard the commotion and were coming to help – whoever was in trouble, and leading the help was the guy in the Browns jacket. Now he was face to face with the intruders.

"Hey, Benny. What's goin' on?"

"Oh nothin'. These boys wanted to see you, that's all. There's Rudy Banick, Leo Coceano, and Murvyn McDowell." He turned to Sam. "But I told you I didn't want someone standing out here all alone looking…"

179

Sam interrupted him. "But you said 'you didn't want someone standing out here all alone looking in – well, I ain't all alone. I brought Leo and Murvyn and Rudy…"

Frank laughed, "Maybe I should leave this Browns jacket at home."

The guys started to go back to the bar.

Frank was the last to return to the bar. He stopped and looked back at his young fans. "You boys, don't ever underestimate a human being, you understand he can do anything." He started to go inside, then turned. "You get your own jacket someday."

Sam, Leo, Murvyn and Rudy walked away to the corner. Sam was jubilant. "See, I told you he would be there."

Gene Autry in Town

That sore throat that Sam had on and off for as long as he could remember, was "on" again in March of 1948, and just about as bad as ever – and at the worst time. Gene Autry was coming to town. No kidding. The Gene Autry was on a countrywide tour and was stopping at the Farmington High School Auditorium. That was one of Sam's favorite cowboy stars, and everybody in town, except Sam Huff, was going to be there. His mother absolutely refused to let him go. He had to stay in bed and doctor the throat, and besides whatever Sam had, Katherine did not want to be spread to other children.

Sam waited at home to get the report from Leo, who had some disappointing information.

"He was shorter than I thought he would be, and chubby, too."

"Short and chubby? Gene Autry? Did he have Trigger with him?"

"No, how could he have Trigger at the school?"

"Yeh, Mr. Cotrel wouldn't like that. Well, what did Gene say?"

"He talked about his movie that's coming to town, 'Loaded Pistols' and then he talked about being a good person, doing what your parents say, making good grades, things like that."

"I wish I could have been there."

"Me, too. Your throat real sore?"

"Even the doctor was here. Doctor Jenkins. He said he should take out my tonsils, but Mom and Dad said 'no, I'll outgrow it.'"

"You better hurry up then," Leo said. "I mean grow out."

"Yeh, I know. He gave me medicine. It makes it feel better. Then it goes away for a while."

The rest of the school year went as expected: Sam passed everything, but not with the grades Leo had, which were among the best in the class. Sam's sister, Mickey, mentioned that it was her last year. She was sixteen and like all of the other Huff kids, Martha and Donald, she would quit as soon as the law allowed. She was planning to get married as soon as possible.

Then the summer was on. There were the baseball games of the Marion County Sandlot League at the Farmington High School field and swimming at the Hough Park in Mannington. Uncle Leroy came in from Akron for the Fourth of July and brought some great new songs with him, including "*Feudin', Fussin' and Fightin'* ", "*Jambalaya*", and "*Peg O' My Heart*".

Sam worked at Manchin's, saved some money, took Mary to the movies, and talked about going out for football. This year he would be a freshman, and freshman could play for the high school team. Rudy Banick did last year and earned a letter. He even scored a touchdown! And Duane Bonnette was in the same grade and he, too, earned a letter. Sam didn't know if he could be that good, yet. He was still pretty small for football, about 5 foot 5 and 130 pounds, but he was counting on growing up – sometime. And he was counting on Leo going out for football, too. It was almost impossible to think any other way. Ever since James Fork Elementary in first grade Sam and Leo were together, on everything, especially sports. Sam had taught the little Italian everything he knew, and in some aspects Leo had passed up Sam. In the classroom, Leo was making better grades, and it annoyed Sam, to think that his one-time protégé, the kid he helped learn the English language, was now doing better in school. But they were buddies, and if Sam was going out for football, Leo had to.

Not so. Sam was mad as hell! "What do you mean, you ain't going out?"

"My mom won't let me."

"Well, my mom won't let me either, but I'm going out anyway."

"She says I'm too small. I'll get hurt."

"You're almost as big as I am, tell her that...oh shit, Leo, you're bigger than some of the other guys."

"I can't disobey my mother."

"Why not?"

"My dad would kill me."

"Well, I'm going out, and you'll be sorry you didn't."

"I know I'll be sorry, but she says maybe next year."

If only Amerigo, Leo's older brother, had been home, things might have been different. He could have helped persuade his mother to let Leo play. Amerigo played football at Farmington in 1943 and 1944 and was very good. After graduation he enlisted in the army and was wounded at Normandy on D-Day. After returning he married and moved away.

Leo's other brother, Dominick, who graduated from Farmington in 1946, didn't play football, so he wasn't too inclined to help Leo's cause, and besides he was in Morgantown getting ready for school to start at West Virginia University, where he was majoring in engineering. Leo's football career was not on his priority list.

"You're going to be sorry," Sam said. "Hell, everyone is going out."

"I know it. I am sorry already, but I can't help it. I just hope I can grow up a little more, then maybe... and maybe Amerigo can come home and talk to my mom, too..."

Sam still wasn't through nagging. "Well, what am I going to do. We been doing things together all the time and now when it comes to the most important thing, playing football, you ain't going to be there."

"Don't make me feel worse than I already am."

"Okay," Sam conceded. "I'm still going out. I told Mary I was and she's going to be in the band and I was going to be on the field...playing."

Leo lowered his head. "I guess I'm gonna be watching."

High school football practice started August 20. Sam hitchhiked to the high school to be there at 9 a.m. when the equipment was going to be passed out. The old locker room was crowded. Sam stood up against the back wall watching some of the upper classmen laughing and talking, while they waited for the equipment door to be opened. A lot of the guys hadn't seen each other since last May, when school was still on, so they had some catching up to do.

Sam was thinking how much better he would feel if Leo were there. Heck, there hadn't been a time since first grade, the two kids weren't playing ball together. Now his buddy wasn't even in the room.

Then a friendly voice, "Hey, Sam," Harry Sopuch, another freshman sided up to Sam. "Ready to go out?" Harry asked.

"Yeh."

"Where's Leo? Ain't he going out?"

"No, his mom won't let him."

Two more freshmen, Ronnie Fluharty and Billy Suarez, joined the guys against the back wall. Sam was happy to see Billy. He was even smaller than Sam, who now stood up taller when Billy came over. But Billy brought bad news.

"I hear there's a new assistant coach...and he's the new math teacher, too."

"Oh shit," Sam said. "He's a math teacher?"

"Yep. It was in the newspaper. My mother told me."

"Oh shit." Sam said again. "That ain't good."

"Why is that?"

"Heck, I don't know, maybe 'cause math is hard..."

Ronnie Fluharty changed the subject. "Any other guys from our class going out?" He nudged Sam. "Where's Leo?"

"Well, like I said, his mom don't want him to go out yet. There's only five of us ninth graders going out."

Rudy Banick was standing alongside some upperclassmen toward the front of the room. As a freshman last season, he earned a letter and the respect of his older teammates, so he felt comfortable being with them. But when he saw Sam behind him, he came over to him.

"Hey, Sam, where's Leo?"

Sam lowered his eyes and started to give his stock answer, but Ronnie and Billy Suarez spoke up in unison. "His mom won't let him come out."

Billy Suarez, all 102 pounds of him confirmed, "Says he's too small."

Rudy laughed, "Yeh, look at you."

The equipment door swung open and Coach Kelly and his new assistant, John Victor, along with equipment manager, Mike Arcure, stood there. The loud din of conversation suddenly stopped. All the attention was directed to the head coach.

Kelly lit up the place with that narrowed eyed beaming face of his. "First of all I want you to meet Mr. Victor. He's going to be the assistant coach this year."

Sam twisted up his face at the news thinking, "he's a math teacher, what's he know about football?"

In contrast to Kelly's always sunny demeanor, Victor was serious – too serious for young boys who intuitively recognized Victor's lack of knowledge of football. Hell, he was a math teacher! But the school system paid one coach for football and basketball – and even sometimes baseball. In the case of Farmington High School, Burl Rinehart was the baseball coach, and a good one, while teaching biology. Kelly, while coaching football and basketball, also taught health. The duties of an assistant coach were handled by teachers like Rinehart and Victor, who received a small supplement for assisting in a sport. Never mind that they might not know much about it!

Kelly continued, "Okay guys. Seniors first. We'll call your name and Mike will fix you up with everything."

By the time Mike got the names of the freshman, the equipment had been picked over and exact fits for freshmen were not possible. Finding shoes, hip pads, shoulder pads, pants, jersey and a helmet for 130 pound Sam Huff was difficult, for 102 pound Billy Suarez, impossible – but he did the best he could.

Rudy slipped the shirt over his head and as is necessary, he looked for help in getting the shirt pulled down over the back of the shoulder pads. He

looked at Sam and turned around. Sam quickly obliged, as if he were

185

honored, Rudy would ask him to help. Sam tugged hard to get the shirt over the pads, then pulled down to give Rudy a good fit.

"Thanks, Sam. Here, let me help you."

Sam pushed his head through his shirt and turned his back to Rudy, who quickly pulled it down over Sam's shoulder pads. It was easy, since Sam's shirt was much too big for him.

The other freshmen, Harry Sopuch and Billy Suarez and Ronnie Fluharty all managed to get dressed and joined Sam and Rudy in the trek down the hill to the field.

"Everybody get a salt tablet."

It was Coach Kelly shouting instructions to keep his young football players alive in the sweltering August afternoon. Sweating so profusely due to ninety plus degree temperature and twenty pounds of a uniform could cause a kid to lose salt, – and a kid could even die of a heat stroke. Nobody ever did, but a salt tablet was the standard operating procedure, just in case.

Coach Kelly walked over to Sam and the other young kids and flashed his fatherly gentle smile. "You freshmen go over there with Coach Victor."

"Oh, shit," Sam thought, "Coach Victor!?"

"Let's run, boys," snapped Victor.

The young boys got into a run and followed him over to a grassy spot on the field. It was plain, this grouping was intended to give the young boys a chance to learn some basics of practice and football.

"Boys, let's run some sprints. Line up right here. First, let me show you the stance for football."

Well, Sam already knew that. He had the picture of Frank Gatski in his drawer back home, and in his mind.

Victor got down in a three point stance, right arm extended to the ground, knees slightly bent. All the boys followed, but he didn't have to tell them. It was something every kid knew – or thought he knew.

186

Victor walked along the line. "Murvyn, that's good... good, Leo...Sam, your tail is too high. Get it down."

Sam did.

"That's better."

Sam knew Victor had to be wrong. The stance he was in was just like Frank's picture – or at least he thought it was.

Victor reviewed the line again. "Okay, that looks pretty good. Now stand up. I'll say 'Ready, Set, Go', – we'll sprint ten yards to the post and back. Ready, Set, Go."

The practice continued with more sprints and hitting a dummy held by Victor, emphasizing the correct position of the body for blocking and tackling, and in each case driving the opponent – the dummy – backwards.

To illustrate this further, toward the end of practice, Victor held the large full-length padded dummy, while each boy took his best shot. Victor would take the impact and give resistance as each kid made contact with him and drove him backward.

Sam Huff couldn't wait for his turn. He got in his Gatski stance. He became Gatski – even Frank's menacing facial expression.

Victor braced himself, "Ready, Set, Go.

Sam lunged forward. Bam. He hit the dummy as hard as he could and drove... his teeth clenched – he grunted and drove his feet forward – and Victor backward.

"That's the way to hit!" Victor shouted. "That's the way to hit."

Calisthenics at the end of practice left everyone exhausted, especially the freshmen. Sam, along with his buddies, Sopuch, Fluharty, and Suarez, moving around in their ill-fitting uniforms, had to expend a hell of a lot more energy to do exercise, like side straddle and running in place.

Sam looked up at the blazing sun. He was getting sick to his stomach, but he wasn't going to let it show.

"Good practice, boys," Kelly shouted.

187

"Yes, good practice," Assistant Coach Victor echoed.

Everybody else was tolerating the conditions a lot better than Sam. The other freshmen walked together, their shoulder pads clacking with each step in a steady, but slow pace from the field, and up the hill to the locker room.

Sam trailed alone clumsily behind everyone. The last one up the hill, but he didn't care – all he was thinking was to keep from throwing up. The dull ache in his stomach was churning.

Coach Kelly and Victor were behind Sam and couldn't help but notice his struggle.

"You okay, Sam?" Victor asked.

"Yeh, I'm okay," Sam didn't want to give the math teacher any reason to doubt his ability to climb the hill.

"If you can't make it, sit down and rest," Victor instructed.

Sam wanted to say, 'go to hell, I can make it' – but he didn't. He simply said, "I'm okay." And he kept going one step after another till he reached the top of the hill. Victor was still giving verbal lack of confidence that Sam did not process, but only heard as a stream of sounds with no meaning.

Sam made it to the locker room and a place on a bench beside one of his freshmen buddies, Harry Sopuch.

"Where did you go, Sam?"

"I wasn't feeling too good, but I'm okay now."

"Damn hot out there."

"Yeh, I didn't eat` no breakfast or anything. I think that was it."

The small locker room was steamy from the showers and had that familiar jock smell of sweat and analgesic balm.

The loud conversation of energetic boys bounced off the concrete walls and echoed with their loud shouts. Manager Mike Arcure tossed towels to them, most of whom welcomed the adversity of tough coaching and high temperatures.

He handed Sam a towel. "You okay, Sam? Someone said you got sick."

"I didn't get sick… who said that?"

"Coach Victor said…"

"Oh hell with… well, I didn't get sick. I just didn't eat nothin'."

Mike wanted to change the subject fast. "Why didn't Leo come out?"

"His mom wouldn't let him, maybe next year."

"I saw him working at Gango's Market."

"Yeh? He didn't tell me that."

"He just started. I think it was just to help out before school. His mom won't let him work during school – it's just to get a little money for school stuff, clothes, and…"

"I'm working, too," Sam said "at Manchin's, except now with practices starting, I don't think I can do both."

Sam stood up and started to take off his jersey, but couldn't get it over the shoulder pads. Mike offered to help.

"Here, bend over," he instructed.

Sam bent at the waist and Mike pulled the jersey up over the pads, so Sam could get it off over his head.

Sam sat down, and took off shoes, pants, and jockey strap to join Sopuch and Fluharty in the shower. They deferred to the upperclassmen for shower time. Now, most of them were getting dressed, and by this time the locker room was a steam bath. The hot temperatures outside had made its way inside and along with the water spray from four shower heads made taking a shower an experience in futility. The dirt of the football field would come off, but there was no possible way to get dry. Sam put his blue jeans on, slowly because he had to force the denim up his still wet legs. He put on his socks and tennis shoes, but didn't bother with the t-shirt till he got outside where there was some air and the hot sun to at least dry him off.

Sopuch walked out with him.

"Supposed to be even hotter tomorrow."

"Well, I'll be here. I ain't quitting. That's for sure."

"Yeh, me neither. You goin' home now?"

Sopuch stopped walking. He lived at No. 8, the coal camp on the other side of Farmington. The two boys were prepared to hitchhike in different directions. Sam turned toward the road to No. 9.

189

"Yeh, I guess I'll see you…Wait a second. Let's walk down to see if Leo's at Gango's Market. Mike said he was working there."

"Sure. That's on my way."

The door jangled a welcome bell inside the small neat Gango's grocery store. The ceiling fans created a gentle breeze that was a welcome change from the heat.

"Nice in here," Sopuch said.

"Yeh, sure is."

Sam looked around. Gango's was not like Manchin's where he was working part-time. Manchin's sold everything.

"Hi ya, boys," the voice was the Italian accent of the owner, Phillip Gango, a small, pleasant man whose round gentle face said 'welcome!' He smiled at Sam and Harry.

"Looking for Leo?"

"It ain't important," Sam said. "We just thought we'd say 'hi'."

"That's okay," Mr. Gango said. "Hey, Leo, your friends are here."

Leo stood up from the milk case in which he was placing gallons of milk. Mr. Gango retreated to the cash register. Leo was a little embarrassed that Sam and Harry would show up after football practice, the place he would rather be, and see him dressed neatly in a shirt and dress pants working in the comfortable, cool surroundings of a grocery store.

"Nice in here," Sopuch said again.

"Yeh, but I would rather be playing football with you guys. I'm just getting some money for school. My mom won't let me work when school starts, but this way I can help a little. Football… maybe next year she says."

Sam understood the need to work. "Mr. Aloi wants me to work more at Manchin's, but with football practice I told him I couldn't. I'd like to get some money to go to the fair next week. Mary will be going with the band and we'll meet up."

The cash register sounded its familiar ring as Mr. Gango rang up a sale and it caught the boys' attention. It also signaled the end of the boys' brief meeting. After all, Leo was working.

"I better get back…"

"Yeh, we better go."

Leo disappeared behind a high counter of canned goods, and Sam and Harry turned and headed for the door.

"Bye boys," Mr. Gango said. "You come back anytime."

"Thank you," Sam said as he opened the door and felt the heat of a hot August afternoon.

Harry and Sam said goodbye and started to head home: Harry to the road to No. 8 and Sam to No. 9. But Sam only took a few steps before he stopped at the corner right outside Gango's Market. He looked around at Farmington. He was standing in the center of town, and he was suddenly aware of the places and people that gave meaning to his changing life: Gango's Market, where he had just left his best friend, Leo, who meant more to him than just about anyone; around the corner was Ben's Circle Bar, the favorite hangout of Frank Gatski, who inspired him to play football; and across the street was Manchin's, where he had begun to work for the first time to make money, and most important, experience the interactions of the Manchin family and their values which gave him a perspective on a new and different life from the one he had grown up with in No. 9.

And he felt like a different boy than the one who had played ball and just worked around the house. Now he had a girlfriend and he was thinking of working and making money. "Was this what you called growing up?" he thought.

And he confessed to himself, "yes". He was feeling more grown-up. That small job at Manchin's made him feel real good about himself. He could do the work, and he liked it. And the Manchins liked him. He enjoyed being able to take Mary out on a date and the intimate moments with his girlfriend sure did make him feel grown-up.

He was going to be fourteen in October and was in his freshman year of high school. He thought, "Heck, Donald quit school when he was sixteen and in his sophomore year and now he's working in the mines. Now I wouldn't want to work in the mines, but I would like to make money like Donald." Sam

191

was in a daydream. He awakened quickly. The troubling dream was not making him feel good. Maybe growing up did that.

"Sammie! Sammie!" The dreamer turned to see Mr. Gango on his steps shouting his name. He woke up quickly.

Mr. Gango went on, "Sammie, over there." He was pointing across the street. "Over there, Sammie."

Sam looked across the street where Big Sam Aloi was trying to get the young boy's attention.

"Sammie, come over here."

Sammie finally woke up. "Yes, sir."

"Don't ya hear me? I shout your name three times!"

"No, I guess I was daydreaming."

The big man got to the point. "You want to help me. I got some stuff to deliver. I need your help."

"When?"

"Now, today, and maybe tomorrow and next few days. People doing things before school start – new furniture and things. What do you say?"

"I'm practicing football now," Sam explained.

Mr. Aloi shook his head, "It's too hot for football."

"Yeh, I know, but I would like to earn some money. The fair is coming up next week, and like you say, school's startin'. But football practice…"

"Okay, football. You think about it. You come here when you decide."

Here Comes the Band

Boom, Boom, Boom, Boom....

The loud pounding of the bass drum of the Farmington High School band clearly underscored the thin sound of a twenty-five member group as it marched along the school's football field. The band started practicing at 9 a.m. but it didn't bother any of the residents around the school, after all that was their kids, and the sound of a band was a note of pride.

Pride was what the practice was about. The band was practicing for their first event of the 1948-49 school year – to participate in the Mannington District Fair Parade. The parade not only featured bands for eight high schools in the county – but junior high schools as well, and bands from as far as fifty miles away; from Clarksburg, Morgantown and Elkins, they came to be a part of the second largest fair in the state.

The two mile parade route would be jammed with thousands, and judges would be there to evaluate each band for the right to a shiny new trophy and bragging rights. Yes, there was a lot to play for.

Coach Kelly, who began football practice at 9 a.m. too, wasn't thinking of the fair parade when he had to scream out callisthenic instructions to be heard over the band. The sound of the Farmington High School march was nevertheless inspiring to players – you could see it. Their movements were more crisp. They couldn't help themselves. There was something about that damn song that got the players going at a higher level.

Sam Huff, in the back row of the players, heard it too. But his thoughts were not football inspired. The sound of the band made him think about the French horn player and about the Mannington District Fair and how he

193

might get to spend a couple of hours with Mary eating some cotton candy and taking some rides and kissing her in the dark shadows around the community building.

"…six, seven, eight, nine, TEN!"

Ten pushups lifting twenty pounds of ill-fitting uniform in the hot August morning was the limit of Sam's physical capability. He collapsed facedown on the green grass. He looked down the row of his ninth grade teammates – Sopuch, Suarez, and Fluharty were not doing much better. Sam waited for the next command from Coach Kelly.

"On your back!" he yelled. Groans arose from the ground as the players turned over.

"Leg lifts!" Kelly barked. "Ready. Up…Spread your legs…Back together…Down…Up…Spread 'em…Back together…Down…"

"Sam, get it up!" a voice sounded. John Victor was calling Sam out again, as if he was picking on him. Hell, Sopuch had his legs down, too, and Victor didn't say anything to him. "Sam, get it up!" Victor demanded. Sam got back in rhythm with the rest of the players.

"Up...Spread 'em…Back together…Down." He was finally getting it. But he just couldn't get Mary and the fair out of his mind. He had to come up with some money to go and he didn't have any. He had a couple of days before the fair and he would have to figure something out between now and then.

The only money he ever made was when he worked at Manchin's, and that job was available now. Sam Aloi was waiting for him. He said he needed him. Getting that money could take him and Mary to the fair in style.

The thought of quitting football entered his mind. These practices had been tough. The weather was hot and there wasn't much for a freshman to do. Coach Kelly spent most of the time with the first and second stringers, and the freshmen were coached mostly by Victor, who had become Sam's mortal enemy.

Damn, Leo. If he had only come out, there would be no chance of Sam giving up football – not even for the money he could make at Manchin's. He knew Leo wouldn't quit, and neither would he.

194

"Boom, boom, boom, boom." The band struck up the Farmington High fight song again.

"Okay, everybody up on your feet." Kelly screamed over the bass drum. "Side straddle. Ready, one, two, one, two."

"Oh shit," Sam thought as he struggled to his feet. He could see the band march by the field and he could see Mary in the middle of the third row march out of her tight shorts with that particularly sweet walk that made him think of the community building shadows at the fair.

When Mike Arcure walked into the locker room, he was surprised to see a uniform set, shoulder pads, hip pads, pants, shoes on the counter. He went to Coach Kelly.

"Coach, did you want me to do something with this equipment?"

"What equipment?"

"The equipment that's on the counter."

"Who put it there?"

"I thought you did."

Then Mike thought that someone may have turned it in, and realized he could check the identifying number he marked on each piece when he gave it out. It was number 35.

"Number 35." He checked his record. "It's Sam Huff. Guess he's quitting."

"I guess that does mean 'I quit'. Do you know why?"

Mike tried to make a good excuse for Sam. "I think he might be working at Manchin's."

Kelly bought it. "Well, I like Sam. I was hoping he might be more interested."

"Too bad," Victor said. "Now that leaves us with just three freshmen, Fluharty, Suarez, and Sopuch."

The loss of one freshman from the roster of the 1948 Farmington Farmers football team would go unnoticed. According to Eddie Barrett,

195

who was writing a preview of all the county teams for the <u>Fairmont Times</u>, the Farmers would begin a slow rise from the county bottom. He began his story: "Up at Farmington, folks believe the time is nearing when Farmington High athletic teams no longer will be at the bottom of the county list. The movement, they say will begin this year even though the Farmers may not hang up the equal of last year's surprising 3 - 4 - 1 record.

He had some good things to say about Rudy Banick…"a sophomore who is short but slim and sturdy and considered the best call carrier…" but then Barrett said of Rudy "…he will have to suffice because there is no one else." Barrett called another sophomore Duane Bonnette "another well-built, second year student who will take care of one tackle position…" and he mentioned Harry Sopuch: "a 136 pound freshman…the best of the sub backs."

According to Barrett, Kelly wasn't counting on Sopuch though, for the coach said, "If any of the starting four gets injured, we're sunk."

In the end there was a dire analysis as Barrett concluded the story with this prediction, "…the Farmers will do well to win three games…"

The Fair Deal

At the Mannington District Fair, Sam got all that he had bargained for. He had made a deal with the money devil, trading ninth grade football for work at Manchin's for fifty cents an hour. In the bargain he got his rides on the ferris wheel, cotton candy and even the kisses from Mary in the Community Building shadows.

But he didn't figure he would have to pay some pride, but he did. For as he and Mary walked down the far midway, Mary spotted Rudy Banick and Duane Bonnette, two of Sam's <u>ex</u> football buddies.

"Let's go over and talk to Rudy and Duane."

That was the last thing Sam wanted to do. But before you know it, Mary was walking in that direction and Sam was in a quick step to catch up to her.

Rudy and Duane were wearing their game jerseys of scarlet and gray, which stood out among the green and white of Mannington, the blue and gold of Barrackville and the red and white of Rivesville and the colors of the other schools in the county.

Because of his success as a freshman, Rudy was idolized by a lot of younger boys, envied by boys his own age and coveted by the young girls who were in love with the young handsome football hero.

Sam, the freshman to be, suddenly in Rudy's presence, felt small. Rudy had already distinguished himself on the football field, even as a freshman, while Sam had just practiced a couple of weeks before, turning in his uniform. He felt a twinge of jealousy at the attention Mary was paying Rudy.

Rudy turned around. "Hi ya, Sam…Mary."

Mary blushed. She felt a rush that Rudy would speak to her. "Hi," she said meekly.

197

Sam wanted to belong, so he spoke up. "You ready for the game with East Fairmont."

"Yeh, ready as we'll ever be."

"Are you gonna make the trip, Sam?"

Sam dug his foot in the ground making a hole he wanted to dive into. "Well, you know I had to quit…"

Duane blinked. "Had to quit?!"

Sam cleared his throat and felt its soremess. "Yeh. I wanted to work some… I could use the money, you know."

Rudy helped him off the hook. "Sure, I know what you mean. I could use some money myself."

While Sam was looking for a way out, Mary inadvertently found it for him. She saw a couple of uniformed Farmington High School Band members running toward the Community Building. It was a sudden reminder that the bus would be leaving at 8:00 p.m. She looked at her watch.

"Oh, Sam, it's quarter till. I better go. C'mon."

Farmington High School band members all jammed together at the bus door, waiting to board for the seven mile trip back to Farmington.

Sam and Mary walked over and waited for a minute. Conversations on top of conversations told of escapades of the last hour spent at the fair. Girls giggled and screeched and laughed. Boys talked about the girls from other schools they met.

Mary took hold of Sam's hand. "I guess I'll see you tomorrow. Want to go to a movie?" Mary asked.

"Sure, I guess," Sam replied, feeling for the money in his pocket.

"How are you getting home?"

"I'll hitch a ride with someone."

"Okay," Mary said as she took her turn to step up into the bus. "Bye." She put her head down to hide her eyes from the other girls.

The door closed behind her and Sam was already on his way back into the midway and looking for a ride to No. 9.

The girls were dressed like they were going to church. The boys took extra care – or at least the parents did, to see their blue jeans and t-shirts were neat and clean.

It was September 3, 1948. The first day of school. Every boy must have had a haircut from the local barber. The part would never look this good again.

The combined student body of seventh through twelfth graders numbered about three hundred. Most kids walked there. A few from Plum Run, Rachel, Ida May and Carolina rode the school bus. A couple of kids whose dads were mechanics at local garages were fortunate enough to have an old car to drive. Drive! The half dozen cars in the parking lot belonged to the principal, the teachers, and a couple of students.

Some of the kids whose families could afford it had gone to Fairmont to the more "exclusive" stores, Jones Department Store and Hartleys to shop for their new school clothes. Others of lesser or more practical means went to Golden Brothers, where the clothes were good, and at a reasonable cost, or to Murphy's Five and Dime or McCrory's, where you could purchase the lowest priced clothing.

The rest did what they could with hand-me-downs from the older siblings or handmade clothes from the hands of a creative mother.

The hallways buzzed with talk. "What did you do this summer?" "Who's that good looking guy?" "Who's that good looking girl?" "Boy, I hate school!" "Where is my room?" "Where is the bathroom?" "What about the new teachers?"

The new teachers. The ones who held the future happiness of students in their novice hands.

The school had four new teachers: Pauline Francis, who taught Physical Education for girls; Music supervisor Edmund Kuhns; Nickolas Klutkas, the new Manual Training instructor; and John Victor, teacher of junior high Mathematics.

Sam had already become "acquainted" with John Victor – on the football field – where he suffered miserably! And besides, anyone who is trying to teach junior high mathematics is a natural born enemy to a ninth grader – so John Victor was at a disadvantage in attempting to be liked by his students. While Sam Huff struggled with mathematics and geometry, the relationship with his teacher became strained. Of course Mr. Victor couldn't teach!

But Sam took an immediate liking to Mr. Klutkas. Could it have been the subject that Klutkas taught? After all, manual training is the course where you began to learn about tools and equipment – the things Sam had been around because of his dad – and where you made a bookshelf and a pump light you could take home to your mother. There couldn't be any adverse relationship with an instructor in that course!

There was something else though. Victor was of a serious nature, and highly critical of students who didn't learn immediately – and he was only a teacher. It was obvious, even to the ninth graders, that he was no athlete.

Klutkas, on the other hand, had been a football player at Florida State and had even played professional football with the Buffalo Bills. The big Russian could relate to boys whose life was playing football and school – in that order.

And besides Sam found it hard to deal with Victor's equilateral triangles and multiplication tables while he was working on Klutkas' bookshelf he would take home to his mom.

Three in a Row!

Paul Brown called Frank Gatski the toughest son-of-a-bitch he ever coached, not just because he could hit hard. That was true, the hard rock-solid miner with a six foot three frame could take your head off with his power and leverage. And Brown wasn't referring to the opponent's inability to move Frank off his block. And Brown wasn't referring to any suggestion of dirty play. That was not Frank Gatski.

The "tough" Brown talked about was in Gatski's head, not his body. He was so tough because he would not be defeated. He was so tough that he was committed to being the best. He was so tough that he never missed a practice – not in high school, college or in the pros and he certainly never missed a game. Injuries were endured, ignored and overcome. Regardless of the situation, Coach Brown and Frank's teammates knew they could count on him.

Gatski to Graham. Every play the Browns ran, started with a center snap, Gatski to Graham. Frank knew that at the other end of that ball was the best quarterback that ever played the game. He was going to be damn sure to be as competent as the guy on the other end of the football. Gatski had to be the best! He had to be! One of the Frank's favorite sayings was "never underestimate a human being. He can to do anything."

In August 1948, when the Cleveland Browns started training camp, several players were concerned about their salary. Not Frank. He never was. He always made enough money for himself. He never needed much. His joy was in the free things of life – hunting, fishing, archery – material things never impressed Frank.

For the two previous seasons his salary was $2000 and that was fine. In fact, to tell the truth, Frank would've played for nothing. He would have and Paul Brown knew that, too. The thrill of playing for a championship team was pay enough for Frank. In the two years of the Browns existence, the matter of money never was negotiated. Brown stated the pay and Frank said okay.

Nothing would change in the third season either; however, Frank's life had changed. Now he was married and was going to be a father. But coming fatherhood did not change Frank's feelings toward the pay scale. And the responsibility of being a husband and father didn't bother him either. He was supremely confident to make his way. He had a college degree now – even a masters degree – and if this crazy improbable football career ended for some reason, he would find a coaching job – or even go back to the mines. Why not? He liked being a miner. And Frank was astute enough to understand the reality of professional football. It was a shaky career – made even shakier by the big news in the world of professional football that there was some concern about the survival of the All-American Conference. If the league would fold, then players would be scrambling: some would catch on to NFL teams; others would never play football again and find some other means of employment. In that regard, most players who had off-season jobs would turn them into year round jobs.

Frank felt confident enough in his ability to compete against any other center for a job on one of the NFL teams; if his "forces" denied him, then he would go into coaching, or even back to the mines.

The sports page headline screamed "Youngest Grid Circuit Faces Decisive Year". Reporters talked about the third season being "The year of decision." New York writer Steve Snider told the story:

"This year would decide whether the junior professional football league can stay in business.

When the fledgling association was formed in the summer of 1944, the founding fathers decided they must be prepared to lose money to compete with the bewhiskered National Football league.

So far, five of the eight teams have made the grade: New York, Cleveland, Buffalo, Los Angeles, and San

Francisco. None has the assets of Chase National, but they are above the water line.

Now what about the other three clubs – Brooklyn, Baltimore and Chicago? All go into the 1948's punt and pass program completely reorganized.

Of the trio, Brooklyn has the best chance for success if Brier Branch Rickey can stand the financial gaff.

Baltimore's football team is now a civic project, usually a very precarious operation for a project so commercial as pro football. But in Baltimore there are encouraging signs. For one thing, the Colts – playing their first season after taking over the defunct Miami franchise – drew the top attendance figure of the three "poor folks" All America conference teams.

Chicago is the weakest of the tiny three. The Rockets are overwhelmed by competition – from the Chicago Bears and the Chicago Cardinals of the National Football league and from the surrounding power of the Big Nine conference."

While Frank was confident he would be able to provide for his family, he wondered if it would be on the professional football field or some high school sideline – or perhaps hundreds of feet below the earth.

The Cleveland Browns opened the 1948 season on September 3 at home with a win over the Los Angeles Dons 19 - 14 before a crowd of over 60,000. Coach Brown always gave players Monday and Tuesday off after a Sunday game. Brown believed in a strong family life and he gave his players the opportunity, at least two days a week, to spend valuable time with their

families. And he also believed it was necessary in order for the players to

203

renew themselves physically. But he worked them hard as hell the rest of the week.

Frank won the starting job at center after distinguishing himself in the 46 and 47 seasons playing behind regular center and all-pro Mike Scary, who decided to retire after the 47 season. Scary's retirement was pre-destined: Frank had his eye on the starting job and was determined. Scary saw Frank's emergence as an exceptional player and decided it was time to walk away.

Frank didn't waste a second of the "off" time. As soon as the final gun sounded on the Los Angeles Dons, thoughts turned toward his wife, Ida. Frank was going to be a father sometime soon. He couldn't wait to see her. The feeling was mutual. Ida, who was working for an awning company in Charleston, arranged with Frank's brother, Paul, who also worked in Charleston, to ride with him and his family to Grant Town and brother Benny's house where Frank had planned to stay before returning to Cleveland.

Frank's homecoming was a chance to celebrate another season with the Browns; for Paul and Benny, a time to enjoy the achievement of their "little" brother whose success could be called their own, after all, they had been his early examples and coaches. By 6 o'clock, Frank was in his car outside of Municipal Stadium heading east.

The lights were still on at Benny's house when Frank pulled in front at midnight. The screen door screeched opened, and a half dozen shadowy figures appeared on the porch.

Frank grabbed a small bag from the front seat. Ida hurried to the car door. She couldn't wait for him to get out.

"Hi, honey," she said as she kissed him.

Before Frank could get out of the car, the others were there to escort Frank into the house where Benny's wife was ready with bread, sandwich meat, cheese and plenty of beer. There was a lot to talk about – the Browns and the baby.

Frank's travel routine back and forth to West Virginia to see Ida, either in Grant Town or in Charleston, continued throughout the season – a remarkable season in which the Browns marched through the Western Division of the

All- American Conference winning fourteen games. They laid claim to be the class of the league - professional footballs' only perfect record team.

Dusk had settled over the great city.

The Cleveland victory train was leaving the Manhattan skyline behind as it headed east out of New York City. It was December 5, 1948. The Browns had just defeated the Brooklyn Dodgers 31 - 21 in the regular season All-American Conference finale at Ebbetts Field.

The New York press called it a "tune-up for the Western Division Champions who will be heavy favorites to defeat either the Baltimore Colts or Buffalo Bills in the conference championship game on December 19 at Cleveland."

The Browns had run up a 31 - 0 advantage at halftime and coasted to the win. The remarkable thing about the game was the size of the crowd. Only 9,821 fans paid their way into Ebbetts Field to see the game. The numbers spoke loudly of the coming demise of the Brooklyn Dodger franchise, just as the headline did "Cleveland Browns Rip Brooklyn to Pieces in Regular Season Windup"

The lights of New York City were now far in the distance. The quiet excitement of the Brown's players subsided in a few minutes. They had become used to winning – and a victory over the lowly Brooklyn Dodgers was expected. No surprise. And neither would be the Brown's claim to another All-American Conference Championship on December 19 when they would face the Buffalo Bills in Cleveland.

Frank settled back in his seat looking out the window. The train plunged into the early winter day darkness of the Pennsylvania countryside. Frank had chosen a seat by the window toward the rear of the car to be alone for a few minutes. The conversations of the players, coaches and the accompanying press were drowned out by the torrent of thoughts that cascaded over Frank.

The thunderous roar of the train went quiet when Frank's mother spoke to him, telling him of her pride in his achievement. Then his father came to

205

his side expressing no doubts now why his boy chose to play the game. Frank smiled. He heard his father warn him again, "Son, you'll break your leg."

Frank shook loose of the vision for a moment to reflect on the long improbable journey he had taken. Impossible! He shook his head. How could this have happened to him in three years? He thanked God for working it all out. He had no other explanation. In his wildest imagination, he could never see this happening this way. And then to think that his one chance to try out happened to be for the very best team – the Browns. Life would have been so different if it had been the Brooklyn Dodgers or the Miami Seahawks. Had their representatives contacted Frank at the state basketball tournament in Huntington, he would not be in a Browns uniform. Had it not been Johnny Brickells who was trying to help build a Browns organization and instead someone from the Miami Seahawks, Chicago Rockets or Brooklyn Dodgers, his life now would be different. He would have signed with one of them for sure, happy to have a chance to play professional football, but would be faced now with the disbanding of the team instead of playing for a team prepared to win its third consecutive championship.

"I would be out of football," he thought.

But now he was a winner and there was no telling when this would stop.

A reflection in the window turned the outside blackness into a suit and tie. He turned away from the window and his fantasy as someone real sat down beside him. It was Otto Graham.

"One more to go, Frank. Great game today…" And as Otto talked, Frank respectfully listened, but couldn't help but be distracted by the image of this "improbable" picture: Frank Gatski sitting with perhaps the greatest quarterback to play the game, who was telling the kid from No. 9 how valuable he was to the team.

As Otto talked, Frank listened and thought about his good fortune. He smiled at the image in the window – the sophisticated Northwestern graduate and the coal miner from West Virginia. What a pair!

Otto, like a professor, was talking about the offensive strategy to be used against the Buffalo Bills. Frank was listening – he really was – but could not keep himself from being carried away by the dream he was living in. He shook his head affirmatively to everything Otto was saying – X's and O's and schemes – for the championship game.

There couldn't be two more different people. Frank had heard Otto's story and read about it. He couldn't help but be in awe of the man next to him.

Otto grew up in Illinois in a home where his father was a high school band director, and Otto learned the piano, violin, cornet and French horn. The high school genius was an award-winning French horn player and an Illinois all-state football AND basketball player. French horn, football and basketball! Frank didn't read a note of music and barely was noticed for his high school football career.

Otto rejected Notre Dame and sifted through other numerous scholarship offers before deciding on Northwestern, the elite school in Evanston, Illinois, known for its emphasis on arts, as much as football; however Otto's scholarship to Northwestern was for basketball, not football. But when football coach, Lyn "Pappy" Waldorf saw Otto play intramural football, he persuaded him to play that sport, too. All Otto did was to set school records, become the Big Ten's Most Valuable Player and an All-American in both sports! Then Otto got drafted into the Navy, distinguished himself as an officer, then later played professional basketball with the Rochester Royals, who won the professional basketball championship in 1946, before agreeing to become the first Cleveland Browns quarterback.

"Is this guy incredible?" Frank was thinking. Why wouldn't he shrink before him? Frank barely was noticed in high school and even at Marshall, where his student life was undistinguished.

"Baby"…the word "baby came through the noise of the speeding train to shake Frank from his revelry, his daydreaming of Otto's greatness.

"Baby, how's the baby?" Otto was asking.

207

Otto, ever the diplomat, the sensitive and articulate man, was asking with sincere concern about his teammate's wife and child. In spite of his enormous achievements and talents, Otto rarely talked about himself.

"The baby is fine," Frank replied.

"And your wife?"

"Fine, too."

Even while Frank was answering Otto's questions about the new baby, he couldn't help but feel the discomfort of the cultural distance between the center and his quarterback.

Otto stood up. "You're the best, Frank. I want you to know that," he said as he gave Frank a pat on the back and turned to join players in another section of the train.

Frank looked out at the pre-dawn darkness. He took inventory of his life again: pretty damn good – a family man now with Ida and little Frank, Jr. back home in West Virginia, on the verge of three straight professional football championships, and the great Otto Graham saying "you're the best."

Frank had never felt more satisfaction and still amazed at the forces at work in his life. He felt his future was bright – he knew he could count on the loving comfort of his mother's arms – and the accuracy of the right arm of Otto Graham.

As expected, the Browns dispatched the Buffalo Bills in the championship game in Cleveland on December 19, 1948 by a score of 49 - 7. Only 23,981 fans showed up to see their beloved team make history. It marked the only time a professional football team had won three consecutive championships. The expected victory, along with below freezing temperatures, kept the attendance low.

The adverse ticket sales affected the Browns player's pocketbook, as well. Each player only took home $594.18. On the same day, the Philadelphia Eagles players were pocketing $1,540.00 for their winning share of the National Football League Championship Game in which they defeated the Chicago

Cards 7 - 0. The Eagles - Cards game was played in a blizzard, but still 36,309 showed up to pack the Eagles home stadium, Shibe Park, to capacity.

The difference in attendance of the rival leagues championship games reflected a concern, once again, for the welfare of the All-American Conference; but still the conference front office in Cleveland insisted that the league was in good shape. There was some concern about the survival of two teams, the Brooklyn Dodgers and the Chicago Rockets, but it looked like the other five teams, the New York Yankees, the San Francisco 49ers, the Baltimore Colts, the Buffalo Bills, and the Los Angeles Dons, along, of course, with the Browns, would live to play another season.

Frank looked at the check for his share for the championship game – $594.18. Not bad, he thought, for a guy who would play the game for free. He didn't envy the players share for the champion NFL Philadelphia Eagle which was more than twice as much – over $1,500.00.

He knew the extra money would come in handy – and just at the right time. There was little Frank, Jr. now two months old, and Christmas was just a few days away. He'd give a couple of hundred dollars to Ida to buy Christmas gifts, and buy Ida a new coat.

The big difference in the playoff money between the NFL and the AAC, though it meant little to Frank, did register with other players and the team's offices in both leagues. Would the two leagues fight over players? Would the All- American Conference fold up completely as the better players went for the bigger money?

Frank was confident the Browns success in its first three years would assure the team would continue, even if the league did not. There was even some discussion of the two leagues agreeing to consolidate.

On December 19, immediately after the two championship games, the press reported that "a peace meeting with the National League had been arranged by the All-American Conference."

Writer Dick Dugan of the United Press explained the reason for the meeting as follows: "…clubs in the rival league have bid without restraint for the series of college stars coming into the pro ranks giving spectacular cash

209

bonuses and fat salary contracts. If the league comes to an understanding on distribution rights to certain players, it will be possible for them to get them without competitive bidding, with a resultant lowering of the disastrously high salary scales."

Cleveland Browns Coach Paul Brown endorsed the idea of the league cooperating. He went so far as to propose that the champion Browns of the AAC and the champion Eagles of the NFL start off the next season with an all-champion game.

Dugan quoted Brown as saying "I think we should start off next year and then have the champions of the two conferences meet every year in a similar game to open both seasons. Everybody knows by now that the 'war' is dying out and there's nothing we'd like better than play the Eagles."

By December 21, Frank was on his way to Charleston where Ida and Frank, Jr. would be waiting. Ida was still staying with her sister. Ida's job with the Charleston Awning Company slowed down in the winter months, so she was glad to take some time off to spend with Frank and her baby.

The plan was to spend Christmas in Charleston, then go to Grant Town and stay with brother Benny while Frank worked his off-season job with the railroad company driving spikes.

Ida's sister was incredibly considerate to allow Ida to stay with her during football season; the generosity helped make the unusual living and moving-around arrangement work out. Financially, it was a big help, especially since Ida's job with the awning company helped with the family's living expenses.

After Christmas, as planned, they headed for Grant Town. Frank enjoyed being with his brother again, and when he wasn't working, he enjoyed doing some hunting, attending basketball games and visiting with old friends at the Circle Bar.

Wherever Frank went, he drew a crowd. At Farmington High School basketball games, it was easy to spot the tall Tarzan of a man with the thick

210

blonde hair and a BROWNS jacket. Sooner or later, the buzz would go around the building that Frank Gatski, the Cleveland Browns center was there. It was hard to hide a guy like Frank in a small gym seating a couple of hundred people. So eventually just about everyone there was looking in his direction or walking casually by to get a close-up look at the celebrity.

The Basketball Team Picture

"Look up here – keep your eyes open."

Flash

"Let me get another one." The photographer spit out the bulb from his camera. It clunked on the basketball floor. He quickly put a new bulb in.

"Ready?"

Flash

The 1949 Farmington Jr. High basketball team was immortalized to be seen in the high school yearbook. And Sam Huff was there. In spite of his conflict with Coach John Victor, Sam had made it at least to picture-taking day.

John Victor wasn't really such a bad guy. He couldn't have been. The math teacher and assistant football coach didn't have anything personal against ninth grader Sam Huff; otherwise, he wouldn't have put him on the 1949 junior high school basketball team. Yes. "Mean old" Mr. Victor was the coach.

Sam hadn't felt good about quitting football after three days in August and was hungry to get in a game. Any game. Even basketball, which he wasn't really very good at. But he had to satisfy his desire to compete – beat someone – beat someone up – win something – and keep up with Leo, who had decided to be on the team, too.

Sam was beginning to realize that basketball wasn't his sport. He played it – just like all the kids played all the sports. But Sam was small. Except for Leo, the smallest player on the team. And besides, he wasn't blessed with God-given basketball ability. The school was small, and even the marginally talented or non-talented players could be on the team. After all, there was a need for at least ten players to hold a scrimmage. Sam was happy – and proud to wear that uniform with FARMERS across the chest.

Sam was a guard. Leo was a forward. The little Farmers opened the 1949 season with a game against Barnes Junior High on January 3. Barnes 20, Farmington Junior High 17. Neither Sam nor Leo scored a single point.

The team wasn't very good – losing 14 games, while winning just two. The scores were lopsided mostly: and painful like losing to the hated Fairmont Junior High Black Hawks, twice 52 - 18 and 44 - 16. The Farmers two victories were squeakers; they paid Barnes back 34 - 26 and beat Mannington, 44 - 39.

Both Sam and Leo managed a good bit of playing time. That was not necessarily a good thing for the little Farmers record. Leo managed to average two points a game. Sam never did score – the entire season.

The basketball season was positive for one thing. It gave Sam a slightly different opinion of Mr. Victor. The coach and math teacher, who was tough on him in the classroom, did put him on the team, let him play a great deal and was not overly critical in spite of the kids less than average talent on the hardwood!

The basketball season also showed Sam chasing Leo once again. While Leo was no Bob Cousy, at least he managed to put the ball in the basket a few times. Twice he scored four points in a game. Sam's scoreless season established, or at least tied a junior high record for futility. Zero points. This was just another example of how Leo, the forever friend and teammate from the James Fork Elementary days was forging ahead of Sam, the one-time leader and mentor of the little Italian immigrant.

Now, Robert Lee "Sam" Huff was trying to keep up with Leo.

While Frank's appearance around Farmington still created interest, local folks had gotten use to the idea of having a professional football player in their midst. The Browns were All-American Football Conference Champs for the third straight year and Frank's fame was now old news.

And even for Sam, the excitement of seeing Frank and the child-like adulation of the man was not quite the same. Maybe he was growing up – thinking of Frank less was, well, like getting rid of toys.

213

Sam's life was changing. Soon he would be fifteen. Playing football wasn't <u>everything</u>, like it used to be. Now he had a girlfriend, and he was working part-time at Manchin's. Sam searched for answers. He was learning to be on his own. He was even thinking that he was just a couple of years from being able to quit school and go to work full time. Was it in his blood? His sisters and a brother, all of his siblings, did just that. Quit. Could Sam make the football team someday at Farmington? Down deep that flame had not gone out. Yet, it just seemed more improbable that a fire could start. After all he did quit in his freshman year and he had to ask himself, "is playing football something I really want to do?"

During the off season, Frank Gatski would stop in Manchins occasionally to shop. If Sam were working at that time he would see Frank – but didn't feel the youthful adulation of a couple years before. It confused Sam. It was like the pain of lost love lessening over a period of time. He wanted to feel the same thrill to see his old hero, but it wasn't quite the same. Was it like all the extreme feelings we have about love and death. Time just won't let us hang on to them.

He had a girlfriend now. It was serious business for a fourteen-year-old. They had even talked about getting married someday. So the same boy that ran around No. 9 hoping for a glance at his hero had changed his focus.

Sure, who wouldn't want to be like Frank Gatski, but Sam had to confess he saw nothing in the near or distant future that would ever make it happen.

Sophomore Slump

As spring came to Farmington in 1949, the ninth grade was buzzing about "The Gingham Swing," the annual country dance at the school where a "Sadie Hawkins" was chosen and in the Lil'Abner tradition, the girls got a chance to ask the boys to be their date.

Mary Fletcher, that fetching French horn player of the band, top student, and popular besides, was chosen by her classmates as Sadie. Her choice of a date was easy. Sam was her perfect Lil' Abner. He even got into his dad's bib overall for a picture with Mary in pigtails, gingham chicken feed dress and saddleback shoes and bobby socks.

The gymnasium/auditorium turned into Dogpatch with banners. The band, right from nearby Dunkard Mill, played some swing and a square dance and country western music while the kids got high on non-alcohol real Dogpatch kick-a-poo-juice.

The dance heralded spring and everyone knew that "The Gingham Swing" marked the "the beginning of the end" of the school year. Just about six weeks to go and this freshmen class would be history – and sophomores.

Life was moving along. Sam continued to spend a lot of time after school with Mary. She was the most important person in the world to him. She kept him interested in school. Because she was popular and an exceptional student, and a class leader, she wasn't going to date the school dummy, that was for certain. So Sam kept up with passing grades, Mary made sure of it.

Sam finished the school year with good grades, not quite as good as Leo, of course, but better than just passing in every subject. By the summer he had grown to 5 foot 9, but he was still skinny, weighing just 145 pounds.

215

He kept thinking about going out for football in his sophomore year. One day, while sitting at the kitchen table, he brought up the subject with his mother.

"You'll get hurt, Sam. You ain't big enough, are you?"

"Yes, I am. Everybody's going out."

"What about working at Manchin's. Ain't you still going to do that?"

Sam hadn't given much thought to giving up the job.

"You can't do both, now can you?"

Sam twirled the salt shaker in his hand. He would miss the few dollars he made there. It sure did help on his dates with Mary. "Yeh. I guess I can't do both. I couldn't work after school – 'cause that's when I would practice, but then sometimes Mr. Aloi would need help on a weekend. I could work then."

Katherine dried her hands on the dishtowel. "You'll have to decide, boy." She placed the towel on the handle on the cabinet door. "I know your Dad is hoping you'll go to work with him sometime down the road."

Sam flashed, "I ain't goin' to work in the mine, Mom…"

"Oh, shush, I didn't mean to bring that up. Heck, you ain't fifteen yet. It'd be a year or so before you decide on that."

"You mean quit school when I'm sixteen…"

"Oh, Sam. I ain't suggesting that, but your brother and sisters all did."

"I know they did, but I ain't gonna quit to work in the mine."

"You'll be in tenth grade this year. What will you do if you stay in school?"

"Well, graduate I guess."

"Then what?"

"I don't know." Then he had a vision. "I could work at Manchin's full time. That'd be better than the coal mine."

Katherine turned toward him and raised her eyebrows, "Except for the pay." Then she laughed. "Don't worry about it now. See what happens."

While Sam pondered his future, the answer to the immediate problem came through the door. It was Leo with an announcement.

"I'm going out for football!"

Sam's decision was made. "See, Mom, I told you everyone was going out for football."

"But, Sam, you went out last year and quit. Leo never went out."

Leo explained, "My mom wouldn't let me, but she said okay now." Then he turned to Sam. "You ain't gonna quit this year, are you?"

"Heck no, I ain't gonna quit."

Leo slapped Sam on the back.

"Well, I'm going to get a letter this year."

Sam laughed. "A letter? Do you know what it takes to get a letter?"

"No, but I'm going to get one."

Sam's explanation was short of the correct information, but "well you gotta play in so many games. Heck you never even went out before."

"That don't matter. I'm still gonna get a letter."

Sam shook his head at his ignorant friend. "Okay."

Sam's superior attitude, born of his short term experience as a freshman football player who quit before the season even started, did not discourage Leo or dampen his enthusiasm. Leo was on fire with the idea and kept moving forward.

"Coach Kelly... He is going to give out shoes to some players who want to get them ahead – so they can practice – I mean before the real practice starts, you know what I mean..."

Sam knew. "Yeh, I know what ya mean." But Sam couldn't help but remember the day he turned in his equipment the year before. Would Coach Kelly remember that?! If he did, would he hold it against him?

Now it was Sam's turn to tell Leo.

"You know what else we have to do. We have to go to the doctor for an examination."

"What's that for?"

"To see if there's anything wrong with us, so we don't have a heart attack or die while we're playing."

Nothing would frighten Leo.

"Ain't nothing wrong with me and I am going to get my letter."

217

Doctor Jenkins put the tongue depressor in Sam's mouth and focused his light. "You got a bad throat, son. You parents ever say anything about it?"

"No, sir."

"Well, what's it feel like?"

"I've had it as long as I can remember. It don't hurt all the time."

"Your tonsils should come out."

"Does that mean I can't go out for football?"

Sam anxiously waited for the doctor's reply. It might solve his dilemma that had him torn between spending time on the football field and delivering for Sam Aloi. On one hand, if the doctor would keep him from playing, it would make things easier.

Doctor Jenkins smiled. "Taking your tonsils out, son, would mean your throat wouldn't be hurting anymore. No, you can go out for football, but tell your parents what I said, okay."

Sam scooted off the examination table and went across the street to Manchin's to tell Sam Aloi he was going out for football again.

Leo was even spreading the news as if his pronouncements would force him to follow through with his determination to win a letter.

On a Sunday morning, even before practice had begun, Leo and Mike Arcure were putting on their cassocks and surplices to serve mass at St. Peter's – and the conversation had turned to the upcoming football season. Leo told Mike then, in no uncertain terms, that he was going to earn a letter.

Now Mike was sounding like Sam, except Mike had all the details. "Do you know what it takes to get a letter? You have to play in sixty percent of the quarters. Sixty percent!" He paused to let that sink in. "That's a lot!" Mike didn't want to discourage Leo, but quietly he felt Leo was aiming too high.

Mike was the team's manager and familiar with the players and he figured it would be hard for a new player to get enough playing time to wear that scarlet and gray "F".

218

Practice for the 1949 high school football season began on August 10. In the locker rooms of all the county high schools, the picture was the same: an equipment manager trying to scrounge up enough shoes, pads, pants and jerseys for all the kids from the nineth grade on, who wanted to go out for football. Some of the kids were just too small for any of the equipment on hand, so they had to do with whatever was there, resulting in some comical picture of little kids in oversized uniforms, but everyone knew that the days ahead of hard contact, tackling and blocking and running laps – and the resultant attrition – would trim the squad down to a manageable level. By the third week of practice in the hot August sun, the squads were reduced to thirty or forty players – enough to scrimmage, first team against second team and to run the upcoming opponent's plays.

By late August, the Farmington Farmers had 45 players still out – an unusually large number – but Sam Huff wasn't one of them. He did what he promised Leo he would not do. Quit! He had lost interest as he languished on third team, a 145 pound, 14-year-old too slow for halfback, too small for the line, and not determined enough to make up for his lack of size and speed – and too much in love with Mary Fletcher and attached to the job he had at Manchin's where he could earn a little money. Money had become an issue in the Huff home because the miners were talking "strike." A major strike would mean "no pay!"

John L. Lewis, the United Mine Workers head, was threatening a walkout of 480,000 miners nationwide, to protest the suspension of welfare and pension fund payments. Refusal of some southern operators to continue royalty payments of 20 cents a ton for every ton of coal mined to the UMW's welfare-pension fund was the latest bad action to make a strike seem imminent. Lewis announced that the pension fund was down to $14,000,000, and he suspended benefits as a "temporary expedient to protect" the fund. Payments to sick and

219

pensioned miners and their families had been made at the rate of $10,000,000 a month.

The Huff's had gone through this before. But the last year had been tough. The miners worked only three days a week since July on the instructions of the UMW president John L Lewis. The wage agreement had expired on June 30, but the miners set aside their traditional "no contract, no work" policy to continue working while an agreement was hammered out.

Sam didn't feel right about asking his parents for money since they were counting every penny now. The miner's strike fund was still able to supply the bare necessities. But trying to keep food on the table, take care of his baby brother was enough to make Sam determined to help out.

Throw that on Sam's plate, and suddenly football wasn't that important, but trying to do his part at home was. He hated to see his mom and dad distressed over the lack of money.

But in No. 9 everyone was in the same boat. Every single household was feeling the same pain, so there was a certain comfort in the solidarity there. But that didn't spend. So everybody hunkered down and waited to see if the union could get everyone back to work full time. Three days a week was better than none. Everyone in No. 9 and in all the county's coal communities feared the worst – a strike!

It wasn't a very comfortable position for Sam – to be spending his time playing football when he could be working and helping out at home.

Leo wasn't buying it. "What do you mean, you're gonna quit football."

"I got to."

"No you don't."

"My dad ain't getting the same pay. I need to help out... and anyway I ain't getting anywhere with football. Victor don't like me. I ain't gonna play."

"You ain't tried yet."

"I tried last year."

"For what, three days? I told you I'm gonna get a letter. I want you to do it, too."

Sam countered, "But I got a chance to make some money."

"That's not important."

"It is to me."

"Sure, sure," Leo said. "You're gonna be sorry, you know that?"

Now Sam was getting mad. "Don't say that, Leo. I ain't sorry, damn it."

"You will be. Everyone's gonna think you're a chicken."

"I ain't no chicken, damn it. I ain't!"

"I know you ain't, but that's not what everyone else is gonna be thinking!"

Sam didn't want to face Mike Arcure or any of the players or Coach Kelly or Coach Victor – not this time. He didn't bother to tell anyone he was quitting. He just couldn't, not two years in a row.

But Mike Arcure, the manager, noticed everything. When Sam didn't show up for practice, Mike asked Leo where his buddy was. Leo shrugged. He couldn't say anything bad about Sam.

Sam didn't want to go to the Mannington Fair this year, but Mary would be there with the Farmington High School band, and she expected Sam to go so they could enjoy the annual fun.

Sam had always looked forward to it before, but this year would be different. He knew there would be a lot of high school players wearing their game jerseys as they prepared for their first game of the season. And worse, he would be forced to face his own Farmington buddies who knew that he had quit again. Most players had little respect for a healthy sophomore who didn't have the guts to stick it out.

Sam had avoided them all as much as possible. But school hadn't started yet and he was safe from the scrutiny of the players. Even at home at No. 9 he stayed away from Leo because it was uncomfortable to think of him practicing with the team and planning on playing. Sam didn't want to think about the bus ride from No. 9 to school when he would have to sit with Leo and hear about it.

221

The fair lights and usual dazzle couldn't keep Sam from the gut-wrenching thought of walking up and down the fairgrounds and seeing the players from all the county schools in jerseys of blue, red, green, gray – all talking to each other – with great excitement, each looking forward to the games they would play against each other.

The calliope sound of the merry-go-round made Sam think of a clown he had seen in a movie. And suddenly he was feeling like a clown. The cool night air of the early September night couldn't keep him from feeling his face grow warm and sweaty as he walked along the midway with Mary – not hearing a word she said, while trying to avoid the looks of anybody in a gray Farmington football jersey.

Finally, the din from the carnival went silent when Mary said, "there's some of the players, let's go over."

Sam stopped. Mary turned around. "I don't want to, Mary."

"Why not?"

"Oh they're talking about the game and football. I don't want to hear that crap."

"Oh why not?"

"I ain't playing, that's why."

Mary tried to be kind. "Well, you're working some now…and that's a good thing."

"Yeh, well I'd be playing if Victor liked me – or if Sam Aloi didn't keep after me to work at Manchin's, but I ain't sorry."

They turned around and began to walk the other way – away from the Farmington players.

On September 3, Eddie Barrett, the Fairmont Times Sportswriter, was in town to obtain information for his pre-season look at the team, one of a series that included every team in the county.

On September 4, the long three column story spoke positively about the team…"But the factor which characterizes this team is its spirit. Pushed by their driving young coaches, Kelly and his assistant, John Victor, the Farmers are an upstart crew who brag they can beat anybody."

Barrett mentioned that the squad was one of the largest in years. There were forty-three players, including fourteen seniors, thirteen juniors, eight sophomores and eight freshmen. Sophomore Sam Huff was not there, but Leo Coceano was.

The Browns Stumble

The 1949 football season for Frank Gatski and the Cleveland Browns began on September 5 and not quite the way they expected. In spite of beating the sixteen point underdog Bills every way possible – in the air and on the ground – the final score was 28 - 28. And the Browns were lucky to get the tie. The New York Times reported it as follows:

> "The champion Cleveland Browns came roaring from behind with 21 points in the last quarter today to tie the Buffalo Bills 28-28, in the local All-America Conference football season opener before 31,839 in Civic Stadium."

Otto Graham, most valuable player in the conference last season, pitched the Browns back into contention, completing 15 of his last 17 passes. All of the Cleveland touchdowns came through the air, Graham completing three scoring passes to Edgar (Special Delivery) Jones. Mac Speedie made the fourth, two minutes before the finish.

The Bills, who never had led the Browns in eight previous meetings, appeared to have the decision in hand as the fourth quarter opened. Graham, who had hit his receivers on the last two passes of the third quarter, took up the string when the visitors gained possession on their 28. He completed six straight as the Browns raced into scoring territory in eleven plays. The last went to Jones for the final seven yards.

The Bills, who were upended in their first start by the Chicago Rockets, were 16-point underdogs. It was Cleveland's first start.

The statistics told a horror story. The Browns out rushed the Bills 177 yards to 80 and out passed them 330 yards to 95. Yet, because of two fumbles, the Browns had fallen behind by twenty-one points going into the final quarter. Thankfully for the Browns, Otto Graham showed his greatness once again.

After the game Paul Brown was furious. His defending champions had beaten the Buffalo Bills the season before, not once, not twice, but three times – and by substantial margins, 42-13, 31-14 in the regular season and 49-7 in the championship game. A combined total of 122-34.

After three years of enormous – yes, even unprecedented success – had his players become complacent? Were they getting old? Almost all of the players had been in the armed service during World War II and many were thirty years old or older.

Otto Graham began his career with the Browns in 1946 as a twenty-five-year-old rookie. Now he was 28. Frank Gatski, now in his fourth year with the Browns, was also 28. But neither of these guys had a problem with age. They were as young as school boys, always in shape, and in love with the game.

Paul Brown didn't care how old they were, or how young. He wasn't keeping anyone who could not produce, and for Brown, that meant winning every game – just exactly what they did in 1946, 1947, and 1948. A damn tie with the Buffalo Bills was unacceptable!

Beating everybody was Browns goal. Being the best football team – not only in the All-American Conference but in all of America was his dream. In fact after winning the championship in December 1948, he went on record to propose that his team play the champions of the old, arrogant National Football League to open the 1949 season – a bold, some thought "crazy" idea, to think that his team, only in existence for three years playing what many considered inferior teams, could compete with the champion Philadelphia Eagles of the established National Football League.

Now, a tie with the Buffalo Bills. He could hear his critics now. "Hell, he can't even beat the teams in his own league." The tie with the Bills was fodder for those NFL owners and fans who would suggest the AAC was a "minor" league that couldn't compete.

He did not want to be near a phone in case one of his counterparts in the NFL would call. He wanted to hide until his reputation was reestablished – and that meant dominating the teams in the AAC as they did the year before.

225

Brown couldn't wait for the Monday meeting with his team. He was at his best here – teaching, but still through his anger, maintaining his composure. Brown's fury did not shout, instead it sliced – like purposeful words from a professor. He went down the list of sins committed on the football field in a quiet rage the players could feel.

No one was left out. He had something for everyone. He wanted to include everyone – because it was a team game – and in the case of the Buffalo Bills, a team tie.

"Mac, you ran that route on 38 pass too deep…Boedecker, that fumble you caused by letting your arms swing out – you have to press the ball in…Otto, you have to hold on to the ball, no matter what…Vlinski, when you pull out on that off-tackle play, run, man, run! You must be quicker…" Even the perfect Frank Gatski felt Brown's wrath. "Frank, we allowed your man to get Otto two times in this game. This can't happen!"

"Men, this is a team we beat three times last year. You are champions. This should have been no contest, yet we had to come from behind to get a tie. When we put this team together, I said then I would only take lean and hungry players. And yes, I said I wanted amateur spirit. But not amateur players. We had no spirit, and unfortunately played like amateurs. You are the same team of champions. So let's begin to play that way."

He turned the page on the easel. "Let's get ready to play the Baltimore Colts!"

Pinball Wizard

School began in Farmington on September 7 and right away the talk turned toward the first football game two days later on September 9. The Farmers were going to play against Benwood Union, a Class A school power located just south of Wheeling – about sixty miles away.

Everybody was talking about it because everybody was involved somehow. Of the total Farmington High enrollment of 120 boys in the top four grades, over a third were on the football team. On Thursday afternoon, the day before the game, the team crowded on the combination stage and basketball court in the small auditorium for the thuse. The thirty-member band struck up the fight song. Three hundred more students, ready to fight for good old Farmington, stamped their feet and cheered.

Sam Huff sat with the other tenth graders feeling jealous at the attention focused in front of him. To hide his embarrassment he grinned and faked his way with false excitement. He managed to draw some attention to himself by his casual non-conformity cheering – poking fun instead. But inside, Sam wasn't laughing. He wanted to be up there with Leo and Rudy. Hell, ever since James Fork Elementary he was the leader in any game – football especially. What the heck happened? Here he was, a sophomore, sitting in the damn auditorium, while all his buddies and his very best buddy Leo, were on the stage. And he was cheering for them?!

Coach Kelly was talking about the game, but Sam didn't hear a word. His fake grin had disappeared and his sad face looked at Mary. She was one reason – and then he thought how things at home kept him from staying out for football.

He sat back in the seat and looked up at the high ceiling. "God damn," he thought. "Those guys are ready to play a football game, and I'm not going to. This is stupid."

227

"It's Farmington High School...It's Farmington High School!"

The loud song made Sam sit up and look around. Coach Kelly had spoken and so had captain Gerald Martin. The thuse was over, and the team was walking off the stage to the cheers of everyone but Sam. He swallowed hard and as he looked around at everyone cheering, he clapped his hands and kept his head hidden.

The bell rang to end school on Friday. Sam picked up his books and headed for the Home Economics room where Mary would be coming out of class. It was the routine now. Even when Mary would have band practice, they would get a chance to see each other for a few minutes before she would join the band and Sam would board the bus for No. 9 – or go to Manchin's and work with Mr. Aloi.

There was an additional buzz to this end of the school day since the Farmers were playing their first football game at Benwood. Everyone was going to the game, so players and cheerleaders, and all the students, were on high energy.

Players and cheerleaders had come prepared to board the big yellow bus parked near the gym. Other students going to the game were quickly heading home excitedly preparing for the trip to Benwood in cars – nearly a two hour journey along Route 250 to Moundsville and then about fifteen miles north on flat Route 2 that runs along the Ohio River to Benwood.

Mike Arcure, football manager, and some players were helping load equipment, uniforms, first-aid cases and a duffle bag of footballs. Coach Kelly and Assistant Coach Victor stood at the bus door checking off names of players of the twenty-two man traveling squad.

Mary and Sam stepped outside into the chilly sun-splashed autumn afternoon. Sam handed Mary back the French horn he carried for her. Down on the football field, band members were forming to practice their half-time routine they would perform at the half time of next week's game in Fairmont. It would be the first half-time performance of the season. It had been decided that a trip to Benwood was out of the question – too far and too expensive for a band trip!

The sound of the band members warming up played a dissonant song as Sam leaned over to kiss Mary goodbye.

"I better hurry," she said. "I'll see you tomorrow."

"Okay," Sam said. "I ain't working today. I could hang around and meet you after band. Maybe we can go to the movies."

"Yeh, okay," she looked down at the band director, who was beginning to form his band in front of him. "I gotta go. Bye."

She turned and hurried quickly down the grassy bank to the football field. He watched her go, then turned and headed toward Farmer's Inn, the student hangout on the edge of the hill above the field to play the pinball machine for a while. If he could win some games, he could kill the hour or so that Mary would be practicing. He felt in his pocket for the two dollars he had for the movie and popcorn. He had some change – exactly twenty cents, four nickels, which would give him four games of pinball.

Before he entered Farmer's Inn, he looked down on the field at the band getting ready to practice. He saw Mary put her horn case down on the ground, take out the horn and play some scales – which only added to the clamor of sound already being played. As he turned to walk the few steps up the street to Farmer's Inn, he saw the football team ready to board the bus for the trip to Benwood.

"Oh shit," he thought. "I got to go past Coach Kelly and the players – Leo and Rudy. Oh shit." Sam wanted to disappear.

He turned around again and walked down the street away from the bus. He looked back over his shoulder and saw Coach Kelly and Victor looking into the bus.

"Damn it, maybe they've already loaded." He was right. Kelly and Victor boarded the bus and it started to move.

"Shit. They'll be coming this way." It was the only road out of town and on to Route 250. Sam just knew the bus would go right by and let the players have a good look at him. Instead, the driver decided to back up, giving Sam a chance to hurry down the street before the bus began to turn around and head toward him. He hurried into Farmer's Inn and looked out the window as the bus rattled past and down the brick street with twenty-two players and two coaches heading for Benwood. Sam turned his face from the window. His heart was pounding.

Just when Sam thought he was safe from any scrutiny, Mr. Welty, the Farmer's Inn owner, spoke up from behind the counter.

"That's the bus going to the game tonight, ain't it?"

"Yeh," Sam said softly. "I think so."

"I thought you were on the team?"

"Well, I was, but I uh quit," Sam nervously found a nickel in his pocket and shoved it in the machine. The balls dropped into the shooters alley. "I'm working at Manchin's and... my Mom and Dad..."

Sam kept up a steady stream of talk hoping to keep Mr. Welty from asking any more questions about the football team. And the machine noise helped. Sam pounded the flippers on the side of the machine to propel the steel ball back up the playing surface. He shook the machine and pounded on the top. The steel ball ricocheted off of the posts lighting up the display and racking up points before it whizzed down past the flippers and disappeared into a black hole. Sam quickly pulled hard on the spring-loaded plunger and shot another ball up the alley and into play. The machine lit up and dinged and rang while Sam kept the ball alive. More points and no more talk from Mr. Welty. Then, "game over".

Sam quickly got another nickel and started over. While the lights danced in front of him, he couldn't help but think of that bus heading toward Benwood.

Sam won some games and managed most of the next hour playing pinball. As the last ball of the last game from the fourth nickel dropped from the game board and the display flashed "game over," suddenly there was silence. Silence. After a constant sound of bells and the ringing of thousands of points, now there was silence.

Sam felt in his pocket. He knew there wasn't another nickel there. There was the two dollars, but they were for the movie date with Mary later on. Sam looked at the clock. But he didn't need to – he could hear the band practicing on the field below. Mr. Welty cleared his throat – and it startled Sam and made him anxious. Sam turned. Mr. Welty got up from the stool and began wiping the counter. He cleared his throat again.

"Yeh, Leo told me he was going out for football. You know he works here sometimes.

"Yeh, I know."

"Yeh, Leo said you and him was going out for football."

"Well, I was out…"

Mr. Welty sat back down on the stool. "And he told me he was going to get a letter."

Sam slammed his hand on the pinball machine. "Yeh, well that's nothing. I could get a letter if I was out."

Mr. Welty changed the subject. "You want a pop? I'll buy… here." He slid open the cooler cover. "What kind?"

"I'll have an orange," Sam looked at the clock. "Another five minutes," he thought, "I have to meet my girlfriend. She's playing in the band."

"I hear 'em practicing," Mr. Welty flipped the cap off the bottle and set it in front of Sam.

"I told Leo he could work for me as long as he keeps his grades up and if he wants to play football, too…"

Sam took a drink of pop. "I'm working at Manchin's with Sam Aloi. He's a good guy."

"Yes, I know him, but too bad you ain't out for football, too… you and Leo are best friends. That's what he says."

"We are buddies. I hope he gets a letter…" Sam swallowed hard because he felt a twinge of jealousy as he said it. "I better finish my pop." He couldn't wait to get out of there. All that talk about Leo getting a letter…

Sam kept talking because he didn't want to hear another word of advice from Mr. Welty. "The band stopped playing. My girlfriend will be waiting." He took the last drink of pop. "Thanks for the pop, Mr. Welty."

The bell on the door jangled and two young girls carrying band instruments came inside. Sam stood aside as they came in. He wanted to avoid them, too, but…

"You goin' to the game, Sam?" one asked. "I thought you were on the team."

By the time she finished speaking, Sam was out the door.

The lights in the movie theatre dimmed, and the small crowd of thirty or so stopped their chatter and settled back to watch the movie. One of Sam's favorite stars was Red Skelton – and this night he was lucky. The feature was Red Skelton in "The Fuller Brush Man".

But there was also a short subject before the main show – a cartoon or travelogue…so what would it be? The lights came up, and the small crowd clapped and cheered as Larry, Shemp, and Mo – the Three Stooges – stared back into the darkness promising fifteen minutes of laughs for their insane antics.

Minutes later, when Red Skelton's name came up on the screen, Sam, for a moment, lost himself in the moment of fun – being with his girlfriend, eating popcorn and watching Red Skelton. He hugged Mary. She reached back to touch his hand and pressed her head on his chest.

Mary laughed and looked up to see Sam's reaction to one of Red's funny lines. Sam was staring straight ahead. He was looking at the screen, but wasn't watching – his head was on the football field in Benwood. Mary moved and the field dissolved into black and white shenanigans on the big screen in front of him. Sam laughed back and took another bite of popcorn.

The Saturday morning <u>Fairmont Times</u> told the sad story in a headline: Benwood 26, Farmington 0. The sub-headline said "Farmington Eleven Outmanned by Union Ironmen." The story followed:

> "Benwood Union had too much weight and roughness tonight for little Farmington High school, and pounded out a 26-0 victory here. The outstanding play by the outmanned Farmers was by little halfback Rudy Banick in the third period. He returned a punt 57 yards to the Benwood 8-yard-line, but the Farmers could do nothing there and lost the ball on downs."

Leo began the first step on making good on his prediction of earning a letter. He got in the game as a substitute in three of the quarters and played well for his first football experience. He even got his name in the paper – underneath the "starting lineup" and score by periods in a small section listing "substitutes". Now there was little doubt – Leo was going to get a letter.

Leo couldn't wait till Saturday morning to go over to Sam's house to talk about the game – to show off some bruises and revel in the fact he had come through the fight, even in defeat. No doubt about it – Leo felt enormous satisfaction and pride in playing.

Sam came to the door and stepped outside on the porch. Leo could hardly express himself. The thrill of putting on a uniform, the nervousness and the excitement brought out the worst in his Italian dialect English. He tried to relive every play – incoherently, almost. Sam finally had heard enough.

"Yeh, well you lost 26 - 0. How did you get beat so bad?"

"Well they was a good team."

"Yeh, but 26 - 0. That's getting skunked! What happened?"

"Shit, I told you. They was good. I hope we do better this week when we play West Fairmont."

Then Leo suddenly realized something was wrong: he was defending his team with someone who didn't even play.

233

"At least we tried," then he looked at his friend. Sam sat on the banister and didn't say anything more about the game.

But downtown in the Circle Bar, it was all the talk. The bar's <u>Fairmont Times</u> newspaper had gone ragged from being read by every beer-drinking ex-Farmer football player. Everyone agreed it was just the first game and Benwood was recognized as a Class A football power. They talked about the bright spots of the young team, especially Rudy Banick, but they also knew that playing West Fairmont at East-West Stadium, the next Friday night would be a mismatch. Farmington, a Class B school, had 120 boys in the top four grades; West Fairmont was Class A with 300 boys in high school and a school with a reputation as one of the big school powers in the state. No contest!

But Farmington High wasn't the only football talk at the bar. The newspaper also reported on the big clash coming on Sunday, September 11 between the Cleveland Browns and the Baltimore Colts. Of course, because of Frank Gatski, everyone in town had become a Browns fan while holding on to their allegiance to the Pittsburgh Steelers in the NFL. And everyone wondered what the hell happened to the Browns when they played the 28 - 28 tie with the Buffalo Bills. The Cleveland Browns were now like the New York Yankees and Notre Dame – never supposed to lose or tie. Since the conference began in 1946 the Browns were 43 - 2 - 1 and they hadn't been beaten or tied since 1947.

The next day in Cleveland, the Browns lived up to their championship reputation by beating the Baltimore Colts 21 - 0. The UPI led off the story this way:

> "The champion Cleveland Browns meshed a powerful passing and running attack today and defeated the Baltimore Colts 21 - 0, for their first 1949 All-America Football Conference victory...
>
> Until today, the Browns had been treated rather disrespectfully in three exhibitions and their

opening league game, a 28 - 28 tie with Buffalo. The
opposition had scored 70 points against them..."

Otto Graham had a good day, which means that Frank had a good day
protecting him and allowing time for Otto to set up and throw. Otto completed
14 of 20 passes for 234 yards and a touchdown pass to Dante Lavelli. The
rushing game was effective, too, with Ara Parsegian, Marion Motley, Edgar
Jones and Les Horvath toting the pigskin.

In Stadium Shadows

East-West Stadium in Fairmont was as intimidating as hell. Seating 6,000, the big, impressive stone structure was home to both West Fairmont and East Fairmont football teams, who arranged their schedules to play there, usually one on Thursday and one on Friday.

The field at Farmington bore no resemblance to the East-West Stadium field. Both were one hundred yards long, marked off with lime in ten yard increments, but that was it!

There was grass at East-West Stadium – green grass and the field, was layed out smartly below thirty rows of bleachers that curved in a half horseshoe configuration from one end zone to the other. Tall modern light poles provided illumination, which made players feel they were on a giant stage. Compare that to Farmington, where two grass banks provided seating and only games in daylight could be played there.

Some of the Farmington players had been to East-West Stadium, and they knew what to expect. Others had never even seen the stadium. One kid, a freshman, said the tall stonewalls reminded him of a castle he saw in a movie. He looked around with awe as he got off the bus and joined with his teammates going into the locker room underneath the end zone bleachers.

The Farmington High School band began arriving at the stadium shortly after the players. Sam decided to hitchhike to the game since Mary would be playing in the band. He couldn't sit with her during the game, but at halftime they could have a coke and a hot dog. And besides, he was anxious to see the game. Not to see Farmington win – or even play well. He didn't want to admit it, but he secretly wanted them to lose – and play poorly. It was a matter of foolish pride. Yes, jealousy. If he wasn't going to be on the team, then he didn't want to acknowledge that the team could be good without him. A loss would justify his decision to quit. And besides, he didn't want to give Leo any further advantage over him. The fact that Leo was even on the team was bad enough!

Hitchhiking the nine miles to Fairmont was easy since just about everybody in Farmington was going to the game.

When Sam got inside the stadium, he walked past the concession stand and through one of the entrances to the seats. Down below to his left he could see a yellow school bus and gray and scarlet clad band members of the Farmington band who had just gotten off. Majorettes in thigh high skirts and military type tops practiced twirling their batons. Other band members were waiting for the instruments to be unloaded. He saw Mary reach over to pick up her French horn case. Since the band wasn't ready to assemble in the stands, Sam walked down the steps and over to the bus. Mary saw him coming and walked over to him.

Sam took the case from her. "Let me carry it."

"Okay," she said. "I'm glad you got here okay. Wait here for a minute. Me and the girls are going to the restroom. I'll be right back."

Mary and two friends climbed the steps of the stadium at the top level where the restrooms were. She looked down to see Sam holding her French horn case and staring out onto the football field. He seemed uncomfortable – holding a band instrument. He wanted to set it down, but he didn't dare. He didn't want to risk having something happen to it. In fact he felt his hand clutching it tightly as if to prevent someone from grabbing it from him. He looked around, hoping no one would see him with the instrument. What if someone would think he was in the band – or maybe a student who was helping the band – or a band manager? He took a deep breath looking toward the restrooms for a sight of Mary, so he could give the instrument back to her – as quickly as possible.

Suddenly, there was the sound of football cleats on concrete and boys' shouts. The big and heavy metal door of the dressing room swung open banging against the concrete stadium wall. The Farmington High School players came

end. Capt. Frank DeMoss plunged for the first extra point and Wilcox went over on the last play of the game for the second.

The victory was by no means an easy one for Biz Dawson's charges as the underdog Farmers battled the Bears on virtually even terms for the greater part of the contest. Led by their rugged center and captain, Gerald Martin, the Farmer line repeatedly stalled the Bears ground attack while their offense was picking up ground through the Fairmont line.

Highlighting the game was the running of little Rudy Banick. The pint-sized Farmer scatback won the approval of the crowd as he shook himself loose for a considerable amount of yardage on a punt returns and end sweeps."

Fight at the Gym

The scuffling of feet and the rattle of lunch bags and paper, the shrill laughter and loud conversation echoed noisily in the large auditorium that served the school in so many ways – basketball games, dances, band and glee club concerts, plays, and lunch room.

Rudy Banick unfolded his paper bag lunch and took out a sandwich and a pint of milk. The auditorium was filling up with students gathering there to eat lunch. Good buddies and football teammates, Duane Bonnette and Billy Pasko came in and sat beside Rudy.

On this Monday, the students at the school, and the folks in town were still talking about the game with West Fairmont on Friday night.

The Farmers lost 14 - 0, but everyone there, including the Fairmont newspaper writers, conceded that Farmington gave West Fairmont all they wanted. The Farmers were quite a surprise, especially after losing to Benwood 26 - 0 the previous week. They played the bigger Class A Polar Bears to a standoff except for a couple of pass plays – one, a last second touchdown that boosted the final score to 14 - 0.

It was a moral victory for Farmington. A win would have been an enormous upset. So in spite of the loss, everyone, players and coaches, knew they had a good team, one that could compete for the Mason-Dixon Championship. If they could play with Class A West Fairmont, they surely could compete with the Class B schools of the Mason-Dixon: Rivesville, Barrackville, Monongah, Fairview, and Clay-Battelle.

Rudy Banick, quiet and unassuming, was so well liked and respected, and probably by now the most popular member of the football team, even though he was only a junior. As he ate his lunch, he became surrounded by students who wanted to be near the school's young football hero.

241

Rudy was not big – just 5' 9", weighing 160 pounds, but he was all muscle. His wiry frame in jeans and a t-shirt showed his tight lithe muscular body. He had a smoothly dark handsome face – almost a Valentino look, but with a pug nose that looked like he had been in a boxing match.

The girls were all attracted to him, but his modest and self-effacing way, his naturalness and leadership on the football field made him popular with the boys as well.

Sam and Rudy had been friends, but in recent weeks, Sam was dating Mary and no longer on the football team, and he didn't have as much contact with Rudy.

Sam and Leo walked in the auditorium together to eat lunch. They were drawn to the crowd that surrounded Rudy and found seats nearby.

The conversations in the auditorium were, of course, about last Friday – the day of the game. Band members talked about the halftime show; kids who went to the game talked about the trip to Fairmont or the stadium; but mostly the conversation was about the game, and how the Farmers had played so well and almost won.

Duane and Rudy and a couple of other players were discussing the two plays that resulted in touchdowns for West Fairmont and the 14 - 0 final score.

"One damn play before the half and one at the end of the game. We're as good as they are," Duane insisted.

"I think we are," Rudy said, "except we didn't score – can't win if you can't score."

Leo and Sam finished their sandwiches and got up and went over to join in the football talk.

Rudy didn't want any excuses. "But the plays they scored on – a reverse play fooled me. It was my fault. And another thing we had four fumbles…"

"Yeh, we held them to fourteen points – both trick plays…damn"

Sam Huff had no business talking, but he did, "Yeh, but we still lost…"

Suddenly there was silence. Everyone there, twenty or more students, turned toward Sam. The comment was completely inappropriate, especially from someone who wasn't on the team. And especially from someone who <u>was</u> on the team, but had quit.

Rudy glared at Sam. Leo sensed the problem. He tried to defend his buddy. "What he means is 'we still lost' that's alright...ain't it?"

Silence.

Rudy didn't budge from his seat. He looked up at Sam. "What the hell do you mean <u>we</u> still lost? You said <u>we</u>. <u>You</u> quit. Twice."

Rudy stood up. Everyone's eyes followed him. "You're chicken shit, Sam. You talk like you know something, but you don't know a damn thing."

Uncharacteristically, Rudy's voice was rising. "Yeh, you quit. You..."

Leo tried to intervene. "Rudy, he didn't mean..."

Rudy brushed Leo aside. "Don't tell me, Leo. You're playing. That's one thing. But Sam, here, he quit, twice. He's not on the team." He took a step toward Sam. There was a collective gasp. "I think you're chicken shit, Sam. Show me on the field or shut the hell up."

The students surrounding Rudy and Sam were transfixed and afraid to intervene. They hoped it would end.

By this time, Sam was feeling like dirt. He knew he should have kept his mouth shut, but it was too late now. Being called "chicken shit" by Rudy, someone who everyone admired was the worst possible thing that could have happened. The worst. By this time Sam was feeling like, well, "chicken shit." He didn't retreat from Rudy, but didn't talk back either. He knew he shouldn't have said anything. The words just came out – in an attempt to be involved. It was stupid and now he couldn't fix it.

The shrill loud lunch bell rang. The students surrounding Rudy and Sam were relieved by the sound and were glad to get back to class and away from the scene they had just witnessed.

Sam stood there while everyone slowly vanished. He lifted his eyes from the floor to see his only friend in the world, Leo, standing there a few feet away. He could hear the echo of conversation and laughter in the hallways, kids heading for class, now talking about the fool he had become.

"Shit, Leo, I didn't mean nothing."

243

"But you said something."

"Yeh, something I shouldn't have said. It just came out. I sure as hell didn't mean to piss off Rudy."

"Sam, you quit the team. It didn't sound too good…"

"Yeh, I know."

Leo started walking to the auditorium door that led to the hallway. "We got to go to class. The bell already rung…"

Sam started to follow. "Now I'm pissed off at myself for ever quitting the team. I mean, I shouldn't have done it."

They stepped out into the hallway now, void of students who had all gone into their classrooms for the 12:30 class.

Sam didn't even remember walking to his next class – Woodworking Shop. As he and Leo walked hurriedly along the empty hallway, he could only think of the altercation with Rudy. "Jesus Christ," he thought, "How in the hell could I do something so stupid as to piss off Rudy, the most popular guy in the whole damn school, by saying something so damn stupid…" The thoughts just kept coming…

"Sam!" a loud voice shouted. Sam was startled. He looked up and in the face of Mr. Klutka, the shop teacher. Suddenly, the silence of his thoughts was broken by the loud whirr of table saws and a planer. Sam looked around, yes he was in shop class, but didn't remember getting there. He was so consumed with his near fight with Rudy.

Klutka lifted the goggles from his eyes. "You're late," he glanced at Leo, "both of you."

Sam looked down at the floor and kicked at the sawdust. Leo stood by his friend.

"Look at me, Sam."

"I'm sorry. Something happened…" He couldn't bring himself to confess his stupidity. "And that's why I'm late."

Leo stood by his friend. "Yeh, that's why…"

Klutka could sense that it was Sam who was having a problem. "Leo, go ahead and work on your project."

244

Leo disappeared quickly.

"Sam, come here." Klutka turned and walked away from the noise into his corner office and shut the door muffling the noise outside.

Sam's ears were ringing as he left the noisy comfort of the shop and entered the relative silence of Klutka's office. Now he wasn't protected by the noisy sounds outside. He could hear his sniffling as he tried to hold back the tears.

"Sit down, Sam," Klutka ordered.

Sam obeyed immediately. He respected the big guy. The former pro football player had become almost an idol to Sam. Sam liked the shop class, and he liked Mr. Klutka. Besides Frank Gatksi, Klutka had become the most influential man in his life.

Klutka never tried to interfere with the football team, even though players knew that the former pro football player knew more about the game than anyone around, except maybe Coach Kelly. He certainly knew a lot more than Assistant Coach Victor, and a lot of players expressed the thought that Klutka should be the assistant coach. But Klutka was a Mr. Nice Guy – and sensitive enough to not interfere or to display his credentials.

Klutka sat on the edge of a table, leaning back with both feet on the floor and his hands down by his side. "What happened?"

"Oh, I did something stupid?"

Klutka smiled, trying to comfort Sam. "Something stupid? You, Sam?"

Sam's lips quivered a small smile.

Klutka turned serious. "What was it?"

Sam told Klutka about the altercation with Rudy, his voice shaking and the words sobbing while Sam kept the tears from flowing. He just couldn't let Mr. Klutka see that he was that weak. Sam finished his story…"and then the bell rang."

Klutka didn't move for several moments. Sam looked up, his eyes reddened and glistening with the tears he kept from falling.

245

Klutka's eyes focused on Sam's, "So what are you going to do now?"

Sam blurted out, "I should a never quit...I should a never quit in the first place. That's the problem."

Klutka asked the obvious. "Why did you?"

Sam rambled, "Oh, I didn't like Coach Victor and I didn't think he liked me either. And then I got a job...'cause I got a girlfriend...and Mom and Dad didn't want me to go out..."

Klutka stopped him, "Do you want to play?"

"Yes, sir."

"Why don't you go back out?"

Sam wiped his wet mouth with his arm. "Coach Kelly wouldn't let me come back, not now..." He looked at Klutka, who didn't change expression, as he waited for Sam to express himself – and Sam waited for Klutka to say something. He didn't. Finally Sam finished his sentence. "...would he?"

Then Klutka spoke. "Sam, you really want to play, don't you?"

Sam shook his head.

"Then you have to ask the coach to come back. You don't have a choice. And you better hope he says 'yes'."

"Man, I'd give anything if he would let me."

"I think he might if he sees you're sincere and you're not going to quit again."

"I'd never quit again."

Klutka stood up and opened the door letting in the din of machinery and pounding in the shop area. He got back to the business of his class. Klutka had to shout over the shop noise. "You're working on that bookshelf, aren't you?"

Sam shouted back, "Yeh, it's for my mom. She knows I'm making it for her."

Sam took one last opportunity to wipe his eyes with his forearm and walked to the section of the shop where his nearly finished bookshelf stood. Leo, who had kept watch on Klutka's office for the sign of something happening, was encouraged to see Sam walking a little taller than he was in the auditorium at noontime.

Sam couldn't wait for the bell to ring and end his shop class. Even though it was one of his favorite classes, the hour had been spent thinking what he would say to Coach Kelly. What could he say to convince the coach to let him come back. He was hopeful, but down deep knew that Kelly would tell him 'no'. And he wouldn't blame him either.

Sam and Leo filed out of the workshop classroom into the crowded hallway. Hurried footsteps behind them caught Sam's attention. He turned to see Mike Arcure, the football team manager hurrying to get to his classroom before the bell. Mike scooted past them. Since Mike ate lunch at home, near the school, he was unaware of the confrontation with Rudy.

"Hey, Sam, Leo," Mike spoke in his raspy, youthful voice.

Leo spoke back. "Hey, Mike."

Sam didn't speak. He was still thinking about Rudy, but as he watched Mike walk away in front of him and into a classroom, he felt a glimmer of hope. Maybe Mike could help him somehow. He wasn't sure how, but he just had to talk to someone close to the coach, sure as hell nobody on the team – because by now, or very soon, everyone would know about his big mouth and Rudy's reaction.

Sam and Leo walked into the English classroom just as Mrs. Davis was closing the door to begin class. While the teacher was spouting Nathanial Hawthorne, all Sam could think about was Mike Arcure.

When the bell rang for a change of classes, Sam hurried to the adjoining room where Mike was in eighth grade geometry.

As the clatter of changing classes rose in the the hallways, Mike walked out of his class looking right at Sam Huff – waiting for him. At first Mike recoiled. He stopped. He wasn't use to seeing Sam, so serious and looking like he was going to pounce on him. Even though Sam was only about 145 pounds and 5 foot 9, he outweighed the little manager by about 30 pounds and Mike knew it would have been a mismatch. Mike waited on Sam, who obviously had his sights set on confronting him.

247

They moved away from the doorway and Sam spoke up, "Mike, I got something to ask you." His words were filled with sadness. Mike, the best kid possible and always one to be helpful, listened intently. It was just what Sam needed.

"Something wrong with you, Sam?" Mike asked looking up at Sam whose eyes began to tear up. "What's wrong...?"

"Do you think Coach Kelly would let me come back out for football? I just gotta come out."

Mike, always the positive one, felt there was hope. Coach Kelly was a wonderful man, compassionate and interested in his player's personal problems. "All you can do is ask him. He might."

A tear trickled down Sam's cheek. It was from happiness, or hope, or joy, just that it might be possible. In that moment, working for Manchin's didn't matter, Mary didn't matter, nothing mattered, except getting out on that football field. So he could redeem himself – in Rudy's eyes and in the eyes of all those who knew by now what a damn fool he had been.

"I don't want anyone to think I'm a chicken. I just need to be out there I know that..."

Mike tried to match Sam's level of concern. "I would sure ask him, Sam. Are you going to do that now, I mean at practice this afternoon?"

"Yeh, I was going to."

"Good idea," Then Mike sent Sam off with even more, "boy I sure hope he says 'yes'."

Sam was the first student in the dressing room after school. He got there as soon as he could. He didn't want the players to see him if he could help it. He walked past the metal baskets that held players uniforms and to the small interior office that Coach Kelly and Coach Victor shared. Coach Kelly was seated on a metal chair putting on football shoes in preparation of practice. Kelly heard someone at the door and looked up. "Hi, Sam," he said cheerfully, his Irish eyes glinting with warmth. The fact that a player quit his football team didn't diminish his genuine feeling for the student.

Sam stepped forward into the office. "Coach," he cleared his throat, "I was wondering if you would let me come back out for football?"

Kelly stood up. He was surprised. That had never happened to him before. Plenty of guys had quit, but none had asked to come back out. Sam was the first. "Coach, I don't even care if you don't let me dress for a game or even if I don't get in a game or get a letter, I got to come back out to show the guys I ain't chicken and..." As much as Sam tried, he couldn't hide the tears coming down his face. "Coach, I just got to come out again. It means everything to me..."

Kelly put his arm around Sam, "You know, Sam, I just can't let you come out and quit again..."

Sam cut him off. "I promise. I won't ever quit again – not ever! Do you know what I mean?"

Kelly couldn't help but admire Sam's courage. "Okay, then promise me you won't quit. You'll make me look real bad if you do."

"I promise. I'll never quit, Coach!"

Mike Arcure walked into the locker room with an arm full of towels he had just pulled from the washing machine. Kelly saw him and asked him to come into his office.

"Get Sam a uniform. He's coming back out."

Mike smiled up at Sam. Sam wiped his nose on his sleeve and sucked up his spit and tried to hide the smile he showed Mike, a smile of tearful joy. He told Mike he was going to do it and now he had.

Sam dressed quickly. He didn't want to be in the locker room when the rest of the guys came in. He would see them on the football field, and they would be busy with practice. There wouldn't be any time for explaining then. The uniform, old game pants, hip pads, and shoulder pads, didn't fit very well, but they would do. Sam stuck his head through the jersey and went to Mike to ask him to pull the back down over his shoulder pads.

As Sam stood there he felt the happiest he had been for a long time. All at once he discovered, or rediscovered, something about his life. He had

been a competitor all of his young life, but in the last two years had drifted

249

away from it. Now he realized how good it made him feel. He would never quit again!

His cleats sounded on concrete and echoed through the locker room as he walked outside and headed down the grassy bank to the field. A weight lifted off his young shoulders as he descended the hill. With each step, the thoughts came. "Shit," he thought, "All this time I let things keep me from this. Even Mary, my girlfriend. Yeh, and I love her, but shit, it ain't worth it. And working at Manchin's... Nothing could mean more to me than this. What the hell happened? I've been wanting to be a winner ever since I can remember. I was the one who chose up at James Fork Elementary and even in seventh and eighth grade I let things and people keep me from playing football and being happy. Hell...I always wanted to be Frank Gatski and I let..."

He reached the field and walked toward one of the few grassy spots. He looked up toward the school where players were beginning to come down the bank. He began trying to figure out what to say when they would see him. He decided he wouldn't say anything. He was more interested in getting ready to hit someone.

Rudy and Duane Bonnette were walking together down the bank and onto the field to join with the other players. Rudy squinted as he walked in Sam's direction. Sam could see that Rudy seemed puzzled. Rudy nudged Duane. "That looks like Sam."

"Shit, it is him. What the hell's he doin' here?"

Rudy's eyes widened and he whispered, "Jesus Christ, it is Sam."

Sam couldn't just stay silent. He cut Rudy and Duane off. "Look Rudy, I ain't chicken shit! Coach let me come back out and I ain't gonna quit again."

Rudy tried to be kind. "Yeh, well I hope so."

Soon the rest of the squad, about forty players, were on the field, and the word quietly circulated that Sam was there. Everyone was good with it. But there were some who thought he wouldn't last. Nobody could know the fire that had just started inside the kid from No. 9.

Whether he wanted it or not, Sam was the focus of attention of players and Coach Kelly and Coach Victor during practice. Everyone knew nobody quit and came back out, especially after a couple of games had already been played. Why did Kelly agree to it? Sam certainly hadn't distinguished himself in any way on the football field. There wasn't time to coddle or give special attention to this two-time quitter that was for sure. And the team had to prepare for the next game just four days away at Fairview. So why did Kelly agree to reinstate Sam? Evidently, the emotion he showed, and the courage to approach the coach with a no-quit promise, somehow convinced Kelly to say 'yes'.

It showed that in spite of the big Irishman's tough squinty-eyed demeanor, he was a warm, gentleman, sensitive enough to feel the pain of a desperate fifteen-year-old.

The players at first dismissed Sam as just another body to be there for practice – someone to fill in on defense while the first string practiced new plays for the Fairview game. But Sam had an instinct for the game. He could get in the proper position, and he was a natural athlete with good footwork and better than average speed. So while he had some catching up to do, that natural instinct and athleticism allowed him to be as good as other second string players immediately. Now throw in the newfound will to succeed and prove Rudy Banick wrong – and you had the making of a pretty good high school football player.

"Death Valley," Coach Kelly shouted.

"Oh shit," a couple of players said softly. 'Death Valley', was a drill with four tacklers, lined up about five yards apart, who would attempt to tackle a ball carrier who would take them on one at a time. Rudy Banick, shifty and quick, could give a tackler a fake and make him fall flat on his face or grab for air. While this was watched by all the other players and coaches, it could be humiliating for the bad tackler – or the ball carrier who would allow himself to be tackled.

251

Dutifully, Rudy Banick, the guy no one could tackle, was the first to pick up a football to challenge the line of four tacklers. Kelly decided to give some young guys a chance. "Bonnette, McIntyre, Morris, Huey…"

Rudy adjusted his helmet and twirled the football in his hands while the four players assembled, one after the other about five yards apart. Rudy tucked the ball under his arm and as quick as one-two-three-four, dispatched each one. The best anyone could do was slap his thigh as he slithered by.

You can't teach someone to run like Rudy, the open-field runner who approaches a tackler and instinctively makes him think he's going in one direction, while he's going in another. The 'fake' leaves the tackler grabbing for air in the spot where he thought the ball carrier was, while the ball carrier is instantly somewhere else, and going past the tackler. It is a talent a runner is born with.

Runners can practice side steps and crossover steps, but in the heat of the moment, you either fake the guy out or you don't. Ask a runner how he did that, and he can't tell you.

The next runner to follow Rudy was Harry Sopuch. Sopuch was no Rudy. That's why he played fullback instead of halfback. The fullback running plays were more north-south, powerful straight ahead moves instead of Rudy's side to side, quick instinctive moves that bewildered would-be tacklers.

The tacklers waiting for Sopuch were relieved. While he tried to be Rudy, he wasn't. Huey hit him hard and bounced off; Bonnette got a good hit, grabbed his legs and pulled him down; McIntyre tripped him up; and Morris challenged him with a head on tackle and got run over. The other running backs took their turns at the four. Players and coaches watched with great interest and reacted to each missed tackle, showing approval for a great 'hit' or a runner's ability to make someone 'miss'.

Now it was back to the top of the running order – Rudy's turn again. Kelly clapped his hands, "Let's get four new guys in there." Sam saw Kelly look right at him with that steely-eyed stare. "Sam, get in there." Sam felt a tingle go up his spine. He gulped a deep breath of air, put his helmet on, fastened the chin strap, and took his position as the number four tackler.

Rudy repeated his magic and even though he got touched, he didn't get tackled. He twirled and danced, slipped and stepped his way out of trouble. Sam didn't tackle Rudy, but nobody else did either.

Kelly smiled that mischievous narrow-eyed warm smile, as he walked past the first three tacklers toward Sam. "Come here, Sam." He took Sam aside and let the drill continue with just three tacklers. The players watching the drill couldn't help but notice the coach talking to Sam. It wasn't very often that Kelly would take someone aside like that – and especially the guy who had just come back out after quitting the team. But now Kelly was coaching and he felt Sam's determination, and he was still feeling some emotion after Sam's tearful request for another chance. He appreciated the courage to ask. Now he was going to do what he could to help him.

"Look at me, Sam. Rudy's a good runner, but he's not <u>that</u> good. He <u>can</u> be tackled." He put his hands on Sam's shoulders. "Look at me." Sam obeyed. Kelly bent his legs in a semi-crouch position. He started to explain. "You can't look at a runner's head. Everyone's looking at Rudy's head or his eyes, or his legs, or his hips. They can all be deceiving, Sam. They can fool you, and Rudy's real good at that. He makes you think he's going left, then he goes right. Don't look anywhere but right here." He pointed at his mid-section. "Right here. Don't look anywhere but right here at his belly button. That ain't going anywhere, but where he is." The words came measured. "He can't fake with that! You understand?" Sam shook his head. Kelly continued with emphasis, "his belly button – bang. Then drive your shoulders right in there." He slapped Sam's shoulder pads again. "You understand?"

"Yes, sir," Sam replied. He slapped a closed fist into his other hand. "God damn it, I'll get him."

"Now get back in there," Kelly barked. He walked back to the group of runners taking their turn. Skip Stewart, a tall, long-legged senior halfback began his turn. Skip stiff armed and whirled his way around the first two tacklers, then overpowered tackler number three.

As he approached Sam, Sam was thinking 'belly button'. Sam made good contact with Skip, right on the belly button, but Skip, who outweighed Sam by forty pounds, won and Sam fell at his feet.

Kelly shouted, "Sam, get that shoulder in there. Hit!"

Sam slapped his fist in his hand again. "Come on, God damn it." Sam whispered to himself. "Get tough."

'Get tough' was right, because it was Rudy's turn to run. Past the first tackler, the second and third…and 'belly button' Sam was thinking – 'belly button'. Bam.

Sam felt the sweet hard contact of his shoulder in Rudy's gut and heard the crack of leather pads smack hard. It felt good. The impact lifted Rudy off the ground leaving him helpless in mid-air and on his way to the ground. Thud. Sam's shoulder drove Rudy into the dirt.

There was a collective gasp from the teammates. Kelly's voice came through loudly, "Way to go, Sam! That's it!"

"Man, nice tackle, Sam," Rudy said.

Sam rolled over and off of Rudy who was still clutching the ball. He knelt there for a second. "I ain't chicken shit, Rudy. I wanted to show you."

"I guess you ain't, Sam. Good tackle." Rudy reached out his hand to allow Sam to help him up. "Yeh, good tackle man," and he patted Sam on his rear.

"Okay," Kelly shouted. He couldn't think of a better way to end practice. "Let's get ready for sprints."

Sam stuck his face into the hot water of a hard shower, happy to be there in a dressing room after a football practice. Finally, he was one of the guys again. That feeling of euphoria – happiness like he hadn't felt before, was too precious to ever let go.

The loud talk, jokes and shouts of guys having fun echoed against the hard concrete walls as Sam toweled off and got dressed. His buddy, Leo, pulled his clothes over on to the bench beside Sam.

254

"Good practice today, Sam."

"Yeh, it felt so good to be out there - and I ain't quitting again."

"I know you ain't …'cause I ain't goin' to let you."

"You don't have to worry 'bout that," Sam said as he pulled his t-shirt down over his head.

The other players paid little attention to Sam's return to the team. It was no big deal. They figured Coach Kelly had his reasons for allowing Sam to come back out. Sam had never played a down of high school football yet. So his contribution was zero. For some players, it was just a matter of time before he would quit again. Others figured he was another body to put out there for practice. The coming week would be spent on preparing for the first Mason-Dixon Conference game at Clay-Battelle on Friday.

Sam didn't know any plays – not one – nor had he practiced any defense with the team, so his participation in any game would have to be very limited, almost certainly, if any at all, only to defense – and probably when the game was already decided.

The Clay-Battelle game would be the third game of the season. Only six more were scheduled. And now practices would be devoted in large part to preparing for each opponent.

Certainly player technique would always be stressed, but a player's role on the team had been determined in pre-season practice – and Sam wasn't there. He had lost out, but because of Coach Kelly's willingness to give Sam a third chance at least he was able to return to the team and prove to his buddies he 'wasn't chicken'. At least he was getting that chance and that was all he wanted – for now.

As Sam and Leo walked out of the dressing room into the chilly September evening air, they heard the voice of Coach Kelly. Sam looked over to see him talking with Mr. Klutka. That surprised Sam. Mr. Klutka never came around football practice – but maybe because of Klutka's talk with Sam earlier in the day, the thought came to Sam that they were talking about him.

Sam and Leo walked around the corner of Main Street to the hard road to No. 9. They were heading home preparing to walk the two miles there,

255

but with each car's headlight shining in the pre-dawn darkness, they showed their faces to the light, stuck out their thumb, hoping to hitch a ride.

After practice on Thursday, the day before the Clay-Battelle game, Coach Kelly posted the traveling squad names on the locker room wall. The trip to Clay-Battelle was a short one, only about twenty miles, near the Pennsylvania state line, so most of the players out for the team got to go. Short trips, like this one and to the other Mason-Dixon Conference schools, were taken with a school bus, which seated about forty, so if there were enough uniforms Coach Kelly was happy to reward the players with a trip.

It didn't surprise Sam that his name wasn't on the list. He didn't expect it. He was feeling lucky to be out there practicing.

The headline on Saturday's paper said, "Banick's Punt Return Spells Defeat for C-B." The story began "A 40-yard punt return by Rudy Banick in the last period gave Farmington a 13 - 7 victory over Clay-Battelle in a Mason-Dixon Conference game before a big crowd here tonight."

Rudy had scored earlier in the game and then capped it off with the kind of thrilling play he was becoming known for.

The line-up showed Coceano starting at left end. Now, Leo wasn't only going to earn a letter, he was even becoming a starter.

The Name on the Bottom

Maybe Sam Huff was the only person in the world that knew how much it meant to have another chance to play football. Anybody would have given the two-time quitter little chance to become a player, but now Sam knew that he was going to be one. The cockiness was returning. The leadership role he had left behind in those elementary and junior high years was now something he quested for again. He was envious of the other players who could talk about the game. Leo did that and it began to drive Sam crazy. Now it was more than just proving to Rudy that he wasn't chicken – now he wanted to be the best player out there. All of a sudden, Sam could tell that the football field was where he could find recognition – and satisfaction for competing and winning – and the attention he was craving.

The fourth game of the 1949 season was against Fairview, another Mason-Dixon Conference foe, located just seven miles away. Fairview's most famous claim to football fame was Fielding "Hurry-Up" Yost, whose point a minute teams at the University of Michigan were the talk of the college football world in the early 1900's.

On Thursday, September 15, the day before the game, Coach Kelly posted the traveling squad on the bulletin board outside of his office. As usual, since it was a short trip, just about everyone on the squad was expected to go. But Sam knew that it wouldn't include him. He had only been practicing for a few days and even though Kelly designated him as a lineman, he hadn't really learned the offensive blocking for any of the plays, so consequently couldn't be used in a game on offense; however, Sam's toughness and desire allowed the coach to consider playing him on defense – when the game was out of reach.

Sam and Leo walked over to the yellow legal pad sheet hanging on the locker room wall. Of course, Leo expected to see his name. Sam stood

257

back, not even bothering to look for his name – 'maybe next year,' he thought. Suddenly Leo nudged Sam, then fingered the yellow sheet where at the very bottom was the name, "Huff".

Leo nudged Sam again! Sam looked – and then sucked in wind and bit hard on his lip to stifle the sound – the sound of tearful joy. It was embarrassing. Sam turned and headed for the door. He wanted to get away before he bawled out loud. Leo followed behind in a hurry.

Outside, Sam exhaled and let loose his emotions. The tears fell. Leo wrapped an arm around Sam's neck. "Hey, you're going, Sam." Sam turned his face away from his friend's eyes. "Yeh, yeh, I'm going." He sucked up some air. "God damn it. I'm going!"

They treated it like nothing special, but Sam leaned back and closed his eyes to revel in the short ride. It meant so much to him to be part of the team – going on a road trip to play football, even if it was just to Fairview and even if he knew there would be damn little chance of playing. At least he was going to be in a scarlet and gray uniform. A chill ran up his leg. Sam's hand felt sweaty. "Damn," he thought, "What if I would get in?" He could imagine Coach Kelly calling out, "Sam, go in there for Bonnette at tackle."

He sat up straight to shake loose of the vision. He looked out the window at the darkness coming down fast. The bus rattled onto the hard road out of the Farmington High School parking lot and in minutes was going past Sam's home and the No. 9 portal and past the Grant Town turnoff.

It took just twenty minutes along the winding, rough Fairview road from Farmington. That short ride was a young lifetime of reflection for fifteen-year-old Sam Huff, as he sat beside Leo and listened to the loud casual talk among the players.

In a minute Sam could see the green and white city limit sign of "Fairview – population 725". There was the rushing excitement chill again. He sat up and looked toward the front of the bus. In the distance he could see the pole lights of the Fairview High School field. The bus turned into the parking lot.

The football field was enclosed by a massive tall cut stonewall built by the same WPA that constructed the 6,000 seat East-West Stadium in Fairmont in the thirties. The Fairview field itself had lights, grass in most places, and stone bleachers that seated about five hundred. It wasn't East-West Stadium, but it was a big step up from the Farmington High field of no lights, no grass, and a tall grass and weed bank for spectators.

The game was another Rudy Banick night. The Fairmont Times headlines read, 'Farmington Surges in Last Half to Trounce Indians in 21 - 6 Upset'. The story began:

> "Rudy Banick's 60 yard punt return for a touchdown in the third period suddenly set off an explosion in the Farmington football team here tonight and before the battle was over, the favored Fairview Indians had wound up on the short end of the a 21 - 6 score."

Rudy was the main offensive weapon again, scoring another touchdown on a 40-yard scamper and setting up the third touchdown with an 18-yard run to the 1-yard line – along with the 60-yard punt return.

Late in the fourth quarter, with Farmington ahead 14 - 6 and victory assured, Fairview called a time-out. Coach Kelly turned to Assistant Coach Victor to ask him who hadn't played. Kelly liked to get everyone in the game, if possible. And now, with just two minutes remaining, with an eight point lead, he felt confident enough to replace the first team. "You want to put Sam in?" Victor asked. "He could take over at tackle for Duane."

Kelly looked over at Sam sitting on the end of the bench leaning forward with his elbows resting on his knees watching the game intently. "Yeh, sure," Kelly said with that smiling glint in his eye. Kelly stepped around Victor and shouted above the crowd noise, "Sam, Sam, come over here. Get a helmet."

Sam jumped up. There was that dizzy rush of excitement again.

"Get a helmet, Sam," Kelly ordered.

Sam picked it up and rushed over to the coach. Kelly put his hand on Sam's shoulders, a calming gesture that did nothing to diminish the excitement raging inside Sam. Sam put his helmet on and nervously snapped on the chin strap.

Kelly's calm voice instructed, "You're going in for Duane." His gentle shove out from the dim sideline onto the bright lights of the field was like releasing a bird to the wind. Sam flew away to the huddle of his scarlet and gray clad teammates with a shaky breathless voice. "Duane, I'm in for you."

Gerald Martin, the star center and captain, took the young bird under his wing. "Right here, Sam," as the official blew the whistle to start play again. Sam got down on all fours. "Over here, Sam," Martin ordered. "Move over." Sam moved.

The ball was snapped. Sam charged. It was a pass play. Intercepted! By Skippy Stewart. Skip returned it to the Fairview forty-yard line. For all intents and purposes, the game was over. Rudy made sure. On Farmington's first play after their interception, he went forty yards for the touchdown. The extra point made the final 21 - 6.

The victory, coupled with Monongah's tie with Clay-Battelle, gave the Farmers undisputed possession of first place in the Mason-Dixon Conference race.

Leo didn't start the game, but played in every quarter. During the season, he had become an important part of the team, even starting one game. In four games, he had participated in fourteen quarters. By Leo's calculation, he would need only eight more in the next five games to get the "F". It was his. He even had his mother buy the sweater to put it on.

On the next Friday, Farmington traveled the short seven mile drive down Route 250 to Mannington and beat them 27 - 7. Mannington, because of its larger enrollment, was a Class A school. It always gave the Class B Farmers great satisfaction to beat up on a bigger school. The game was especially thrilling for Leo Coceano, and not just because he got in another four quarters toward his letter "F". He scored a touchdown! In the fourth quarter, with Farmington leading 14 - 0, Skippy Stewart, junior halfback, called a pass play to Leo. Leo got himself free, caught the ball on the fifteen-yard line and scampered over.

Sam Huff walked from the bench and cheered with everyone as the touchdown pushed the lead to 20 - 0 and put the game out of reach of the Mannington Big Green. Leo came off the field to be congratulated by everyone. Coach Kelly held out his hand to Leo with that wide grin and narrow-eyed smile and said, "Nice play, Leo." Players gathered around to slap his pads – Sam reached in, too, with a hard slap on Leo's shoulders, then returned to the bench. He felt that twinge of jealousy he hated, but couldn't help. "Hell," he thought to himself, "Leo wasn't just going to get a letter, now he was scoring touchdowns! Jesus, before you know it he's going to be a star...and here I am riding the bench." He shook loose of the nonsense. "Oh shut the hell up!" he said to himself as he returned to the bench.

"Sam!" the voice was Kelly's. "Get a helmet – Let's go!"

Browns Streak Ends

The Cleveland Browns team that had been unbeaten in all fourteen games of the 1948 season; the team that won the 1948 AAC championship; and the team that had been clearly the cream of the Conference since it's inception in 1946 wasn't there yet in 1949.

After the shocking opening game 28 - 28 tie at Buffalo on September 5, the Brown's managed to get back to their winning ways even though they hardly looked like their former selves. They managed a victory at home September 11 over the Baltimore Colts 21 - 0, and another win over the New York Yankees September 18, 14 - 3 and a 28 - 20 win at Baltimore on September 25. The biggest early season test would be a home game on October 2 with the Los Angeles Dons who would challenge the Browns for first place in the Conference. Finally, the old Cleveland team showed up to clobber the Dons 42 - 7.

"That's more like it," Brown shouted in the locker room. "This is the Cleveland team that I'm familiar with!"

But just a week later, across the country, Frank Gatski and the Browns were shockingly getting the beating of their lives. After the hope gained with the pasting of the Los Angeles Don 42 - 7 the week before, the San Francisco 49ers, led by quarterback Frank Albert, was handing the Browns their first loss since the 1947 season. The score was 56 - 28.

No Paul Brown team – not the one at Massilion High School, at Ohio State, at Great Lakes during the war, or in the pros had ever given up fifty-six points. The N.Y. Times reported the game like this:

"Led by brilliant Frankie Albert who set a new
league record by throwing five touchdown

passes, the San Francisco team ran up 21 points in the first 10 minutes of play.

With a wildly cheering crowd of 59,770 looking on, the 49'ers scored their first triumph over the Browns since 1946 and, with the victory, took over the league leadership.

It was the first setback for the the Browns in 30 games. They had last tasted defeat on Oct 12, 1947, when they bowed to the Los Angeles Dons, 13 to 10.

Graham didn't have his usual "bucket defense" and the San Francisco line kept charging through to knock him to the ground for considerable lost yardage."

When Otto Graham gets knocked down because the Browns "...didn't have their usual bucket defense...", the blame falls first of all on the center of the bucket – in the Browns case, Frank Gatski.

But when the Browns fell behind 21 - 0 after just 10 minutes, the 49ers began an all-out rush on Graham, knowing he would have to start passing. Frank was backpedalling all day trying to protect his quarterback, getting outnumbered and allowing the opponent to get to Otto. Nevertheless, Otto had a "good" day completing 13 of 26 passes for 281 yards.

Otto's stats didn't matter to Coach Brown. He was only interested in one stat. It was a loss, and he hadn't lost for two years!

In the dressing room, Frank was his stoic self. The indestructible, untiring giant of a man never complained and never showed his tired side fatigue. This was no different; however, inside Frank was experiencing the same disappointment over the loss. All of the Browns players were subdued. Quiet. This was a wake. Something had died. The streak had ended. After thirty games, the Browns had finally experienced defeat.

Coach Brown didn't rage. He would do that after a win, or a tie, but not after a loss. Brown was philosophical. "Gentlemen, it had to end. It

263

doesn't feel good to lose, but we played a good team today, who jumped on us early. We have work to do, and let's get back on track next week."

The Brown's next opponent was the Los Angeles Dons, just five days later on October 14. Since the Browns had traveled to the West Coast to play the 49ers, the organization decided to stay there rather than return to Cleveland and then have to travel cross country again for the Dons game on Friday right.

Frank looked at the calendar. After the Dons game there was an open date – no game, for sixteen days before the Browns would host the San Francisco 49ers in Cleveland on October 30. While wanting revenge on the 49ers for ending the Brown's record-breaking streak, Frank welcomed the respite and the time off. Usually Coach Brown gave some vacation time during an open date, and Frank was looking forward to spending time with Ida Mae and one-year-old Frank, Jr. at his brother, Benny's house in Grant Town.

That Jacket Again

On the afternoon of Friday, October 14, 1949 the Farmington Farmers played host to the Barrackville Bisons for a 3:00 p.m. game. The game would be the only one played on the Farmington field during the 1949 season.

The bright white lime of the ten yard stripes painted a gridiron on the brown dirt and intermittent green patches of grass. In a strange way it coordinated well with the uniforms of both teams, the blue and gold of Barrackville contrasting with the scarlet and gray of Farmington, each not flashy and slick, but rough and patched together with rolls of tape.

Barrackville, an even smaller school than Farmington with just ninety-five boys in the top three grades, came just five miles up Route 250. They had dressed for the game in Barrackville and came on a school bus ready to play.

The game was an old story – a Rudy Banick story. The <u>Fairmont Times</u> sports page headline summarized the afternoon: "Banick Scores Three Against Barrackville". Rudy was doing it again, enhancing his reputation as the best halfback in the county and drawing more attention from college scouts. The final score was 27 - 0. Coach Kelly used all the players who dressed for the game, twenty-five in all. It was a great opportunity to allow everyone to play on their home field with all their families and friends there. Sam got his usual four or five minutes of action, even a couple of plays at offensive right tackle.

Later that same night, three thousand miles away in Los Angeles, the Cleveland Browns responded to the shocking San Francisco defeat by beating up on the Los Angeles Dons 61 - 14. It was the most points ever scored by the Browns and gave the team the shot they needed to prepare for the home game with their now bitter enemy, San Francisco in two weeks on October 30.

After the game, Brown announced there would be no practice on Monday, and because of the open date on October 21, he would give them the Friday off to allow the players to enjoy a long open date weekend.

Frank, Ida Mae, and Frank, Jr. arrived in Grant Town on Friday afternoon just in time for Frank to drop them off at Benny's, who joined Frank for the drive to Rivesville to see the Farmington-Rivesville game.

Rivesville had no lights for their football field either, so the game was played at 3:00 p.m. after school. Frank and Benny managed to get there just in time for the kickoff and found a spot alongside the wire fence surrounding the field.

Farmington beat the Rivesville Rams 27 - 0 for their fourth Mason-Dixon Conference win. The Rivesville coach, Deacon Duvall, stacked his defense to stop the running game of Rudy Banick; it left him vulnerable to the pass, which the Farmer's took advantage of with four touchdown passes.

Frank's presence at the game drew some attention. No one could ignore the tall rugged looking blonde wearing the Browns jacket. As the word spread that Gatski was around a number of old friends, and even folks he didn't know, came by to shake his hand. After the game, Frank headed back to Grant Town to have dinner at Benny's.

Sam got a few more minutes of playing time in the Rivesville game since the final twenty-seven point spread allowed Coach Kelly to use substitutes more freely in the second half. But Coach Kelly was beginning to notice Sam's steady improvement as he got more accustomed to being on the playing field. The kid's determination was beginning to get the coach's attention. Even though Sam was still learning the plays, the natural physical ability, speed and quickness was apparent to Kelly – he was beginning to see in Sam someone who could contribute to the team, and not just someone who he rescued to escape the cajoling of his peers.

Sam and Mary left the Farmington Movie Theatre after watching "She Wore A Yellow Ribbon" starring John Wayne. As they got closer to Mary's house, Sam slipped his arm around Mary's waist and Mary responded by pressing her head to his chest. He could feel the soreness in his arms from the Rivesville game the day before, but it was a good feeling. There was something satisfying about the hurt and pain from the game. Sam took a deep breath of the October night. He was finally feeling happy with himself. He was on the football team. He had a girlfriend. His schoolwork was pretty good – Mary made sure of that. The game of football was getting easier. At first he was scared, but the game experience, even in the role of a sub and playing mostly in the third and fourth quarter when the game was settled, made him feel he could play the game. It was almost like a secret he knew. He could feel his body responding to the plays, and his innate ability somehow allowing him to succeed. All of his teammates knew he had quit the team before – and for that he would have to pay the price – but he still knew he was gaining on some of the players ahead of him. Soon he would be better.

The night sky was filled with stars as Sam looked up. He thought of that "wish upon a star" saying when he was little. Unconsciously, he began wishing to be first team. Then he looked down, shook his head to rid him of that foolish thought, knowing it would take more than just wishing. He was damn lucky to even be on the team after his double quit. He quietly thought of Coach Kelly and his willingness to take him back. "He wouldn't do that for just anybody," he thought. "He must think I can play or he wouldn't..."

Mary's voice sliced through his mindless rambling. "What are you thinking?"

"I was thinking how lucky I am to be playing football."

"Oh," Mary answered with some disappointment.

"And about you, too."

"That's okay, Sam. I'm glad you're playing."

267

"Yeh, at least I'm playing, even if it ain't very much…but I'll bet next year I will be."

The street light on the corner by the Liquor Store lit up the corner of a lonely Main Street. In front of them was the neon light of the Circle Bar.

Sam remembered when his football dreams were rising a couple of years before when he and Rudy and Leo and some other eighth graders stood against the wall of the Hardware Store across the street to stare at Frank Gatski and his Cleveland Brown's jacket. He remembered seeing the letters on the back that spelled B-R-O-W-N-S.

"Damn," he thought. "It must be the stars, I'm thinking all these weird thoughts."

The buzz of the neon sign grew louder as they approached the bar. Sam's attention was drawn to it thinking it sounded like a swarm of bees. He didn't want to be seen by the window light as he walked by. Anybody there who knew him could mention it to his Dad – or tease him. He guided Mary to cross the street into the shadows near the Hardware Store where he and his buddies stood a couple of years before. He couldn't help but look back toward the Circle Bar to remember. He couldn't believe what he was seeing. "Jesus Christ, Mary, oh I'm sorry, Mary. I didn't mean to…" He pointed. "Look!"

Mary turned her head toward the window of the bar. "B-R-O-W-N-S"

Sam whispered nervously, "That's Frank Gatski. He's got that Brown's jacket on. Jesus…it was just like this before."

Sam hugged Mary tight. "I gotta be a football player."

"I know, Sam…"

"I mean I got to be…like him!"

Sam turned Mary to him clutching her arms. "Okay, Sam." Mary took a deep breath. "You're hurting me."

"I'm sorry. I'm telling you, Mary, damn it. I'm going to be a football player."

"You already are, aren't you?"

"Not like that. I mean I'm going to be damn good. You watch next year."

"Next year? You have more games to play this year, don't you?"

"Yeh."

"Why wait till next year?"

"I don't have to, do I? C'mon, we better go. The last time I saw Frank in there, they came out and chased me away."

They turned to walk toward the corner, and Sam took one last look at Gatski in his Brown's jacket. He kept his gaze on Frank until he walked out of sight of him. As he turned his head toward the night, he couldn't help but recall that menacing look on Gatski's face in that old newspaper picture in his dresser drawer.

Sam couldn't get Gatski out of his mind. And on Monday he couldn't wait for the end-of-school bell at 3 o'clock to get to football practice. His Gatski-inspired determination and his growing confidence were being noticed more and more by Coach Kelly and Coach Victor.

This was the week of the Monongah game. Practice was intense. The mood suited Sam perfectly. He was intense, too and went full-out and played as hard as he could.

Kelly noticed. After practice on Wednesday he turned to Coach Victor, "You know whose looking pretty good?"

"Yeh," Victor replied casually, "Sam."

Kelly laughed. "Yeh, Sam, and is it my imagination or is he growing up…getting taller right before my eyes. Sometimes I look out there and I think it's a senior…Hell, it's Sam. Too bad he wasn't out all year. He could have helped us."

Everybody for miles around was talking about the Monongah-Farmington game coming up on Friday, October 26.

Farmington had four victories in the conference and no ties. Monongah had four victories also, but a tie with Clay-Battelle. A win by Farmington or a tie would give them the Mason-Dixon crown.

269

The game was scheduled for Farmington's no-seat, no-light field at 3:00 p.m. Coach Kelly was seeing dollar signs. The drumbeat for the game was deafening. There would be no way the game could be played in Farmington. The enormity of the game demanded another venue. Kelly and Monongah Coach Jim Feltz agreed to move the game seven miles away to East-West Stadium in Fairmont – and on Thursday night, when it would be the only game in the county.

The excitement continued to build throughout the week. On Thursday, a pre-game thuse was held at Farmington at 11:00 a.m. followed by a parade through the small business district of Farmington. Mayor John Manchin proclaimed Thursday "Farmington Farmer's Day."

The game lived up to its billing. The newspaper headline read: "Farmers Clinch M-D Title Before 4000 in Thrilling Battle". No, Farmington did not win. The game ended in a 6 - 6 tie, but that was all Farmington needed to jump ahead of Monongah, who had that one tie with Clay-Battelle.

Writer Emlyn Thomas of the Fairmont Times described it beautifully:

> "With a partisan crowd of more than four thousand cheering wildly, Farmington and Monongah battled to a 6 - 6 tie at East-West Stadium last night, but the outcome was a victory for the Farmers for it enabled them to clinch the cherished championship of the Mason-Dixon Conference...very few substitutes were used as the two first teams engaged in a big defensive struggle...lines of both teams making it impossible to gain ground, the battle settled down to a punting duel. Both teams only managed to score in the final quarter and both failed to convert the extra point.
>
> Both teams played sterling defensive ball with the Lions holding Farmington's Rudy Banick down

270

considerably but having the same treatment
applied to their own Benny
Salopek...Defensively it was difficult to single
out any performance on either side as both lines
charged ferociously and made every tackle with
a fury that was little short of vicious. Every
man on both sides literally played his heart out
through the contest...The two teams continued
to slug it out between the 30-yard stripes with
neither able to make any headway through the
enemy line except for one occasion when
Salopek broke through tackle for 19 yards for
the only first down registered by either team in
the first period of play."

Leo started and played almost the entire game. Sam
did not play.

The Farmers, now enjoying their very first Mason-Dixon Conference
Championship returned the following Friday to Fairmont's East-West Stadium
to face the East Fairmont Bees in the season finale.

The Bees, a Class A school, usually trounced Class B schools like
Farmington, but not this time. East Fairmont's John Hando scored two
touchdowns in the first three minutes of the game, then the Bees had to hold on
for a 12 - 6 win.

Eddie Barrett of the Times wrote:

"Farmington plainly outplayed the Bees the
remainder of the game. Four times did they
drive within East's 30 yard-line before finally
scoring in the final period...A small crowd saw
the action on a muddy, though not unnavigable
field. Sturdy little Rudy Banick for Farmington was equally as

271

shining as Hando, and their opposing each other
last night probably convinced local fans that
these are the two finest backs in Marion County.

The third star of the contest was the
unheralded Farmington punter, freshman Jimmy
Antolock. Two of his kicks carried – from
scrimmage – 37 yards, and the other rolled out
of bounds on the East 3 yard line.

The Farmers' performance was all the more
impressive considering that two of their regular
backs, Jim Parrish and Skippy Stewart, were out
with injuries. Their 1949 record – now
completed – shows five wins, three loses (to
Class A schools) and a tie with Monongah. In
addition they earned their first Mason-Dixon
conference championship."

The season ended abruptly for Sam. He didn't play in the Monongah
game and saw just limited action against East Fairmont. Both games were too
close for Kelly to substitute freely. Leo, however, played a major role in the
final two games, just as he had all season.

"He Really Did Make the Team!"

The 1949 season was over. For Farmington, the first Mason-Dixon Conference championship made the team proud. John Manchin began planning a banquet to celebrate and honor the team. The Manchins were always ready to celebrate an accomplishment.

Coach Kelly called John Manchin to tell him to hold off – there may be one more game.

Romney High School in the eastern panhandle was looking for an extra game. The Pioneers had finished their season undefeated, but just a few percentage points away from being able to compete for the Class B State Football Championship. They needed another win over a team with a pretty good record.

Romney High School coach, Dick McElwell, called Farmington High School principal, John Cotrel on Tuesday to see if the Farmers would be interested in playing his team that Saturday in Romney.

After consulting with Coach Kelly, Cotrel advised McElwell that the answer was "yes, Farmington would be there."

Short notice, but that didn't bother Kelly. And he knew the boys would want to play.

The word went out quickly – to players and the school. For the players it was a thrill to be able to suit up one more time. The sadness felt by the seniors who thought they had played their last game at least could be delayed.

And they had a great challenge playing the undefeated Romney team who was trying to play for a state championship.

The Farmer's record was four wins, three losses, one tie and they had won the Mason-Dixon Championship. But they did lose their final game against East Fairmont. Although it meant nothing regarding the Mason-Dixon

273

Conference, it left the players with a bitter taste. Here was a chance for redemption.

Because of the long distance of 150 miles to Romney, the traveling squad would be small and the trip would be made in cars instead of school buses, which were used for games around the county.

Coach Kelly immediately got hold of manager, Mike Arcure, who was in the locker room putting away the equipment and uniforms for another season. The final game at East-West Stadium had been played in the rain and mud leaving Mike with an enormous job of clean-up. Mike had laundered the uniforms and was in the process of putting them away along with the equipment.

Kelly informed Mike of the Romney game and handed Mike a list. "Here are the twenty-two players who will be making the trip. Get their equipment ready. We'll practice tomorrow, Wednesday, Thursday, and Friday and leave Saturday at 8:00 a.m."

Kelly went into his office while Mike got out the duffle bags to match each of the players on the list. The duffel bags were used throughout the season to organize the equipment for each player. Hip pads, shoulder pads, helmets, and shoes were all numbered to identify each player's and kept in the bags which were all tagged with a player's name.

Mike knew the traveling squad list. He had filled those duffel bags eight times this season, but this list was abbreviated – only twenty-two players would be going. That would be the twenty-two best players. He read it quickly. It was the expected – Banick, Stewart, McIntire, Bonnette, Martin, Sopuch, Coceano, and so forth, and at the bottom…Huff.

Mike smiled and felt a rush. "Damn," he thought. "Huff!" Sam finally made the team! "He really did make the team!"

The Romney High Pioneers got what they wanted out of the extra game with Farmington – a convincing win of 32 - 6 and enough percentage points to put them in the Class B State Championship game.

Coach Kelly played everyone. Sam played in the second and fourth quarters of the game. The two quarters he played in gave him a total of fifteen quarters for the season. That was far short of the sixty percent of quarters, or twenty-four, required to get a letter. Leo, who had even become a starter in some games, fulfilled his expectations and pre-season boast of getting a letter. He played in almost every quarter. Leo got his "F".

In spite of the loss to the high-flying Romney team, the Farmers came home to a small town filled with pride for the Mason-Dixon Conference Champs. In December, John Manchin, Jr. got his chance to honor the team with a football banquet.

The Mason-Dixon Championship trophy arrived in March. The school's yearbook staff photographer took pictures: one showing seven members of the team, one of which was Leo, in championship jackets; another was of the Letterman's Club's twenty-four members – yes, including a smiling Leo Coceano.

Meanwhile, the Cleveland Browns finished the 1949 season the way they had the previous three – by winning the All-American Conference Championship.

It wasn't quite as easy as in previous years when they were absolutely unbeatable. In 1949 they had been beaten badly by the San Francisco 49ers 56 - 28, but revenged that game in Cleveland with a 30 - 28 win. They were tied twice by the Buffalo Bills, but beat them in a playoff game 31 - 21 before beating the 49ers 21 - 7 in the championship game.

Thank You Doctor Jenkins

Dr. Jenkins, the "small-town doctor" who treated just about everyone in Farmington, was making his rounds – seeing patients in their homes that he knew were sick or that he had treated.

The doctor had an office in downtown Farmington, but if you couldn't get there, he would come to you. The Huff house was on his list this day. Yes, Oral and Katherine, after years of hearing complaints from Sam about "my sore throat," finally took Uncle Leory's advice and had Sam's tonsils removed.

Doctor Jenkins pulled his 1947 Ford up to the front of the Huff house, got his bag, and proceeded to the porch. He knocked on the door, expecting to see Katherine Huff in a moment. Instead he heard hurried footsteps from inside coming toward the door – and then a hand on the knob. The door swung open. Jenkins blinked. On the other side of the screen door stood Sam – and something was wrong! Blood was coming out of his mouth. Jenkins jerked the screen door open.

"Sam, what is wrong with you?"

"I don't know."

The doctor gently guided Sam inside to the couch where he sat him down. "What happened to you? Where is your mother?"

Sam pointed, "She went to see Mickey about something. I was lying down till I heard you..." He rubbed his hand on his mouth and saw blood. "Geesh, I'm bleeding, ain't I?"

"Just sit down here...stay right here." He stepped quickly into the kitchen and grabbed a dishtowel and came back to Sam. "Here, hold this over your mouth. You're coming with me."

Quickly he walked Sam to the car and in a few moments he had turned around and was heading to Fairmont.

"Where we going?" Sam asked through the cloth over his mouth.

"We're going to the hospital and get you fixed up. Now don't worry. It will take just a few minutes."

Dr. Jenkins exceeded the speed limit down the two miles to Rt. 250 and seven miles to Fairmont General Hospital. At the admissions desk, Jenkins ignored the objection that Sam's parents weren't there to give permission for his admittance.

"We can't waste time. This boy is suffering a hemorrhage from a tonsillectomy. I think we need to go. Just make the arrangement – and now!"

"Now" wasn't any too soon, either. Dr. Jenkins said later that Sam could have easily bled to death without immediate attention.

Sam couldn't talk, but his moans from pain and his young eyes expressed to Dr. Jenkins a big 'thank you' for saving him.

Miracle at Mods Run

His name was Roy. But everyone called him "Monk." Roy "Monk" Hartsell, Katherine Huff's brother, invited his nephew, Sam, to spend the summer of 1950 with him on his small farm at Mods Run.

Mods Run wasn't that far from No. 9: by the way a crow flies, a couple of miles; by the hard road it was four miles down Route 250.

Roy convinced Sam it would help him get in shape for football. Sam took the deal. Monk's farm was the perfect place for a fifteen-year-old who had begun to believe he could actually earn a football letter "F". The boy was tossing hay to feed the cows and horses; the twenty acres needed mowing every week; the large garden, a full acre of potatoes, tomatoes, beans and corn, required planting, digging and daily attention; and it was isolated, – nowhere near trouble or a distraction. No. 9 was isolated, too – from other little camps; Mods Run was isolated from the world. So a boy's whole day was work in silence. It was boot camp in Monk's world.

Coincidentally, in that summer of 1950, Mods Run became home. Katherine's parents had left her and Oral their farm place of fifteen acres right next to Roy's. Oral Huff had enough of the mining life, and after forty-two years, decided to give it up. He wasn't through working, but now he decided to work on the ground instead of three hundred feet below! He had always wanted to farm and now he was going to.

Sam was glad to leave No. 9. Now, at least, there would be less inclination for his dad to push him into a life of mining coal. And the boy would show his dad just how good he could be above ground.

Sam worked both properties from morning till night. His uncle Monk was right! It was the perfect setup for a boy going into his junior year of high school trying to build himself up so he could make the football team – and at the same time keeping occupied in the most positive way while avoiding the distractions of a civilized society – like girls and beer and pool.

And a miracle was happening – the work was turning Sam into a strong, raw boned farm boy, six foot tall and 180 pounds of muscle, while the detachment was focusing his thoughts on what had began to fire him up – football.

Did the removal of his tonsils – that sore throat he lived with all his young years, set his body free to gain his growth potential and center his thoughts?

At the end of his sophomore season he had begun to realize he could play the game. Now he was determined to be the best player on the field. He didn't say it out loud, but he was feeling it, deep inside where it mattered.

Now Sam had an energy he never had before. He somehow felt the sore throat left behind with those bad tonsils had unleashed something inside him. He was growing. He could feel it. He was getting hard. Something was coming.

On the practice field, Coach Kelly did a double take when he saw Sam Huff. Where in the hell did he come from?! Kelly saw Sam's strength and quickness dominate his teammates. He shook his head and smiled, and wondered, "Could this kid be that good in a game?" Hell in the middle of last season this boy was crying, literally, just to be on the team. Could this scrawny cry baby be the same person he was looking at now?

In spite of what he saw, Kelly suppressed any thought of future star status for the boy. When Eddie Barrett came to Farmington to prepare the Farmington story for the pre-season football preview for the <u>Fairmont Times,</u> he already knew about Rudy Banick. Rudy was an established star, having been a starter since his freshman season. Now Barrett was calling him the "classiest back in the county." He raved.

"If you doubt the respect we are paying this
little guy, just listen to the coaches of teams he played against.

They all say the same thing – Banick is in a class by himself. He scales only 152 pounds and stands 5 foot 8. Many backs his size have the scrap, but he also has the ability that puts it to use. He's hard as nails, has plenty of speed, and after three previous seasons as a regular, has learned to shake off tacklers or run through them. Devastating is the word for Rudy Banick."

Kelly downplayed his team's chances which led Barrett to write; "Kelly is not optimistic about his chances…" Barrett continued with some small mention of Sam, still referring to him by his birth name: "The guards have not under gone a baptism of fire. Tom Harker and Bob Huff are big enough, however, to come out alive."

And there was a bow to Leo, saying he was a "tough letterman." That label was important to Leo; and, he acted like a letterman – taking charge on the line, even telling his inexperienced friend, "Bob" or Sam Huff, where to line up in certain situations. Sam did not appreciate instruction from Leo. That little Italian bastard had been his surrogate all his life, and now, just because he earned a letter, he was telling Sam what to do. Sam took it though and didn't correct his old buddy, but deep inside he knew soon he would be telling Leo what to do just as he had when they were kids.

The next day Kelly read the Fairmont Times story and smiled. The day before, that "Bob" Huff was tearing up the practice field at Farmington High. Kelly knew he had a surprise in store for the 1950 season opponents. Six days later they would find out.

The bus pulled out of the Farmington High School parking lot and headed through town and out to Route 250 for the long, hard three hour drive to Benwood.

The school, located just south of Wheeling, was a Class A school, who defeated the smaller Class B Farmers last season 26 - 0. It had been no contest for the powerful Trojans, who warmed up on Farmington in preparation for their Ohio Valley Conference season. Benwood would never have agreed to play at the Farmington field, no lights, no seats – consequently Farmington would have to travel to Benwood to play them there…again.

Coach Kelly saw the game, win or lose in a positive light; it gave his team a hard game before playing the Mason-Dixon Conference games and the other Marion County competition; and besides, the percentage of the gate at Benwood was a money maker for the poor Farmers, who were forced to play most games on visitor's fields.

Sam had grown in confidence through the practice sessions, but still felt his stomach churning over the thought of starting his first game. Leo, sitting beside him, was more than happy to give advice to his old buddy. After all, he had started nearly every game as a sophomore the previous season. Sam didn't need to be reminded, but listened to Leo and nodded silently and nervously.

Throughout the bus, there was silence mostly, except for the quiet conversations between those sitting close to each other.

Sam's nervousness was calmed when the two guys seated in front of him, Duane Bonnette and Jim McIntyre turned to talk to their underling. Bonnette and McIntyre, both seniors who made the All-Conference team the previous year, would be lining up on the same side of the line with Sam: McIntyre at right end; Bonnette at right tackle; and Huff at right guard. If Sam could come through in a game the right side of the Farmers line would be damn good.

McIntyre and Bonnette wanted to reassure Sam that everything was going to be okay and to talk about the defensive play Coach Kelly had put in in an attempt to block a Benwood punt. Kelly instructed Sam to blast the man in front of him, remove him, and let either Bonnette or McIntyre loop around and run through the hole to the punter. The three knew exactly what to do, but talking about it reinforced everyone's role and served to calm Sam.

In the dressing room, Sam and Leo turned to each other to pull their jerseys down over their shoulder pads. A hard slap said 'let's go'. They both sat down on the bench to wait for Coach Kelly's pre-game talk. Instead, Kelly came over to Sam and slapped him on his shoulder pads.

His eyes narrowed and his smile beamed, "You're going to do great, Sam."

"Yes, sir," Sam replied feeling proud that Kelly would single him out at that moment.

Kelly addressed the team. "This is Benwood," Kelly said. "Most of you were here last year when they beat us bad, 26 - 0. I hope you remember that."

They did, and they said so loudly.

Kelly shouted, "Let's go out for warm-ups."

The pounding of cleats led from the dressing room into the Benwood night where the Trojans and over two thousand spectators waited.

"Farmington High's Farmers gained sweet revenge on Union High of Benwood here tonight defeating the Trojans 26 - 0, the same score by which they lost last season."

The opening paragraph of the Fairmont Times brought the news to county fans with an early morning delivery not long after the team arrived back home from Benwood at 2:00 a.m. Saturday.

The Times continued with the summary:

> "Farmington's great halfback, Rudy Banick again was the big gun in the attack, scoring two of his team's touchdowns and sparking the offense throughout the game. One of his touchdowns came on an 80-yard punt return in the second quarter."

The defensive scheme Kelly installed for a blocked punt worked perfectly, not once, but twice. Sam blasted his hole in the offensive line and Duane Bonnette poured through to block one punt; Jimmy McIntyre blocked the other. It was just like they planned.

Leo Coceano had some success, too, scoring the third touchdown on a 34-yard pass play.

The Farmers came home to a jubilant Farmington High School on Monday. The talk was about the Benwood game and the upcoming game on Thursday against West Fairmont at East-West Stadium.

West Fairmont, another perennial big school power scheduled Farmington early in the season as a tune-up for its big school schedule.

The bus of Farmington players was filled with confidence during the short seven mile ride to the stadium in spite of the Bears reputation as a state champion contendor and a school that sent players on to college careers at the University of Kentucky, West Virginia University and other name schools.

When the team got off the bus at the stadium locker room entrance, players grabbed their duffel bags and stepped onto the paved parking lot. Sam stood there for a moment as other players filed past him. He looked around at the now empty stadium remembering how a year ago before this same game against West Fairmont, he stood right there – almost in the same exact spot – holding Mary's horn case. "God damn it," he thought. "Where in the hell was I?"

In the seconds that he stood there, he assessed his relationship with Mary. Now he was seeing it differently. For a while, she became everything to him, shutting out everything else, even football. He knew he still liked her. He felt he loved her. But now football had become the number one thing in his life and had pushed Mary aside – but not away. He didn't like it, but he couldn't help it.

"Sam, let's go!" The voice was Coach Kelly's intruding in Sam's look back.

"Right, coach. Sorry."

"You okay?"

"Yeh."

"Nervous?"

283

"Yeh."

"That's good."

Emlyn Thomas of the <u>Times</u> called the win by West Fairmont a

> "stirring 20 to 12 victory...twice the valiant Farmers, again sparked by the great scatback Rudy Banick fought back to make a game of it...The crowd had scarcely settled back into its seats when Banick grabbed Brzuzy's kick on his 15-yard line, headed for the sideline and broke into the clear. Just as he hit the 40-yard line, Banick shot through a host of Bear defenders and scampered the rest of the way. Sam Huff's kick was short, tying the count at 6-6."

Yes, Sam in his growing confidence, was even trying to kick extra points. In a team tryout, he was chosen by Kelly – but his first attempt failed.

As the game went along, the bigger, more experienced and talented big school Bears were too much...and eased ahead 20-6. Rudy scored again late in the game to make the final score 20 - 12.

Sam Huff was mad as hell. He wasn't willing to accept the fact that Farmington was "supposed" to lose the game, even if the opponent was West Fairmont. And even though the West Fairmont game was only his second start, he was assuming full responsibility for the loss. He couldn't take it, losing just wasn't in him. He wasn't sure where that came from. He knew he didn't like it. Maybe it was arrogance – after all, who in the hell was he? The other guys took the loss in stride – knowing they would win their share, but a single loss, even to a big school, was a bitter pill for Sam to swallow.

Browns Biggest Game

September 16, 1950. It was the biggest game of Paul Brown's life. His Cleveland Browns would open the 1950 season with his greatest challenge – against the Philadelphia Eagles, Champions of the National Football League!

The All-American Football Conference had folded. After the 1949 season, owners took stock and took action, took their financial losses and either folded up their teams or took them to the other league – the established National Football League. Only three teams from the AAFC survived. In addition to the Browns, the Baltimore Colts and the San Francisco 49ers still lived and were absorbed into the NFL.

Gone were the Los Angeles Dons and Chicago Rockets from the Western Division and New York Yankees, Brooklyn Dodgers, and Buffalo Bills from the Eastern Division.

Obviously, football fans who had believed the All-American Football Conference had inferior players would now believe the teams that were left – Cleveland, San Francisco, and Baltimore – would have a difficult time winning against the big boys. Sure, the Browns could beat up on the likes of the now defunct Chicago Rockets and Brooklyn Dodgers, but could they compete with the NFL champion Philadelphia Eagles? Sure the Browns could have a four year record in the AAFC of 52 - 4 - 3. But that would never happen playing in the NFL. Neither would they achieve a string of 18 straight wins, and neither would they ever win four straight championships as they did each year from 1946 to 1949.

No, when the Cleveland Browns got ready to take the field in Philadelphia to play the Eagles, everyone was convinced that frankly, the team from Cleveland was going to finally experience the reality of professional football – everyone, but Paul Brown and his players. The point spread made Cleveland a fourteen point underdog.

285

In the locker room, Frank Gatski was seated on a wooden bench leaning back resting his head against the concrete wall. Beside him was quarterback Otto Graham. They and thirty-one others were thinking the same thing, that this is the time to show the football world the fabulous record of the last four years was achieved by a <u>great</u> team, not one of mediocrity playing in a mediocre league – and the Cleveland Browns could play with the very best, yes even the best in the NFL.

Outside in Municipal Stadium, the players could hear the loud constant drone of 72,000 fans, nearly all of them from Philadelphia, ready for an expected Eagle victory.

Then sudden silence and the faint sound of the Star Spangled Banner found its way into the room. The sound of Coach Brown's shoes clipped on the concrete as he paced the floor. He had rehearsed this talk many times over and over in the previous days. He wanted to say just the right things to motivate his players, to play their best. He knew he could win this game, even against what some would say would be insurmountable odds, but the coach never went into <u>any</u> game, regardless of the strength of the opposition – in high school at Massilon, in the service at Great Lakes, at Ohio State, or with the Browns – that he didn't believe he would win. He knew he had the personnel and the strategy to win every game. No exceptions!

Frank's eyes focused on Coach Brown as he walked past. There was absolute stillness. The hard heels of his polished shoes clacked against the floor. The always professional gentleman with his classy Fedora and immaculately pressed pants and tweed sports coat looked out of place with the rugged and tough 33 men in football uniforms. Brown's professional manner commanded respect. The players sat up erect, almost at attention, as they prepared to hear the coach's words before the biggest game any of them would ever play.

Coach Brown stopped his pacing and stood in the center of the room, his hands on his hips in a typical Brown posture. He looked at his players, making eye contact with everyone as he spoke slowly. "Men, this is the game you have been waiting for. I know we have prepared to win this game, if we can execute the game plan as we have discussed. This is the biggest game of <u>all</u>

of our lives. You know what is at stake. We started together four years ago in 1946. We must win or the great accomplishment of the last four years will be diminished, no question about that. Some people believe that the worst team in the NFL could beat us. This is the opportunity to prove otherwise." He stood up tall. "Everybody up. Let's Go!"

The dressing room door swung open. The crowd's noise silenced the clatter of cleats on the concrete as the Browns ran out of the dressing room and onto the playing field. The scattered cheers from Brown's fans seated in the end zone were drowned out by a Philadelphia welcome of boos for the visiting team. As the Browns ran to the visitors sideline, the boos turned to a loud deafening roar of cheers when the green and white clad Philadelphia Eagles appeared in the tunnel ready to run on the field.

Football fans expected a mismatch. And that's what they got, except the result was upside down. The Browns dominated the favorite Eagles 35 - 10 in a monumental upset.

Coach Brown had devised a system of gradually increasing the spacing between his offensive linemen so that eventually he could nullify the middle guard in the Eagle defense. It set them up for a trap play run by fullback Marion Motley up the center for big gains – right off Frank Gatski's butt. And when the Eagles tried to close up the line to stop the big bruiser, Otto Graham – behind an offensive line led by Frank Gatski, riddled them with passes.

No one now questioned that the Browns could hold their own with the old pros of the NFL. Frank was in the middle of it all, whether it was for a trap play run right off Frank's hip where Frank had to make the important block; or when Otto Graham could set up in comfort behind the center to look for his receivers.

After this game, the Browns had truly established themselves as one of the very best teams, if not the best in pro football, and Frank Gatski had finally gained for himself the reputation as the best center in the game.

Before Frank left with the team for the Eagles game in Philadelphia, he told Ida to get ready to go to Grant Town as soon as the team got back. And she did just that. The train pulled into Cleveland Station at 2:00 a.m. and after sleeping in their Cleveland apartment, Frank, Ida, and two-year-old Frank, Jr. were in the car heading for Grant Town and brother, Benny's home.

Frank and Benny spent Monday afternoon shooting the bow. It was an important part of their athletic life and the time they spent together. After all they had to maintain their reputations as the county's best archer. Frank won individual honors in the combined Northern West Virginia Field Archers Shoot and Marion County Tournament in July with a score of .479 and the Grant Town Club, of which he was a member, won the team division championship. Benny was even better than Frank, establishing the record of .569 two years before in 1947. Being a former champion, he was ineligible for the individual prize, so leaving it for Frank was okay with him.

Both Gatski boys, tall and muscular, effortlessly pulled the high tension of the large bows propelling the arrows to the center of the target time after time. In between shots, they talked of family and football.

After spending the afternoon on Benny's archery range and dinner with the family, Frank and Benny headed for the Circle Bar to catch up with old friends. There was no better time to do that than right after being on the winning side of the game every writer in the country was referring to as "the most important or significant game in professional football history". And who would have ever believed it? The Cleveland Browns from a defunct league, some called counterfeit, beating up on the champions of the old established NFL! Revolution, that's what it was!

The sight of the neon lights of Ben's Circle Bar sent a small shiver up Frank Gatski's back as he pulled his Chevy in front of the place.

He couldn't explain it. But Ben's was part of being home, part of what he was when he was a miner a mile up the road. It was always a warm welcome home. He looked forward to seeing his old buddies here and talking football. He still wanted to be in Farmington and Grant Town more than any other place on earth, so when the Browns had a day off, usually after a game, the Gatski's were heading to West Virginia.

The guys in the bar let out a roar of welcome when Frank and Benny walked in. It was as deafening in this small place as the roar of the 70,000 in Philadelphia Stadium just two days before.

Frank couldn't help but smile, that rare broad smile that showed his perfect teeth. He knew the guys were proud of him, and he felt the warmth of their affection.

Ben Bennett slid open the beer cooler door and clicked off the caps of two Carling Black Label beers as Frank and Benny sat down at the bar.

Accolades fell from the lips of Frank's old beer buddies and embarrassed him. After commenting briefly on the game, he deflected further discussion by asking his own question, "how are the high school boys doin'?"

Everyone at the bar replied at once with a chorus of positives – "Damn good…best team in a long time…gonna win a lot of games" – together sounded like noise, but it was a sweet tune to Frank's ears.

The review continued. "They beat Benwood bad, 26 - 0, got revenge for last year," one said, "and they almost beat West Fairmont this past week." Everybody on the team came in for at least 'honorable mention' from the bar crowd. Rudy Banick was given special treatment. "The best damn halfback we ever had…should make all-state."

Eventually they got around to Sam. "That Huff kid is a big surprise." Frank blinked. "You mean Sam? That little kid?"

"He ain't so little anymore. He's at least 6 foot and 180 pounds." Then the superlatives followed: "He tore Benwood up…we blocked two punts 'cause of him…he's everywhere…fast as hell…he'll knock your head off…"

Frank smiled. "He must have grown up."

Ben Bennett, from across the counter, began to reminisce. "Do you remember when he was standing outside gawking through the windows looking in here at your Browns jacket – just staring – and scared the hell out of us?"

289

Frank laughed, "Yeh, I remember, and you chased him off...him and his buddies."

Ben got two more Carling Black Label beers from the cooler. "He said he wanted to be like you." Ben clicked off the bottle caps. "Maybe he's gonna be."

Frank always downplayed his talent. "I don't know about that. Hell, he could be a lot better than me someday. You never know."

Where is Sam Huff?!

By the third game of the 1950 season Coach Kelly realized he had
another good football team. He had the best halfback in the county, maybe the
entire state, in Rudy Banick. And he had a terrific defense led by his two
seniors, Duane Bonnette and Jim McIntyre, along with this new Sam Huff!
Nobody ran against their side of the Farmington defense. In fact, the next two
opponents were shut out: Clay-Battelle 6 - 0 and Fairview 18 - 0. Mannington,
one of the larger schools in the county and a Class A school, along with West
Fairmont and East Fairmont, managed just seven points, but won 7 - 0.

In the sixth game of the season, Barrackville went down 27 - 6. The
Farmers were 4 - 2 with both losses to Class A schools. They had given up a
total of just thirty-three points all year, an average of just over five points a
game.

The right side defense of Bonnette, McIntyre, and Huff was so
dominate that Coach Kelly began to take advantage of Sam's speed, quickness,
and strength by moving him around on different plays or allowing Sam to "free-
lance" – decide himself where he should be to stop the next play. On one play
he might switch to the left side, then to linebacker or to a spot directly over
center. Pretty soon, Sam Huff was everywhere, chasing a back down on an end
run – or defending a pass – or blasting through the line to get to the passer in the
backfield.

McIntyre and Bonnette, because of their deserved All-Conference
honors, were getting a great deal of attention for leading the Farmington
defensive charge. But coaches who were preparing their team to play
Farmington were wondering "How the hell do we stop Sam Huff?" The guy
was everywhere and around the ball on every play. It was frustrating for
coaches to try and guess where Huff would line up. They often realized their

291

best hope was to run plays away from him – if they could. He was driving the opposing coaches crazy.

The seventh game of the season on Friday, October 20 was a home game against the Rivesville Rams played after school at 3:00 p.m. Rivesville was one of the two teams, along with Farmington, who were still in contention for the crown. The other was hated rival Monongah who would play Farmington on the following Friday. Beat them both and Farmington would repeat as Mason-Dixon champs.

The Farmers did have one other game, but with Class A non-conference foe, Doddridge.

Rivesville, a small community of 800 people, was just five miles away from Farmington. They had a college prospect fullback, Bob Toothman, and a great young coach Harold "Deacon" Duvall. Beat Farmington and they, not Farmington, would be in the driver's seat to win the crown.

Farmington High field was overflowing with fans– some standing, some sitting on the grassy hillsides crowding the field on both boundary lines. Everybody in both small towns was there. The game was a thriller with Farmington winning 27 - 26. Rivesville ran plays away from Farmington's right side, and with considerable success. Sam became a hero in the game. In the fourth quarter with Farmington holding on to a slim 20 - 19 lead and Rivesville on their own three-yard line, he broke through, caused the Ram back to fumble, scooped up the ball, and scored a touchdown. The extra point made the score 27 - 19 essentially putting the game out of reach. Rivesville managed a late touchdown and extra point to make the final score 27 - 26.

Sam took over the game and seemed to be in on every tackle. When the score was 19 - 13 in favor of Rivesville, Sam dropped the halfback for losses on three straight plays, the last of which resulted in the fumble which Sam picked up to run in for the go ahead touchdown.

Sam's impact on a game was becoming apparent. He had literally come out of nowhere this season. The newspapers were still calling him "Bob" even though his friends called him Sam. Somehow he had the ability to do all the things necessary to dominate a game. All the physical attributes had been given to him in the last year – and with it came confidence and leadership skills as well. With an almost magical sense of knowing where the ball was and the speed and strength to get there, he took over. If Sam thought the play would be run to the left, he would shift to that side, barking orders to players to adjust their positions. He took special satisfaction when he would holler orders at Leo. Up to this season, his old buddy had taken the lead role from him on the football field, while Sam languished, initially not even on the team, and then as a substitute. But this was a new season and a new Sam Huff. Now it was like old James Fork Elementary days when Sam was telling Leo what to do again.

It wasn't very often that a coach came into an opponents' locker room to congratulate a player. But Rivesville coach Deacon Duvall, a gracious man, winning or losing, was there to shake Sam's hand, because he had just witnessed the greatest defensive performance he had ever seen in his ten years of coaching high school football.

Ed Shockey of the West Virginia University coaching staff had come to scout Bob Toothman and Rudy Banick but went away with the name of Bob Huff scribbled on his note pad.

"One more game! One more game!" The shouts of a couple of dozen Farmington players filled the locker room after the Rivesville win.

Kelly came over to Sam to shake his hand. "Congratulations on your first touchdown. It came just in time."

"Thanks, coach. I'm sure glad we won."

"Keep up the good work." Then Kelly turned to join the chorus of "One more game!"

Sam was happy to see his coach satisfied with his play. He had come to love Kelly. In giving him a football life, he had given Sam everything. Everything! Sam showered and left the locker room feeling the best he had ever felt in his life!

Night had fallen and Mary was waiting for him, still in her band uniform and carrying her horn case. She hurried over to Sam who was

293

walking gingerly nursing the bruises from the afternoon. She reached up to kiss him on the cheek. She touched her hand softly on the redness of his temple.

"Does that hurt?"

"Naw, we won. That's all that matters."

Sam couldn't help but think back to last year, just one year ago, when he was lost. Even though he had Mary then, he was still lost, because he wasn't playing football. What a change! Now he was not only playing, he was confident that he was among the best, not just on his team, but in the entire county. He heard people talking about him. He heard the congratulatory remarks from other coaches and players, and he had read his name in the paper. Sam was a little annoyed for being called "Bob" Huff in the paper. Even though his given name "Robert" would lead people to call him Bob, he preferred his nickname "Sam". Mary would make sure he saw the papers. She was saving all the clippings.

As Mary and Sam were walking toward the Farmer's Inn for post game coke and hot dogs, Duane Bonnette walked quickly by and repeated the cry for the coming week, "One more game!"

Sam smiled and slapped his back as he went by, "Yeh, one more!"

Sam got a ride to No. 9 and was there long enough for dinner and conversation about the game with his mom and dad before taking off with Leo and Billy Pasko to watch Mannington play their hated upcoming opponent, Monongah.

Senior Billy Pasko was 17 and had a driver's license – and tonight he had the family car. Several other players said they were going to the game. It was very satisfying to go to another football game after a victory. It was one of the good things about playing an afternoon game – you were able to see other teams play that night.

For some kids it was an ego trip, to wear that scarlet and gray Mason-Dixon Champ jacket from 1949 and be together – three, four, five, maybe more – all seated together and knowing some in the crowd knew who they were.

Sam hurried out of the house to Billy's Chevy. Billy had his Mason-Dixon Championship jacket on. So did Leo. Sam wore his khaki jacket, a little jealous that he didn't have a jacket like Billy and Leo, but easily dismissed it, happy to be the player who might be responsible for everyone else getting one this year.

The door of Billy's car slammed shut and he screeched the tires as he pulled out onto the hard road, past the No. 9 tipple, all lit up with halos of coal dust. The car lights flashed by the tall gray timber structure and into the night and toward the lights of Mannington's Hough Park.

.

Billy, Leo, and Sam got to Hough Park just in time to see the Mannington High School football team run through the arches of the Community Building onto the field. Across the field, the band, playing from a bandstand beside the bleachers, struck up the fight song, "Fight Green and White."

The bleachers seating about five hundred fans were packed. Another two or three hundred lined up along the Community Building at one end and along the sideline behind the visiting bench.

As the three Farmington kids walked along the end zone at the Community Building, the scarlet and gray jackets worn by Billy and Leo let everyone know that some of the Farmers were in town.

On the bandstand, Mannington High majorettes, in their thigh-high skirts and tight fitting military style waist jackets strutted their stuff to a march. Billy gestured with a motion of his head to go in that direction – of course, where the girls were. Sam lagged behind the two championship jackets, not wanting to magnify the fact that he wasn't wearing one.

They got to the spot on the sideline between the bleachers and the bandstand where they could watch the game and at the same time look the majorettes over, and also provide the girls of Mannington the opportunity to check out the 'best of Farmington'.

What was it about majorettes? The uniform is revealing enough to show bare thighs, and tight enough to show curves, while calf high boots hide any leg deficiency so that just about every majorette looks good.

The boys glanced repeatedly up at the majorettes. That was fair. They were on an elevated bandstand for the purpose of being seen. The girls looked back, their eyes acknowledging the stares, but did not miss a beat of their bandstand routine to each of the musical numbers.

The game progressed through the first quarter. In the middle of the second quarter, the band members began to assemble on the field for the halftime show, leaving the bandstand by the steps that led right beside the "Farmington Three".

A smile…cologne…short skirts…those bare legs…and boots. The boys watched them go, looked at each other and smiled.

Billy hung his head in embarrassment – then suppressing a smile, looked up at Sam. "What are you laughing at, Sam. She looked right at you!"

Sam shot back. "I ain't got a jacket like you. She wasn't looking at me."

Leo chimed in. "I think both you guys are right. She was looking at me."

In ten minutes, the halftime show was over and the band was heading back to the bandstand. The girls marched smartly in front of the Farmers, then kept time in place until the drum major blew the whistle to signal "halt". The band broke rank and the majorettes broke character, laughed, and avoided any glances as they walked off the field. They welcomed the few minutes break before the second half during which time they were allowed to do what they wanted – go to the restroom, get a coke, or even talk to the three boys from Farmington. Two of the majorettes stood close by waiting for the band members to disperse. It gave Billy a chance. He spoke…nervously.

"Uh…nice show."

Leo and Sam backed him up. "Yeh…nice…"

The girls smiled and like a chorus replied, "Thanks." But their nonchalance wasn't fooling anyone. They were impressed being approached by guys from another school, and with jackets, no less.

The pretty strawberry blonde spoke up. "What's the jacket for?" Then she moved in to look. "Oh, Mason-Dixon Champs."

Billy scrolled the logo with his finger. "Yeh, we won it last year...Uh, what's your name?"

"Nedra Smith" and she pointed to her partner. "This is Patty Santee."

"Hi."

Nedra turned to go. "We gotta get back on the bandstand. The team will be coming out for the second half and..."

Billy was hooked. "Where do you go after the game?"

Nedra started up the steps. "Steve's Dairy Bar."

Sam gave Leo a jab with his elbow. Billy spoke, "We know where that is."

Nedra just smiled. "C'mon, Patty."

Nedra was a petite five foot strawberry blonde with delicate, almost patrician features. Her bandmarch step with her chin up gave her an elegance that belied her flirtatious nature–you could feel the orneriness in her laughter. Her body was small but perfect with long legs for a small girl and taut, toned thighs. You could tell by the way her short majorette skirt moved as she walked away that what was unseen had to be perfect, too.

Patty was short, too, about the same height as Nedra, but her stockiness and overly muscular legs made her seem shorter. Still, in a majorette uniform – bare thighs, boots...

Steve's Dairy Bar

Steve's Dairy Bar on Buffalo Street, the main street running through downtown Mannington, was the meeting place for school kids. The school, which housed all grades 1-12, was just a couple of blocks away. Kids walking from school made Steve's a stop. And at night it was the place to meet up with friends. Steve's had it all in it's bright red and grey vinyl interior: on the right, a long dairy bar with stools where you could get served ice cream cones, sodas, shakes, and sundaes, as well as fountain cokes, bottled pop and Steve's famous hot dogs; in the center, a section of booths, each of which could seat six kids crowding in together; and on the left side, a display case and counter providing a variety of necessities from toothpaste to school supplies.

You could walk through the main dairy bar area to a smaller room in the rear where kids could dance to juke box favorites: Elvis, Frankie, Tony Bennett, Dean Martin, Patti Page, and other hit-parade songs.

Inside Steve's, Sam and Leo were sitting on one side of a booth and Billy Pasko was sitting on the other with his eye on the door. They each ordered a coke and waited. The clock on the wall was pointed at ten o'clock.

Sam shook his head. "They ain't comin'."

And just at that moment the door swung open and the jingle jangle of the doorbell mixed with Nedra's contagious laughter at something Patty had said. Billy's face lit up. Sam and Leo jerked their heads around to see.

The girls had gone home to change clothes. Now, both were wearing jeans, plaid blouses, bobby sox and penny loafers.

The girls came over. Leo got up quickly to let Nedra sit between him and Sam. Patty quickly sat down beside Billy who became embarrassed that he didn't get up first.

Nedra eased herself into the booth and when Leo sat down, Nedra moved over and pressed her thigh up against Sam's. Sam recoiled at first, but then edged his leg back over so he could feel her against him.

Then Sam thought about Mary and moved as far into the booth as he could – but Nedra filled the space between them quickly.

In the next thirty minutes, everybody learned each other's names. The girls drank a coke and invited the boys to a party on Wednesday at Nedra's house.

When Billy, Sam and Leo told Nedra they would be at her party, Billy Pasko, the only one who could drive, didn't know that he wouldn't be able to get the family car on Wednesday. Big brother, Bob, had his own plans. So if Sam and Billy were going to go to the party, they were going to have to hitchhike. Leo had other plans – or at least his parents had other plans for him. He would be staying home and doing his homework. Billy and Sam were on their own.

Getting there at 7:00 p.m. was no problem. It was still daylight when they started out, and they easily got a ride the seven miles to Mannington. Now the problem was getting back, in the dark, at a time when the only guys on the road were working the midnight shifts at the coal mines at Barrackville and Four States. And the boys had stayed at the party too long, even for most of them. Now the traffic heading back to Farmington and No. 9 was down to nothing. Maybe one car every ten minutes.

Sam was getting nervous, "Thank God, Coach Kelly won't see us here. We'd get benched for sure."

"For damn sure," Billy confirmed.

Sam had an idea. "You think we should walk? We'd be there in three or four hours."

"No, no," the senior said to the junior. "We just gotta be patient." Then he cleared his throat nervously and stood looking into the vast darkness up ahead. "We'll get a ride."

"Yeh, where in the hell is it?!"

299

The headlights of a car flashed its' beam on the curve, then appeared in the turn to the left that guided the bright lights into Sam's eyes.

Sam squinted and held out his thumb. "Please pick us up," Sam thought.

"Damn," Billy Pasko said as he watched the car speed by.

Sam was close to despair! "Shit, Billy. What time is it?"

"I'm not sure, but I heard that school clock ring 12 o'clock. Shit, a long time ago."

"Damn, we gotta get a ride."

So Sam and Billy caught up in the invitation of Nedra Smith and Patty Santee to a party, had found themselves about a mile from Nedra's house on Route 250 at the edge of Mannington in front of a dark Esso Station where most people hitch hike from, trying to get back home – Billy seven miles to Farmington; for Sam an extra mile to No. 9.

In between the infrequent times a car came by, Sam and Billy talked about the girls, comparing their notes on each one. Both of them had their moments in game of 'spin-the-bottle'. The game was played with the party seated on the floor in a circle, alternating boy-girl-boy-girl-and so on. Each person took his or her turn to spin a bottle on the floor and the person of the opposite sex to whom the bottle pointed would leave the room with the bottle spinner, go to another room or designated dark closet and kiss or engage in whatever they might-fully clothed in 60 seconds or less. Usually both came out red-faced amid some laughter and bad jokes. One of the problems with the game was that you could get matched up with someone you didn't care to kiss – in which case a hurried peck on the cheek and thirty seconds of a delay tactic sufficient to allow all the players to think something hot was going on avoided embarrassment for someone not worth ten seconds.

Sam got lucky, with Nedra, twice, and each time she kept him beyond the time limit, which resulted in some kids clearing their throats and making other noises that would suggest the 'time was up'. Sam forgot Mary in that dark room with Nedra. He even forgot football. He had never been kissed quite like this. Nedra kissed with her whole body, pressing it all up against Sam's and pulling him to her.

Sam and Mary kissed a lot and played around, but they never went all the way. Mary knew better and held off Sam because she knew of the tragedy that could result from getting pregnant: the humiliation, not just for her or for her parents, but the disruption of school. No! Absolutely there was no way Sam was going to get in her pants and make her pregnant.

Up until Sam kissed Nedra, he was ready to leave the party early. He knew Coach Kelly's rules – be home by 11:00 p.m. during football season. No exceptions. And that was Sam's intentions, but in the arms of a sweet senior from another school, anyone can forget the rules!

The smell of oil and gasoline from the Esso Station brought Sam back to the reality of being seven miles from home at one o'clock in the morning and still counting on some complete stranger to take him away and save his life! Could his parents be upset? They knew he was going to the party. Damn, could Coach Kelly find out? Sam shook loose of the consequences of that happening and stuck out his thumb.

The car's lights flashed around the bend and lit up Billy's grey and scarlet football jacket. Sam jutted his thumb toward Farmington. The car sped by, then slowed up! Sam and Billy froze for a moment in anticipation. The car stopped, its red rear brake light shining a bright beacon of hope.

"Damn, let's go," Billy cried out.

The sound of their strong legs pounded swiftly on the black asphalt, moving faster than they ever did on the football field, to get to the black 1946 Chevy.

They didn't even bother to look to see who the driver was. It could have been the devil himself or the biggest drunk in the county. None of that mattered. The car was heading home!

Billy hopped in the front seat, Sam in the back. There was the immediate smell of coal dust in the car and the sweet aroma of chewing tobacco. Mail Pouch or Beech Nut. The boys knew it from chewing those brands on the football field.

301

The man took a can from between his legs and shot a loud 'clang' of spit into it. "Boys care for a chew?"

"No thanks," they both replied.

The man pressed the gas pedal, shoved the stick into second gear, then third. He shouted over the engine noise. "Where you boys goin?"

Billy answered, "I'm going to Farmington." He nodded to the back, "he's going to No. 9."

"That's where I'm goin,'" He looked at Billy. "I saw that gray jacket, looked like Farmington. Went there myself. You play football?"

"We both do," in unison.

"What's your names?"

"I'm Billy Pasko"

"I'm Sam, er, Robert Huff," the voice shouted from the back.

"I know your families real good and I know Coach Kelly, too."

"You do?" in unison.

"Yeh, Coach and me go hunting together – a lot." The can, spit, clang.

In the ten minute drive to Farmington, Mr. Six was spitting and talking, spitting and talking, and sharing the stories of his small world with the two young strangers.

As they approached Farmington, Mr. Six had to ask the question the boys didn't want to answer. "What are you boys doin' out so late?" He didn't wait to hear the answer because he knew it might embarrass his young passengers. "You're might lucky I came along. There ain't much traffic tonight. The only reason I'm on the road was I had to go to Mannington to pick up some tobacco after my shift at Rachel. Heck, I'd already been home." He spit in the can and kept on talking.

It was alright with Sam and Billy. The less they had to say, the better. In fact, there was the uneasy feeling that they had said too much already. They were only interested in getting to their homes – and in bed – as if that would eradicate their actions of the last few desperate hours.

The win over Rivesville meant the game with Monongah the following Friday would be for the Mason-Dixon Championship. Originally scheduled for the Monongah field – another no light, no grass, no seat facility – the game was generating such high interest that both schools agreed that the game should be moved to East-West Stadium. The intense interest, the rivalry, seating capacity of 6,000, and the resultant gate receipts said 'move it'. However, there was a problem: the game between East Fairmont and Clarksburg Victory was already booked at the stadium for Friday night.

Monongah coach, Jim Feltz, wanted to play on Wednesday, but Coach Kelly objected. He wanted more time to prepare and insisted on Friday. If necessary, Kelly argued, the game could be played as the first game of a high school football double-header: Farmington vs. Monongah at 6:30 p.m. followed by East Fairmont vs. Clarksburg Victory at 8:30 p.m. Finally, Coach Feltz agreed, and the "game of the year" was on.

Teachers were just trying to get through the day. It was no use. The Farmington-Monongah game had taken over every student's brain. The rivalry between the schools separated by just three miles of narrow road, and the Ida May and Carolina coal mines was intense.

The early kickoff at 6:30 p.m. further complicated matters at the school, since it would be necessary to allow students to go home earlier in order to be in Fairmont at game time. Bus schedules had to be moved ahead, in fact, everybody's schedule moved ahead.

Principal Joe Cotrel gave up, dismissing school at 1:00 p.m. Sam and Leo rode the school bus home to No. 9, and then returned back to the school at 4:00 p.m. to catch the team bus to the stadium in Fairmont.

Kelly stood at the door of the bus and checked the thirty players in. Each player had his equipment duffel bag, which was loaded on the truck used for hauling equipment to away games.

Sam swung his duffel bag down off his shoulder and on the ground by the tailgate. As he turned to walk to the bus, he caught the eye of Coach

303

Kelly. Sam noticed he didn't get that sunny Irish look back at him. What happened? Coach seemed to be in a serious mood and that didn't happen to him on game day. He always seemed relaxed – maybe to convey that attitude to his players. But not today.

"Oh well," Sam thought, "you don't play Monongah every day for the championship. Maybe that was it!"

Maybe not.

As Sam started to board the bus with the other players, Coach Kelly took him by the shoulder and calmly asked him to stand aside. Then he did the same with Billy Pasko. After all the other players had boarded the bus, Coach Kelly walked around the corner of the school building out of sight of the players. Sam and Billy followed, looking at each other with the look of knowing that this had something to do with their 'pleasure trip' to Mannington. It had to be. Kelly had found out. They were right.

"I understand you boys were not at home last night at 11 o'clock."

"Yes, sir," they replied in unison.

Old Bill Six, spitting and talking, had talked to his old hunting buddy and had just shot bullets through the hearts of two Farmington football players.

"You know the rules. I should kick you both off the team. This is serious. But I'm taking you to the game. It won't be fair to the rest of the team. They need you both…but you're not starting the game, neither of you."

Sam pleaded, "Coach, we're playing Monongah. I gotta be in there…"

"Sam, we could be playing Notre Dame, and I wouldn't start you today. You broke the rules. Don Poundstone is going to start in your place."

Billy Pasko stood there and took his medicine. Sam, almost breathless, managed to speak. "Will I get to play?"

Kelly remained stern. "Poundstone is starting. We'll go from there. Now board the bus."

The sweet kisses of Nedra Smith that kept Sam in Mannington too long, now were tasting like poison. He could feel the heat rise up in his head as he made his way to the bus, where he got on board and into the front seat with

Billy Pasko and Coach Kelly. The bus driver slammed the door shut. Sam bit his lip to keep from crying in front of his teammates.

East-West Stadium was packed for the 6:30 kick off. Everybody from Farmington and Monongah and thousands of other area football fans were there. Some would stay to see the second game, when East Fairmont and Clarksburg Victory would play. But the second game didn't matter. The first one did! It was Farmington vs. Monongah again! For the Mason-Dixon Conference Championship again! Just like last year. Since Monongah had lost one game in the conference, and Farmington was undefeated, a Lion win would allow them to share the crown with the Farmers; however a Farmington win would give them the crown outright. Just like last year!

And just like last year, Sam Huff sat on the bench. But last year he sat there because he wasn't very good. This year he was on the bench because he screwed up. The sixteen-year-old had become one of the best players on the team, and a leader, too, but it didn't matter to Coach Kelly.

Sam looked up at the lights of the stadium, which shimmered through the tears in his eyes, as the team ran out from the sidelines to take their positions for the opening kick off.

He could hear the buzz of the crowd and he could hear his name being spoken. They were talking about him, probably wondering why he wasn't in the game. The public address announcer had given the line-ups and when he heard "Poundstone at left guard, he winced. "What the hell would people think? Where was Sam Huff? Was he injured?"

Players on both sides stood up against the sideline to watch the kick off. Sam numbly followed his teammates, then after the kick off retreated back to the bench. As he did, he walked past Kelly who paced back and forth in front of the substitutes.

When Monongah gained possession of the ball again, Kelly looked in Sam's direction. Then quickly turned his attention to the action on the field.

Sam could hear the roar of the crowd and while he gazed at the field, he

305

wasn't really seeing the action, just a blur of bodies in one play after another. He kept his mind's eye on Kelly, hoping to get some indication from him that he wanted him in the game. Sam looked at the stadium clock on the west end zone. The big bold lights were ticking down the time in the first quarter.

Seven minutes gone. "God damn it," Sam said softly to himself, "put me in."

Monongah mounted a march. Behind the excellent running and passing of star halfback Benny Salopek, the Lions had reached the Farmington twenty-four yard line. Kelly paced the bench past Sam as he watched the action. He turned and came to the bench. Sam looked up at his coach, his knees flexed to stand for the order to 'go save the day'. Kelly walked past him to another player, Dick Shenal, who stood up and grabbed his helmet. "I want you in for Poundstone." Shenal strapped on his helmet as Kelly walked him to the sideline with final instructions.

"Jesus," Sam thought. "Damn, that's my position. Hell, he's substituting for my substitute."

On fourth down and one yard to go on Farmington's twenty-yard line, Duane Bonnette and Jim McIntyre ganged up on Salopek and held him for no gain. Farmington's ball!

Kelly took a deep breath. His team had held the Lions, and without Sam Huff. Good lesson. On that last play Sam was hoping for a Monongah first down. He knew it was wrong, but he couldn't help himself. It would show the coach how much he needed him in there.

Sam looked at the clock. Two minutes to go in the first quarter.

A strong hand grabbed Sam by the shoulder pads. Coach Kelly stood him up, "Sam, you ready to play?"

"Yes!" Sam blurted out. Coach Kelly grabbed Sam from running out on the field. "Get your helmet!"

Sam dashed out to join his teammates to stop another Monongah march. It was Benny Salopek again. A pass to Eugene Tartell to the Farmington twenty-eight, another to the seventeen. Salopek ran to the eight.

Then Farmington held for four downs. Farmington's ball again. First down.

The <u>Fairmont Times</u> reported the next one minute of action this way.

> "After one play had picked up a single yard to the nine yard line, Rudy Banick strutted his stuff. The might-mite went around his right end, cut back sharply and raced all the way down the far sidelines to score."

The 91-yard jaunt put Farmington ahead 7 - 0.

Salopek led Monongah to a score in the third quarter to tie the game 7 - 7. As the game entered the fourth quarter, Skippy Stewart, the Farmington halfback and play caller, had to leave the game with a bloody nose. That left Farmington with no play caller and no passer, so Rudy Banick called the plays – fourteen straight running plays, and the Farmers charged down the field for a touchdown in the final quarter to a go ahead 13 - 7.

Monongah's turn. A touchdown and extra point would win the game. Salopek got the snap from center and ran to his right – to throw a jump pass just like the pictures of Johnny Lujack. Bam! It was Sam! Huff's shoulder sank deep into the mid-section of Benny. The ball fluttered free. Sam drove Benny down and into the ground. Sam could hear the air go out of Benny. Sam got up. Benny didn't. The crowd roared, then instantly grew silent as they noticed Benny writhing on the ground. Monongah Coach Jim Feltz and the Lion manager dashed out onto the field to tend to Benny, while Bonnette, McIntyre, and the rest of the Farmers slapped Sam on the back for a great tackle.

In a minute Benny was walking off the field with his coach. He wouldn't return, leaving the last minute of the game in the hand of some fresh sophomore. Game over. Farmington won 13 - 7 and became Mason-Dixon Conference Champs for the second straight year.

The <u>Fairmont Times:</u>

> "Farmington High school successfully defended its Mason-Dixon conference football championship

last night, defeating Monongah, 13-7, in the first half of a double-header at East-West stadium as the Farmers fleet halfback , Rudy Banick made his most determined bid of the year for a position on the Class B All-State team."

As the victorious Farmington players headed for the stadium locker room, they passed the East Fairmont and Clarksburg Victory teams running out on the field for the second game. The roar of cheers in the distance for the Bees and Eagles was drowned out in the Farmer's locker room by the loud, boisterous, and joyous shouts of victory.

The din reverberated into a constant cacophony of happiness against the hard concrete walls. As the boys were shouting to be heard, Coach Kelly and Coach Victor were walking around to each player slapping them on the shoulder and praising them for their play.

Players began to undress removing game shirts and shoulder pads, which were scattered around on benches.

Kelly had a special hug for Rudy Banick, not because the star running back had stolen the show again, but because he stepped in to take the leadership role when halfback Skippy Stewart had to leave the game with a bloody nose.

"We ran it down their throats," Rudy shouted over the noise, referring to the fourteen straight running plays he called that led to the winning touchdown. "I had to do it that way, Coach," he said, "I ain't no passer."

"It worked," Kelly shouted back. Sam, undressing beside Rudy was next for Kelly to congratulate. The Coach ignored any reference to the first quarter suspension, feeling his actions had spoken for him. "Great game, Sam." Kelly looked him in the eye. "I'm damn proud of you."

Sam stood up to embrace Kelly. He bit his lip, trying not to cry. He was sorry for having offended the coach he truly loved. "Thanks, Coach, I didn't want to let you down. I'm sorry for all that stuff I did... I, uh..."

Kelly broke in, "It's not alright, Sam...but now you know.   Just remember, okay...Again, I want you to know how proud I am of you."

"Okay, Coach," Sam said as he sat down.

Kelly moved to Leo and Duane Bonnette and Jim McIntyre and Jimmy Antolock and every other player congratulating them in a voice trying to be heard above the joyful noise echoing all around.

Some players had taken off their uniforms and were in the showers where the sound of sprays of water on concrete floors made their conversations unintelligible and just echoes of conquest.   The clamor in the dressing room eventually subsided, and you could hear the cheers of the crowd and the public address announcer as the second game went on out on the East-West stadium field.

Suddenly the attention of players near the entrance of the dressing room was drawn to Monongah Coach Jim Feltz as he walked in – not casually, but with determined purpose.   Rudy Banick noticed and thought the defeated coach's demeanor was odd.   Players in other areas of the dressing room didn't notice Feltz's entrance.   And neither did Coach Kelly.   While opposing coaches did visit opponent's locker rooms to congratulate an opponent as a show of good sportsmanship, it wasn't Coach Feltz's mission this time.

Amid the sounds of shouts and singing and happiness, the angry words "dirty football player" sliced through the din.   Kelly heard it again.   That caught his attention.   He turned to see Coach Feltz standing over Sam Huff pointing his finger at him.

"You're a dirty football player, Sam," Feltz repeated.

Sam was at a loss.   Anybody else pointing a finger at Sam with angry words accusing him of being "dirty" would have to fight.   It looked like Coach Feltz wanted to.   Sam's mouth hung open in complete disbelief.   He didn't know what to do.   "What the hell is going on," he thought.

He knew in a flash, Feltz was upset at the tremendous tackle he made on the Monongah star halfback, Benny Salopek, that knocked him out of the game.   But Sam knew it was a clean tackle.

309

"I didn't do anything," Sam stood up. His quick movement caused the bench to tip over. The sound of the wooden bench clattering on the concrete floor caused everybody to look. Rudy and Leo backed away. Kelly rushed over to grab Feltz by the shoulders and force him back and away from Sam.

Feltz came to his head and realized he was out of line, and after a moment of resistance, walked away escorted by Coach Kelly to a far corner of the dressing room, away from the players who suppressed their further desire to celebrate in the presence of Coach Feltz.

"Jim, you should know better."

"It looked like a dirty play to me, Coach."

Kelly calmly shook his head. "No, that's not it. It was a clean tackle. Sure, I know you're upset about losing the game. As far as Sam goes, your boys just can't handle him, but that's alright. Nobody can. Not one team we've played has been able to do anything with that boy. He's just too good."

Feltz acknowledged it, "Yeh, he is good."

An official, Frank Securro who refereed the game, walked by and overheard the conversation. He wanted to help out and jumped into the conversation.

"It was a clean tackle. I was right there on the play. I heard you talking. I wanted you to know."

Kelly smiled. "Thank you, Frank."

Then Kelly gave Feltz the bad news that he already knew. "And he's only a junior. He'll be back next year and even tougher. Heck, Jim, he's just learning how to play the game."

"Well, we have our work cut out for us, don't we," Feltz acknowledged.

Coach Feltz wanted to disappear, after having made a public spectacle of himself and in a way that suggested he was a bad sport and a poor loser. Kelly walked with Feltz to the dressing room door. As Feltz turned to leave, he stopped. "Coach, tell Sam I'm sorry. He played a great game. We'll get you next year!"

310

With a 6 - 2 record and both losses to bigger Class A schools, West Fairmont and Mannington, Farmington was rated and in contention for the Class B State Championship. Two games followed, both against Class A schools: East Fairmont on November 3 and Doddridge on November 11. Victories in one or both might give the Farmers enough points to put them in the playoffs.

On Friday, the day of the East Fairmont game, rain poured down in torrents to turn the often used turf of East-West Stadium into a mudbowl. The game was postponed due to the rain and the impossible field conditions and was set to be rescheduled at a later date.

Big problem. East Fairmont had its "biggest game of the year" against cross-town rival West Fairmont set for November 11. November 11 was Armistice Day and the football game between East and West had been an Armistice Day tradition for years, one that allowed all of Marion County to celebrate the armed forces with its day that included the game always at a packed stadium.

East vs. West! This game would be played and any thought of a rescheduled East Fairmont-Farmington game would be in relationship with the East-West game.

East Fairmont, with a 4 - 5 record, would try to salvage its season against a good West Fairmont team. East Fairmont Coach Ken Harris wasn't really interested in rescheduling the game with Farmington since it was of no importance to the Bees; however, the game would be of monumental importance to the ratings hungry Farmers looking for points and a ticket to the playoffs. So the decision was made for East Fairmont to play Farmington sometime after November 11, the scheduled day of the East-West game, as well as the Farmington-Doddridge game. If Farmington takes care of Doddridge, then the game with East Fairmont could send them to the state playoffs.

311

Surprise! Doddridge took care of any possible ratings controversy by beating Farmington 19 - 12. The loss also now made the East Fairmont game irrelevant as far as points for a playoff were concerned.

West Fairmont beat East Fairmont 14 - 6. The East Fairmont game with Farmington was never rescheduled, and the Farmers finished the season with a 6 - 3 record. All three losses were to Class A schools, which didn't affect their number one goal – the Mason-Dixon Conference Championship. The season also gave birth to an emerging superstar, Robert "Sam" Huff.

Farmington placed three players on the All-Conference first team. Rudy Banick made it, of course. So did Jim McIntyre at end and tackle Duane Bonnette.

"Bob" Huff made the second unit.

Sam bristled at his name in the paper. They were still calling him "Bob" – when everyone else in Farmington knew him as Sam. And he didn't appreciate being on the second unit All-Conference team. His confidence had grown from zero to a hundred throughout the 1950 season, and he felt he was the best lineman around. Few would disagree. In fact most fans and writers believed he was the most underrated player in the county – probably because he was a complete unknown before the season started and had to contend with those who had already established their names in previous seasons.

Returning Hero

Thanksgiving of 1950, November.

The gang at the Circle Bar was waiting for Frank. The word was around that he was in town and the regulars were expecting him to show up sometime. The Browns had just beaten the Washington Redskins on November 19, 20 - 14, to maintain first place in the conference. They weren't scheduled for another game until December 3, when they would play the Philadelphia Eagles in Cleveland.

The two weeks between games gave Coach Paul Brown the opportunity to give the players some time off and at the most opportune time – Thanksgiving week. And it gave Frank the chance to make a leisurely trip to Grant Town and enjoy Thanksgiving with his brother, Benny.

At the bar, the owner was waiting with two Carling Black Label beers and the good news about Farmington winning the Mason-Dixon Conference Championship.

Everyone else chimed in with a season review: "Did great…won the Mason-Dixon Conference Championship…great win over Monongah to cinch it!...the Monongah Coach Jimmy Feltz wanted to fight Sam Huff after the game, said he was a dirty player…boy, Sam was a killer in that game…he didn't start…" and the conversation continued with the Nedra Smith saga that benched the starting star left guard and finally…"I heard a radio man saying that Huff was going to be the best player to come out of Farmington since Frank Gatski."

Frank smiled and hung his head, a little embarrassed. "Does he think that's good, comparing him to me? Everybody's his own man. You fellas know that. I just play the game the best I can – And I feel damn lucky to be doin' it."

The conversation at the bar always deferred to Frank. When he spoke, the room grew silent, as everybody hung on his every word. It made Frank a little uncomfortable. He still wanted to be just one of the guys. He looked at football as another aspect of his life – not his total life.

He turned the Black Label in his massive hands and thought back to how he had never tried real hard at being a professional football player. It had come to him – somehow. He recalled his mining days at No. 9 and how he was perfectly happy doing that...and when a coach from Marshall College looked him up and invited him there for a tryout...and how after the war Coach Johnny Brickles invited him to a training camp at Bowling Green University to tryout for a new football team, the Cleveland Browns...

He shook his head slowly in silent disbelief, and then he caught sight of himself in the large mirror on the wall, looking lost, when he should have been paying attention to the conversation.

Frank took a drink of his beer. The question was about the two losses, both to the Giants. "I take responsibility for that," Frank said, "both of them. We didn't even score in the first game. We lost 6 - 0, and I should have blocked better. In the second game we lost 17 - 13. We fumbled three times, and Otto got tackled three times. That's my job to protect him." He stood up taller on the bar stool. "You know we could play them again in the playoff. It could work out that way."

And it did work out that way.

Three weeks later on December 17 in Cleveland Stadium, the Giants kicked off to the Browns to decide the 1950 Eastern Division Champion of the NFL. The two teams had ended with identical records. This time the Browns won it 8 - 3.

The win over the Giants left the Browns one win away from the National Football League Championship. That was remarkable, since it was their first year in the league.

The Los Angeles Rams had defeated the Chicago Bears setting up the match between the Cleveland Browns and Los Angeles, the old Cleveland team once called the Cleveland Rams that left that city in 1945 for Los Angeles. The game matched two of the most spectacular offenses in football, and both had to deal with their biggest opponent – the weather. The thermometer read

314

eleven degrees, and there was a harsh, frigid wind blowing through Municipal Stadium off Lake Erie.

With the football season over for Farmington High and with local colleges, Fairmont State and West Virginia University, having finished their season in November, everybody in No. 9 and in Marion County turned their attention to the big game in Cleveland.

Radios went on in bars throughout No. 9. Sam Huff and Leo got together at Leo's house to listen, hoping they would hear Frank's name over the air. And they heard it a lot. The announcer would say, "Gatski over center..." or "Gatski snaps the ball to Graham..." or "Gatski leads the Browns from the huddle..."

Each "Gatski" made a smile grow across the faces of the two buddies who had known their hero all their young lives and found it hard to believe. This was the guy being talked about over the radio all the way from Cleveland!

The Browns won in a thriller 30 - 28, with the deciding points a field goal by Lou Groza. Coach Paul Brown's team had done the impossible – winning the NFL championship in their first year in the league.

The football critics had to acknowledge the Browns' win over the Rams put them on top of the football world. The question asked before the season, "can these All-American Conference teams compete with the National Football League?" had an answer. Yes!

Frank Gatski didn't waste any time in heading out of Cleveland and to Grant Town. He was looking forward to the holiday season, especially with Ida and his two-year-old son.

Frank appreciated the bonus for winning the title. However, the weather kept the crowd down to 29,751, which reduced the payoff for each player. Each member of the Browns took home just $970.50. It would still make a difference, especially at Christmas.

315

He and his teammates had achieved their goal, and now it was back to the other part of their lives. For Frank that meant spending time with Ida, raising his son, and of course checking on his off-season job, working on the railroad driving spikes January through June.

Just like in all the other years, the job was waiting for him, and he checked in immediately. He had to keep a paycheck coming.

Breaking Up

She slammed the door in his face and told him to go home – Mary was mad at Sam again. He stood there staring at the doorbell. He wanted to ring it or push his way in, but decided he shouldn't – not at ten o'clock at night, not with four people asleep in the house.

Sam had stayed too long at the Circle Bar – playing pool and eating hot dogs. This was not the only time Mary had exploded recently. Football practice at Farmington High had just begun for the 1951 season, and some of the guys stopped at Ben's place for pop and hot dogs. The owner generously fed the football players – this day Sam stayed too long. He mentioned going to the movies to Mary, but a game of nine ball can make a guy forget.

As Sam contemplated a break-in, he turned away and walked across the railroad tracks and to the corner to hitchhike home to Mods Run.

He was looking forward to the football season. Everybody in the county and other parts of the state, even the coaches at West Virginia University, were looking forward to the kind of season Sam Huff would have. He was on everybody's "can't miss" list and opposing high school coaches "hit list".

He saw his shadow lengthen beneath the single incandescent street light. Walking the quiet street of Farmington, he was thinking how suddenly everything was going to hell in August when it was just fine in July. Why was Mary so mad at him all at once? He was on the verge of really making a name for himself this football season, but right at this moment that didn't matter. Tomorrow at football practice he would feel better, but the anger aimed at him from someone he loved made him forget everything else.

They had broken up before and kissed and made up, but this was different. It was like she was fed up with him. Had she found out about his

317

messing around with other girls? Maybe. But for Sam, it was just that – "messing around." The real girl in his life was Mary, and only her. As August moved along, with Mary staying at a distance, Sam lived to be on the football field.

In between football practices – sometimes two a day – Sam worked at Manchin's stocking shelves, and now with a driver's license, delivering groceries or furniture. Owner, John Manchin, who had become like a second father to Sam, took advantage of his size and strength to take on the big deliveries. He could count on Sam to get the goods there, whether it was a bedroom suite delivered to sombody's third floor or a rush delivery of baby diapers.

Because Sam felt such fondness for John Manchin, he thought of asking for advice about the problem he was having with Mary. Sam felt the need to talk about it. He would value John's advice, but he just didn't feel right about discussing it with him – yet – so he managed to keep it to himself.

Frequently Sam went to the Fletcher's house and knocked on the door, hoping Mary would talk with him. And she did, once, but she told him she didn't want to see him again. The end.

Thank God for football and Manchin's. The football field was Sam's home now, and it was there he was happiest, and it was only there that he could forget the churning inside that was Mary's absence in his life.

Work at Manchin's was a constant reminder of a different side of life outside the coal mine life of his father and brother – and he was drawn to the new possibilities as much as he rejected the idea of ever working in the mines.

The days passed, but there wasn't a moment that Sam ever forgot the look of Mary's face or the touch of her hand – when he wasn't on the football field.

The excitement was building for the 1951 football season. Nothing –
not even Mary's absence – could stop it. In late August, sportswriter, Eddie
Barrett of the <u>Fairmont Times</u> came to Farmington to write the pre-season
preview of the Farmers, one of a series of reports on all the schools in the
county.

His story was filled with references to Sam and Leo, both returning
lettermen, who would be the keys to the team's success.

"Undefeated in the M-D Conference for three
seasons, Farmington's string is running out.
The loss of 14 lettermen, including Rudy
(Panick) Banick practically precludes another
championship…The classy matchless Banick
graduated and the main topic for bull sessions is
the college's giving him the run-around. The
folks up here are hot because West Virginia
University didn't invite Rudy for a tryout…

Only three 1950 regulars form a nucleus, end
Leo Coceano, tackle Bob Huff, and halfback
Jimmy Antolock…The gridders in general are
medium – small except for big and agile Huff.
This 6 foot 1, 197 pound husky star for
Farmington's sandlot baseball championship
contenders, shows no awkwardness for his age
and runs like a truck. He easily took on 31
pounds in stride since last season. An all-
conference choice in our book…Huff and
Coceano lead a stout line…"

Barrett concluded his story with this:

"…All in all, it's a very young ballclub. Three
sophomores and a freshman may be in the
starting lineup at Wellsburg Friday, which
should be a rough night for the Farmers.

319

...Farmington's second foe, Fairmont West,
will be just as bad, but they play in their own
league, thereafter. They should be going strong
late in the season. After that, wait till next year.
A long-range prediction says the Farmers will
regain the MDC title."

Sam Huff had gotten use to winning. He had always tried like hell to win – from James Fork to Farmington High. He hated losing.

A week before the season started, he wasn't happy with the way the offense was playing. That's right! Sam Huff, just 16-years- old, was making judgments regarding the effectiveness of the Farmington High offense. But, hell, this was his senior year. He was filled with confidence, not only for his own playing ability, but that the team would go undefeated. Losing was not acceptable anymore. And since that was the case, Sam decided he better do something about it!

He had noticed his old buddy Murvyn McDowell was floundering as a third string fullback but felt he could benefit by switching positions and at the same time help the team. During a break, Sam went to Murvyn, "Hey, Murvyn, we need help on the line."

"I'm playing fullback," Murvyn insisted, "My brother played fullback, too."

"Yeh, but we got two fullbacks, Sopuch and Ronnie Blankenship. There ain't no use you sitting on the bench. We need someone to play guard."

"Heck, Sam, I can't play guard."

"You ain't tried."

"Well, yeh that's right. I haven't tried..."

"You're big enough – bigger than John Collins. Heck he's only a shrimp. What's he weigh, 130 pounds?"

"Something like that."

"It seems to me like you're never gonna beat out Sopuch or even Ronnie, so you come and play guard, and our line will be damn good."

"What will Coach say?"

"Let's go ask him."

"You kidding me? We can't go..."

"C'mon!"

So Sam and Murvyn went to Coach Kelly, who was talking with assistant Coach Victor. Kelly saw them coming. It appeared to him that Sam was bringing Murvyn to him for some reason. And he was right.

Sam Huff was taking charge. And Coach Kelly didn't mind listening. It was astonishing to Kelly to have watched Sam develop from a sophomore who begged to return to the team after quitting to a junior who had begun to dominate games. Now as a senior, Sam was being regarded as one of the best in the county and maybe in the state.

Kelly learned that Sam's instincts for the game led him into positive situations and winning decisions.

Sam's confidence in himself had grown. During his junior year he began to take charge on the field – putting players in position to defend certain plays and suggesting offensive plays. His growth in leadership had developed, too, and now he had the respect of his teammates, and it paid off. Now they counted on him – and listened to him.

Kelly smiled as he saw Sam and Murvyn walk toward him. What would this be about? "Anything wrong?"

"No, Coach," Sam said, "but we had an idea."

"Oh, you did?"

Murvyn stepped forward, "I'm here to play guard."

"Guard? You're a fullback, aren't you?"

"Yeh, Coach, but we got two fullbacks and I think, well, Sam and I was talking and I think I could help the team if I play guard."

Sam agreed, "I think that would be great, Coach."

"You do?"

Murvyn and Sam answered together, "Yes we do!"

Kelly smiled, his Irish eyes squinting and his face lighting up over the interest to help the team. He had never had anything quite like this happen before.

321

"Alright Murvyn, you'll have to learn the plays."

"I'll help him, Coach," Sam said.

Over the next few days, the new guard, Murvyn McDowell, became good enough to be the starter. And just in time.

Farmington would open the season at Class A Wellsburg on September 7.

While everybody talked about their summer vacation, the real buzz around the school was about Mary and Sam. The couple who had been going steady since eighth grade had broken up! Impossible!

No one in school could imagine one without the other. And for both of them, moments with their friends were awkward, filled with silences and irrelevant talk. No one mentioned the break-up. They didn't have to.

When Sam and Mary passed each other in the hallway during a change of classes, she would hurry by hoping he wouldn't stop to talk with her. And he didn't, even though he wanted to. It was easier for Sam. He had football and football had him – consuming him, saving him.

The first game was at Wellsburg, a Class A opponent in the Northern Panhandle of West Virginia – a three hour bus drive away.

The Farmers battled big-school Wellsburg to a scoreless tie. The Fairmont Times said the game "was restricted to the area between the respective 30-yard stripes." It also noted "Sam Huff, Farmington's right tackle played an outstanding game on the line…"

Farmington returned home feeling they could compete with anyone on their schedule. The Wellsburg game had given them confidence. They would need it. Next Friday they would be at East-West Stadium playing the West Fairmont Polar Bears.

The Fairmont Times sounded the warning:

> "Fairmont West, with its best team since the
> 1946 state champions, are figured to be too
> much for the Farmers, who are a rebuilt club after losing the

322

mainstays of the two-time Mason-Dixon titlists. The score was close last year however, 20 - 12 and the rugged Farmington eleven may be expected to put up a good fight."

They did better than that! The headline screamed, "Farmers hold Polar Bears to 6 - 6 tie." Writer Eddie Barrett:

"Scoring with a 76-yard pass play on its first try from scrimmage a rugged under-rated gang of Farmington heroes played vaunted Fairmont West to a 6 – 6 tie last night before 3,000 stunned fans in East-West Stadium."

Barrett's story continued,

"After the Farmers were stopped on the enemy goal-line by a pass interception in the last minute of play, the Big Bad Bears were quite willing to settle for a tie. They even punted on the next-to-last play of the contest.

For a ballclub that wasn't supposed to go anywhere – having lost eight regulars, including Rudy (Panic) Banick from the 1950 class, Farmington has insured a successful season already. In their opener, the Farmers played a scoreless tie at Wellsburg, the club which dead-locked the conquerors of powerful Wheeling last week.

Farmington played a slam-bang ballgame, and while the Polar Bears were below par, richly deserved to tie Fairmont's best team since the 1946 state champions. Outweighed some ten pounds per man, the inspired Farmers came within a hair of winning in the last minute, dog-tired though they were. Coach Ray Kelly admitted at halftime

323

that his team was 'tiring fast,' but he was not
reckoning with their indomitable
determination."

Sam Huff was everywhere. The Times story went on:

"Charley Thomas shot through left tackle to
the 23, but Huff – then stopped Spadafore for a
two-yard loss…

Huff stopped Thompson's try on his side for
the extra point and the tie remained…Spadafore
gained six around left end, but Huff and
company threw Reese back to the 18 and
Brzuzy threw two incomplete passes…Huff and
Coceano were the line standouts for
Farmington, with Antolock, Coceano, Sopuch
and blocking back Shenal getting most of the
work in the backfield."

Leo scored Farmington's touchdown in spectacular fashion.

"The Farmers caught the foe completely
unaware on the first play as Jimmy Antalock
passed 50 yards to end Leo Coceano on the
Fairmont 35. Although Buzuzy was keeping
pace with the receiver, Coceano put on a burst
of speed which Brzuzy did not even try to
match. When Brzuzy gave up the chase less
than five yards behind, Coceano romped easily
to the goal."

The story looked to the future:

"Among the onlookers was Line Coach
Harold Lahar of West Virginia University, who
is very much interested in Huff, the fine-looking
200-pound 6 foot tackle prospect. Lahar also
was impressed with the contestants' aptitude for contact."

The game was Sam's "coming out," a demonstration of the best, toughest line play in the county and beyond. Barrett called him "ferocious".

The other newspaper in Fairmont, the West Virginian, couldn't be outdone with praise for Sam:

> "West, although expecting fairly stiff
> resistance from Farmington, didn't expect what
> they got. Sam Huff, the Farmers candidate for
> Class B All-State honors was all over the field,
> getting in the way of the Polar Bears backs
> constantly. In the game, he very definitely
> stamped himself as All-State timber."

On the following day, Clem Hamilton, in his sports column for The West Virginian, echoed the sentiments saying, "Huff will distinctly be a candidate for the Class B All-State team this year."

Coming off the 6 - 6 tie over West Fairmont, Coach Ray Kelly quietly was feeling that this could be his very best team. He began the season in unusual fashion with two ties: Wellsburg 0 - 0 and West Fairmont 6 - 6. The significance, though, was that both were Class A schools, each rated to have its best season in years. Yes, there was good reason to be optimistic.

This season wasn't supposed to be that way. He had lost key players from the year before, especially in the backfield. The great Rudy Banick graduated and was off to Potomac State College. The leader, play caller and best passer, Skip Stewart, also graduated. So did top lineman Duane Bonnette.

But having Sam Huff return with his extraordinary physical gifts, toughness, and must-win attitude was forming the team, giving everyone confidence, and inspiring everyone to play better. And behind Sam was Leo, pushing Sam, inspiring the big guy, just as he had since James Fork Elementary.

Leo had become a terrific player, too, recognized as one of the best ends in the county. His presence was a constant reminder to Sam to "not let up" to "lead on," "keep getting better," or he would take over.

"No damn way," Sam thought!

325

Sam literally took over the games. He became a coach on the field shouting orders to everyone. He continued to feel great satisfaction in ordering Leo around. It showed his old friend who really was in charge. In a game when Sam anticipated a run to Leo's side, he shouted out, "Damn it, Leo, get your ass over there. They're coming through here."

But while everyone else deferred to Sam, Leo never did give up his right to be Sam's equal – and Sam had no choice but to try harder to keep ahead of Leo.

What's Wrong with Mary?

By mid-September, the Farmington Farmers and Sam Huff, were the talk of the county, and their story was even being heard around the state.

Sam was on top of the world – or he was getting to the top. It was only Mary's absence that kept him from being there.

On one unusually warm September day, Sam was with a group of guys outside the school at lunch time. Boys who brought their lunch would wolf down a couple of sandwiches and chocolate milk, then go outside to watch the girls coming back from having lunch at home. Sam was standing near some of his football buddies when he thought he saw Mary walking slowly...at least it looked like Mary – but this girl was all bundled up in a long jacket.

Jack Shenal, the football quarterback snickered, "Hell, it's eighty degrees. What the heck is she doing wearing that stupid coat?" He didn't see Sam standing behind him. "Hell, she must be pregnant." Jack laughed again, but this time alone. He turned to see Sam and forced an embarrassed grin.

Sam blinked, then it clicked in. "My God," he thought, "that's it. That's why she's been so mad at me!"

Sam wanted to slug Jack for being a foul mouth bastard, but he was too stunned by the truth in his words.

Suddenly everything made sense. "Damn it," he thought, "we didn't 'do it' but one time. Oh my God..." And as he saw Mary walking on, his feelings for her welled up inside of him. He choked back a sob and hid it away from the guys, walked across the grass to the sidewalk and stood there with her for a moment, just looking into her eyes. He took her books. She held on to them. He pulled them gently, but forcefully from her. He looked at her and didn't say a word. Then they resumed walking toward the school together.

The next day, after football practice, Sam went to Manchin's instead of hitch hiking home. John Manchin saw him walk through the door. "I didn't think you were working today."

"I ain't, but can I talk to you?"

John Manchin was Sam's lifeline – the only person in the world who Sam thought could help him now. John took Sam to his small cluttered room, which served as an office.

"Something wrong, Sam?"

"I messed up," he began and then he took a deep breath. "I got Mary pregnant."

John didn't change expression. He was too calm and always in control for that. Sure, he was surprised, but he didn't want to push Sam down any farther. And that old Manchin problem-solving mechanism began to kick in. There was always a solution. Flashing through his mind were the possible terrible consequences…Here was Mary, bright student with a future as a teacher and Sam, just 17, in an All-State football season with a major college scholarship waiting: both lives full of potential, facing a tragic circumstance and humiliation.

"Did you tell your parents?" John asked.

"No, are you kidding? They'd raise some hell, probably tell me to quit school, get married, and get a job in the mines…"

"Let me ask you, Sam, do you love her?"

Sam didn't hesitate. "Yes, I do."

"Would you marry her?"

"Well, I guess I have to, don't I? She's gonna have a baby. I don't want to see her messed up anymore 'cause of me."

John Manchin was determined not to let this destroy their lives. He found himself in a position to help both kids, and the parents, make the best of a bad situation. "I have an idea. Let's get everyone together – you and Mary, your parents, her parents, and talk about it. I promise you, Sam, we'll work it out someway."

The next afternoon, after football practice, Sam and Mary and their parents were crammed into the small office. John proposed that Sam and Mary get married as soon as possible. He went on to suggest Mary quit school. He knew the humiliation of staying in school would be too much to bear. Mary would come to work for Manchin's until spring when the baby would be born. That would give the couple an income, along with the money Sam would make there.

The parents all agreed it was the best possible option.

Sam felt relieved. It wasn't the end of the world, as he thought it might be. Mary was back in his life, and although life had changed, he could still move on with football, just like always, and pursue a college education, something no one else in the family ever did. These seventeen-year-olds were going to grow up a lot quicker than they had ever dreamed.

Sam certainly wasn't ready to get married, but he felt relief that everything was now out in the open. It somehow focused him on school. His grades even improved. He made better use of his time. He became a member of the Future Teachers Association and even tried out for a role in the Senior Play, "We Shook the Family Tree."

The director of the play, Social Studies teacher, J. Walker Thomas, persuaded both Sam and Leo to audition and gladly cast them – knowing it would help the box office and create additional interest in school among the students and in the Farmington community.

Rehearsals took place in the evening…after football practice. Sam couldn't help but think how strange it was…here he was going to be a father in the spring and now he was acting in a play about family.

He put the script up to his head trying to remember his line, but his thoughts wandered to his future real life family. He thought how football and whatever success might be derived from it had now become something necessary. It was no longer just for fun. Family life had suddenly been thrust upon him. He saw ahead the need to take care of Mary and the baby. Football could mean a scholarship and an education, which meant a decent job and

financial security. For sure, the seventeen-year-old was growing up!

329

His life change reinforced his desire to play football at the highest level...which was too bad for the opponents.

The 1951 football season became the Sam Huff and Leo Coceano Show. The Fairmont Times reports went something like this:

September 21, Farmington 32 – Clay-Battelle 6

"Antolock tossed two touchdown passes to end Leo Coceano and another one to Sam Huff, who played at end, at tackle and in the backfield on offense and all over the field on defense...On the first play of the second quarter, Coceano ran another one over from 20 yards out...Antolock passing to Huff who hauled the ball in on the 20 yard line and went the rest of the way. The play covered 50 yards...Antolock hit Coceano for 30 yards and another touchdown... in the last frame Coceano snagged another Antolock pass on a sensational catch on the goal line to score. Huff went around end for one point.

September 27, Farmington 27 – Fairview 0

"Jimmy Antolock threw a long pass to Leo Coceano for a touchdown, and Sam Huff moved to the backfield from his tackle slot long enough to plunge for the extra point...Antolock threw another touchdown pass to Coceano from nearly midfield. Huff's try for the point was good..."

October 5, Farmington 19 – Mannington 7

"...Antolock passed to Coceano for the touchdown...Strongman All-State candidate, Sam Huff was all over the field, keeping Mannington away from the goal line."

330

After the Mannington game, in the dungeon-like locker room of Mannington's Hough Park gymnasium, Sam was showering. He closed his eyes to the hard warm spray and started singing in a loud voice, "I'm getting married in the morning." He was going to be okay.

The next day, on Saturday, October 6, 1951, Sam and Mary were married.

Talk about change! The new Mr. and Mrs. Sam Huff took up residence in the house of the the bride's parents, located on Railroad Street behind St. Peter's Catholic Church in Farmington.

Mary's parents sure didn't want their daughter to move out, so the only solution was to have Sam move in. Mary's room became theirs, and Sam divided his time between the Fletchers in Farmington, his parents place at Mods Run, Farmington High School, and work at Manchin's.

It didn't take long for the scene to change. Corby Fletcher grew to dislike Sam very quickly. Why wouldn't he? Sam's presence was a daily reminder that his daughter had done the unforgivable – and Sam was the culprit. Animosity soon became anger – and one day after a particularly heated argument, Sam convinced Mary they had to move out. So they did – but not far – just across the tracks to an apartment over Gango's grocery store. Mary was still within shouting distance of her home, and Sam was out of sight of the man who now hated him the most.

The football season rolled on.

October 12, Farmington 19 – Barrackville 14

"...Big Sam Huff headed the defensive forces for Kelly's gang and it was his blocked punt which set up the first Farmington score...Huff smeared Migialo for an 11-yard loss...Late in the second period Huff spilled Neville for a 16-

331

yard loss…Huff barged through to block the punt…Antolock passed to Coceano for 38 yards…"

October 19, Farmington 21 – Rivesville 7

"…Big, strong Sam Huff was the defensive standout for the victors as he threw repeated Rivesville backs to the turf before they could get under motion…Huff blasted through to throw Lambert for a one-yard loss…"

A couple of days after the Rivesville game, Bill Evans, the sportswriter for the Fairmont Times, mentioned Sam and Leo in his Sport Talk column, noting that

"Leo Coceano at end is not only an excellent pass receiver, but an all around terminal" and "then, of course, there is Sam Huff, the bulwark of the forward wall…On defense it has been proved next to impossible to run against him…The youngster on whom several talent scouts already have had their eagle eyes on, got married a couple of weeks ago, but up to now the happy life of a newlywed hasn't seemed to affect his slam-bang play."

The Farmers were undefeated with five wins and two early season ties, both against Class A schools, Wellsburg and West Fairmont.

Two games remained: one with hated rival Monongah; and a final non-conference game at Romney.

Leo's Rebellion!

On October 25, 1951, the auditorium was in an uproar – with hands clapping in unison to the Farmington High band playing the school fight song. The team lined up across the stage. Head coach Ray Kelly and assistant John Victor stood to the side of the stage with Principal John Cotrel, while the band played on and the student body sang out, "...*hail to Farmington High School, hail!*"

As the band's last notes echoed through the auditorium, the chant began in the back. "Beat Monongah, Beat Monongah, Beat Monongah, Beat Monongah..." It grew louder as it proceeded like a wave from the back to the front of the stage. Now it was deafening.

Mr. Cotrel looked at his watch. Coach Kelly saw him do it and decided he should proceed with the thuse. As he and Victor strolled to the center of the stage, the "Beat Monongah" chant turned into a loud constant roar. Kelly held up his hands and a wave of sound retreated to the back of the auditorium, which in a few seconds grew quiet.

Kelly smiled that wide Irish grin. "This enthusiasm is going to help us beat Monongah – it means as much to these boys as playing the game..." The auditorium erupted in noise – kids yelled, and the drum section of the band banged the drums. "We've been fortunate to win two consecutive Mason-Dixon Conference Championships and tomorrow, with your help, we're going to win our third straight!"

As another roar from the seats died down, Kelly glanced over to see Joe Cotrel looking at his watch again. Cotrel looked up to catch Kelly's eye with a look that said, "You're taking too much time." Kelly also knew that the principal delighted in having a minute or two on the stage for his "moment"

before the student body. "Frustrated actor, turned principal," Kelly thought.

333

Kelly hurried on. "Two of the seniors who haven't addressed you at a thuse before will today." Kelly looked at Mr. Cotrel, "and I believe Mr. Cotrel will say a few words, too."

There were a few suppressed laughs from the back that quickly went silent. Cotrel smiled and nodded his approval, then looked at his watch as Kelly continued talking. "Murvyn McDowell, our right guard, has been a big reason for our success. He was willing to play a different position to help this team, and I'm really proud of him."

Sam, who was standing beside Murvyn, gave him a gentle slap on the back that sent Murvyn into the spotlight at center stage.

Murvyn adjusted his glasses and cleared his throat as he stared into the silent student body. "Like Coach said, I played a different position, fullback, uh, and I gotta thank Sam for, well, making me do it, you know, play guard, but I'm sure glad I did – and tonight we're going to bring back another Mason-Dixon Championship."

The drums banged and the kids yelled as Murvyn stepped back to the line. Sam nudged Murvyn his approval of the speech.

Kelly applauded Murvyn then turned again to his audience. "Another senior who has played an important role this year is Jack Shenal, who plays quarterback. Our quarterback has to do a lot of things – block, handle the ball, even run the ball sometimes. Jack learned that position this year and has done a great job."

Kelly motioned toward Jack. The noise for him began. Jack wanted no part of making a speech, and while the students yelled and the drums banged, Jack said his few words – nobody heard a single one – and retreated back to the comfort of his place in the line.

Kelly looked at Cotrel, who nodded and proceeded to center stage. The students grew silent. Cotrel enjoyed this. He was known as a man of good humor. He could kid, and he projected a self-deprecating attitude to play down the idea of winning – so as to not be disappointed if you lost. Some children do that. Cotrel still did it.

"I can't imagine these boys could win a third straight championship. Monongah is a very tough team. Always has been. But anyway, I want to wish our boys well. Maybe they can win another trophy for our trophy case. You notice I said 'maybe'." He turned to the team behind him. "Do you think you boys can do it?"

The entire line of players smiled at the foolish question and kind of nodded – all except Leo Coceano, who was fighting mad at his principal's luke warm push to victory. He couldn't help himself. He spoke up.

"No, Mr. Cotrel, we are going to win – and that's for sure." His Italian dialect was as clear as a bell. "Ain't no maybe!"

You could hear the entire student body gasp then grow silent. All of the players, Coach Kelly and Coach Victor stood dumbstruck as they waited for Leo to melt into the stage. Suddenly the students came alive and came to Leo's rescue with a loud cheer that moved the drum corps to bang the drums – and sent Cotrel and his lukewarm rhetoric away to stage right. Cotrel stopped, smiled, looked at his watch and nodded to the band director, who promptly turned and shouted to his musicians, "*Fight Song.*"

The players filed off the stage as the band played on and the students finished the song, "*…hail to Farmington High School, hail!*"

The headline declared "Farmers Thump Monongah," then a subheadline "Farmers Win Third M-D Title in Row, Beating Lions 34 - 0." The newspaper story first paragraph summarized:

> "Farmington High School's Farmers left no
> doubt in the minds of an estimated 2000
> spectators at East-West Stadium last night that
> they are the class of the Mason-Dixon
> Conference as they ran roughshod over
> Monongah 34 - 0 to gain their third straight
> conference title and wind up their fourth
> consecutive undefeated league season."

335

There were more raves for Sam and Leo:

"Big Sam Huff was once more the defensive
stalwart for the winners. Nearly every
Monongah play which gained ground, went to
the other side of the line, away from Huff…a
pass from Antolock to Leo Coceano who made
a miraculous diving catch on the four-yard line
and carried to another touchdown…Coceano
blasted through to block the kick."

The locker room echoed with shouts of victory. The Farmers had won
a third straight Mason-Dixon title and were undefeated with six wins and just
two ties, both against bigger Class A schools, Wellsburg and West Fairmont.
One more game remained – against Romney on November 3. A win would
complete the first undefeated season at Farmington in 17 years.

As important as this last game was, Sam and Leo were drawn to
distraction by another school event – the Senior Class Play.

"No, no, Leo. You got to hit Sam – stop fooling around. Hit him!"

Those orders didn't come from Coach Kelly's mouth on the
Farmington High School football field, but instead they were stage directions
from J. Walker Thomas, social studies teacher and the director of the Senior
Class play, "We Shook the Family Tree."

Sam and Leo both were auditioned – recruited by Mr. Thomas – who
couldn't resist getting the two football co-captains on the stage. It would
certainly draw attention to the play – dampen the suggestion that plays were for
sissies and improve the box office.

Leo was cast as Freddie Shermer, "mother's little boy" and Sam was
playing Ernie, "the irresponsible brother."

Mr. Thomas had the wisdom to also cast the football right guard
Murvyn McDowell as the father of the perfectly normal family. This was type

casting. Murvyn was the only kid in school smart enough and adult enough to play the father.

Sam and Leo both lived with their play scripts, especially during the final days of rehearsals. The play, a one performance run, was scheduled at the worst time – Thursday, November 1 – the day before the team would leave for Romney for the game on Saturday.

The play was getting into Sam's brain. He kept running over his lines – even during football practice. Mary helped by making Sam run his lines with her over and over.

On Thursday night, the play went on – in front of students, family, and friends, and of course, everybody loved it. By Thursday night at 10 o'clock, it was all over. But the lines Sam had rehearsed for the last weeks stayed.

The football game with Romney had become a tradition. The school located one hundred twenty miles away in the Eastern Panhandle had a great program. To play them – and to beat them – was a feather in anyone's cap. This year the undefeated Farmers had a lot at stake. Two years before, in 1949, Romney needed an extra game to boost its rating. Farmington agreed to the game, traveled to Romney, and got whipped 32 - 6. Romney went on to play for the Class B State Championship.

This year, things were reversed and the Farmers record of six wins and two ties – both to Class A opponents – had them rated. Now a win at Romney would complete an undefeated season and keep them in contention for the playoffs. Quite a feat. The last time Farmington was undefeated was seventeen years before in 1934.

Because of the distance between the schools, the trip was accomplished by having the visiting team's players stay overnight with the players of the home team. Farmington's itinerary was to have a thuse on Friday, then travel to Romney driving Friday evening, stay overnight and play the game on Saturday afternoon.

337

First, the thuse. Coach Kelly introduced all of the players one last time and then asked co-captains Sam and Leo to speak. They both promised the complete destruction of the Romney team and an undefeated season.

Kelly, with his eye on Mr. Cotrel, faded back into the team row of players as the principal walked to center stage. The team collectively displayed a lack of attention expecting the usual disparaging remarks. But not Leo, he was ready to pounce.

Mr. Cotrel spoke, "I want to congratulate the team on the wonderful record, so far, and for winning the Mason-Dixon Conference Championship again." Then he took a deep breath. "But you know, they're playing Romney. Why, that team won the State Championship two years ago. I don't know whether we can beat them, but I expect our boys will give it a good try."

A distant, faint rumbling sound of opposition rose from the audience. Cotrel held up his hands shook his head and suggested the worst. "If we don't get killed over there, it will be a moral victory."

The students, now on to Mr. Cotrel's obtuse sense of humor, booed loudly. Again Cotrel held up his hands to quiet them. Then, the principal made a mistake. He said laughingly, as if it were a joke, "Why if our boys do win, we might call off school for a day." The boos instantly turned to cheers! But Cotrel cautioned them, "But I don't expect I'll have to worry about that."

The last few words of Mr. Cotrel's speech were drowned out by Coach Kelly clapping through it – his way of bringing the thuse to an end before the principal completely demoralized the team.

But Leo, standing right behind the principal, heard every word he said.

Maybe it was the hangover from "We Shook the Family Tree," but the Sam Huff - Leo Coceano era at Farmington High was coming to an end with a lethargic performance on the Romney football field made muddy with a day long rain. By halftime there was no score as the teams went to the locker room.

Sam was mystified. "They're killing me, Coach. I beat the guy in front of me..."

Kelly interrupted, "I know, Sam. They're trapping you."

"Yeh, just when I get the tackle, I get bumped…"

Kelly reassured him. "Just keep charging in. Something good will happen." And it did.

In the fourth quarter, Sam burst through again, but the pulling guard, who was going to trap him, got there late. Sam had the quarterback, the ball fell to the turf. Sam pushed the quarterback aside. The ball bounced up in Sam's arms. Thirty yards. Touchdown!

Farmington won the game 6 - 0. They had achieved the near impossible – an undefeated season. That included three games with Class A schools. The <u>Fairmont Times</u> headline shouted "Farmers Complete Undefeated Season." Then a smaller headline, "Huff Scores TD on Recovery of Romney Fumble."

The story began as you might expect:

> "Sam Huff, Farmington's High Schools' candidate for Class B All-State honors, picked up a Romney fumble early in the fourth period here this afternoon and rambled 30 yards to register the only score this dreary mud-filled football day."

Later the story summarized the Farmers' season:

> "The victory gave Farmington a clean sweep in Class B competition. Wins were scored over Clay-Battelle 32 - 6, Fairview, 27 - 0, Barrackville, 19 - 14, Rivesville, 21 - 7, and Monongah, 34 - 0. In addition to today's win, a scoreless tie was played with Wellsburg and a 6 - 6 tie with Fairmont West in Class A competition…and the Farmers registered a 19 - 7 win over Mannington in Class A."

A caption underneath a team picture explained that "the Farmers were in contention for the Class B State Championship playoff."

339

The bus trip back to Farmington was one jubilant ride. The Farmers finished the season undefeated, the goal of every athletic team.

On the bus ride back, Leo Coceano began making plans. Jubilation turned into an arrogance of power. Leo was feeling it. He was going to make Mr. Cotrel pay for the statement he made during the thuse.

At first he quietly discussed it with Sam. He reminded him of Cotrel's statement, recalled in Leo's Italian dialect.

"Look, Sam," Leo began, "he said, 'if you boys donna get a killed, it's a gonna be a moral victory. If a you beat 'em, you gonna get a day off.' That's what he said, and that's what we're gonna do."

Sam tried to calm down his friend. "He ain't going to go for that."

Leo insisted, "Oh yes he will. We're gonna make damn sure."

As the bus continued on the two-hour drive back to Farmington, Leo marshaled the forces to join him in the rebellion.

When Mr. Cotrel arrived at school on Monday, he sensed something was wrong. The building didn't sound right. There seemed to be a silence from adjacent classrooms. There was the absence of wooden floors creaking and distant classroom sounds of teaching. He knew the beat and rhythm of his school and right now it was out of tune and out of sync. He pushed back his chair and stood up, ready to go investigate. At that moment his door swung open and Mrs. Davis, the English teacher hurriedly entered. Gasping for air, the excitable woman was delivering the worst news. "The students are all – every single one of them – in the auditorium. No one is in class!" She took a deep breath and wrung her hands.

Mr. Cotrel crossed his arms. "What the heck is…"

"They say they are not going to class today," she swallowed hard. "That you said it was okay."

340

Mr. Cotrel blinked then blew his stack. "I did what?! They said...Who is <u>they</u>?"

"Well, Leo Coceano seems like the ringleader. He said, you said if they won..."

The door rattled opened and Mr. Johnson, the biology teacher, came with more news, "When I came through town, I saw two large signs hanging between telephone poles that say..." He scrolled the words in the air for Mr. Cotrel to see. "DO NOT GO TO CLASS. GO TO AUDITORIUM." Johnson delivered the same Coceano message. "The kids are saying, you said if they won they wouldn't have to..."

Cotrel shook his head. "I was kidding! Now what?!"

Johnson further implicated Leo. "The rumor is that Leo Coceano did it."

The <u>truth</u> was that Leo Coceano did it.

Leo, fed up with Cotrel's disparaging remarks, took to heart the principal's promise. He had a plan. Step one was to enlist Sam to commit to the effort. After all, if Sam Huff, the football hero, was involved, it had to be okay. Hell, Sam Huff could have run for mayor and been elected. Sam was on board. Leo made sure of it.

After they returned from Romney, Leo, Sam and their buddies went scavenging in Manchin's store trash. They found large cardboard boxes that were used to transport refrigerators – perfect for large signs. Then some black paint for the "DO NOT GO TO CLASS, GO TO AUDITORIUM" message, and clothes line rope to tie the signs up high would complete the mission.

They chose the only two intersections in town, so that just about every kid coming by bus or walking in would see them. The few that didn't, got the word quickly and gladly joined the rebellion.

Inside the auditorium, packed with 350 students, peaceful revolution was in the air. Since everybody was joining in, there would be no way to penalize any one person. The kids were too savvy to mention any name – to protect the guilty. Cotrel didn't care to cast blame, he just wanted to get the kids back to class and the school back to normal. He entered the auditorium

341

with the teachers and went to the stage. Respectfully, the kids quieted down.

"Is this because I said there would be no class if we won?"

That's as far as he got. A loud cheer went up and right through Cotrel's head. He held up his hands and got them quiet.

"I know you have to celebrate the undefeated season, but this is not the way…You will have to go back to class…"

"Noooo!" A resounding 'no' filled the air – and it was followed by laughter from students in the rear of the auditorium.

The reaction made Cotrel retreat a step, where he clumsily bumped into Miss Davis, who winced and asked, "What are we going to do?"

The loud chorus of 'no' – not angry, but still determined, – hung in the room, keeping Cotrel from continuing. He shook his head and marched off stage right, followed by the teachers. Together, they gathered in the hallway outside the auditorium. They could still hear the sound of triumphant laughter from inside. Mr. Cotrel headed down the hall and disappeared into his office.

The teachers looked at each other – some amused – some with serious concern, while they waited for the decision to be rendered from the office down the hall.

Mr. Cotrel was on the phone to John Manchin. Why not? John Manchin, the former mayor was also unofficial counselor, financier, and problem solver to just about everybody in town. Cotrel had a problem. Call John Manchin.

"John, I got a serious problem here in school. Thought you might help me out." Then he went on with a discussion of the problem, playing down his role in creating the situation in the first place.

Manchin, with his resources and his valuable contacts, in both the financial and political community in the county, could solve just about any problem. He thought for a minute.

John Manchin was on the student's side. "Joe, since this is about winning the game and finishing an undefeated season, I don't think you can do anything but celebrate. It was your idea in the first place."

Mr. Cotrel felt a surprising twinge of pride. "Well, uh yes, I did say…"

John Manchin was clever. "Well, we'll have to celebrate, just like you said."

Cotrel clenched the phone and wiped his brow, "But we don't have any way to handle this… We didn't make any plans…"

John Manchin calmed him. "Let me make a couple of phone calls. I'll call you right back."

Mr. Cotrel was being saved by John Manchin, whose nimble maneuvering turned the auditorium mob into a celebration that gave them their promised "day of no classes". At John Manchin's suggestion, Mr. Cotrel called the band director to prepare for a thuse and a parade. City Line buses – quite an upgrade over regular old school buses – compliments of John Manchin, were quickly contracted to take the entire student body to Fairmont, where Joe Carunchia, a friend of John Manchin and owner of the Fairmont Theatre, would entertain them with a free movie and all the popcorn and pop they could consume.

The thuse, the best Farmington ever had, went on at 11:00 a.m. The band, wearing their usual school clothes, instead of uniforms, struck up at noon and hit the streets of Farmington, where most of the five hundred residents came from homes and stores to join in the impromptu festivities. Students – dancing, skipping, and bunny hopping behind the band, proceeded beneath Leo's signs that began the day.

City Lines buses pulled into the school parking lot at 1:00 p.m. The kids happily piled into plushier digs to take the twenty-minute ride to downtown Fairmont. A smiling Joe Carunchia welcomed the buses and opened the theatre's doors to the Farmington High School kids, who watched a movie, ate his popcorn, and drank his pop in honor of the 1951 undefeated season, a celebration called for by the principal, Joe Cotrel.

The movie was "The Magic Face." The marquee shouted "See Hitler Killed!" starring Luther Adler and Patricia Knight. "The Magic Face" was about an impersonator who murders Der Fuehrer and takes his place. It wasn't exactly what the kids would have ordered, but it was a day away from

343

school and anything was better than a day of trigonometry, biology, and physics.

Sam's Reflections

On November 4, 1951, the day after the Farmington Farmers completed an undefeated season at Romney, the Cleveland Browns were securing their lofty position in the National Football League.

The opening paragraphs of the Fairmont Times described it this way:

"Cleveland's Browns recovered four Chicago Cardinal fumbles, intercepted one pass and scored after each break today to ramble to a 34 to 17 triumph before 19,742 fans shivering in 21-degree temperature in Comiskey Park."

The victory left the Browns alone in first place in the American division of the National Football league with five wins in six games.

Quarterback Otto Graham had another all-pro day, which meant that Frank Gatski played pretty well, too, since the center is Otto's main protector.

Graham completed 15 of 21 passes for 210 yards and a touchdown, while scoring two himself on short runs.

The Browns won again the next week, beating the Philadelphia Eagles 20-17 in a hard-fought contest, then welcomed an open date on the weekend of November 18 – prior to the final four-week charge toward another National Football League Championship.

Frank was always happy to have an open date. Once again, he could head back to West Virginia for a few days with his brother and his family. He longed for those West Virginia hills, and he didn't waste time getting there. The Browns wrapped up practice on Thursday, November 15. On Friday, Frank headed home.

Railroad Street, which led from U.S. 250 onto the Main Street in Farmington, was crowded with parked cars. The street ran between St. Peter's Catholic Church and alongside the B&O railroad tracks, on which long trains hauled coal from No. 9, Ida Mae and the Carolina mines to industrial America out there somewhere.

Not only was Railroad Street crowded bumper to bumper, but so was Main Street and Mill Street, which ran in front of St. Peter's. No funeral or wedding or even Midnight Mass ever jammed the streets surrounding the church like this.

Many of the cars were strange to Farmington. Late model Buicks, DeSotos, and Oldsmobiles in Farmington had to belong to visitors, there for a most important occasion.

Finally, John Manchin was getting his chance to throw another party – this would be the biggest party the town had ever seen – to honor the 1951 undefeated Farmington High School football team.

The town's largest hall for such a dinner, the basement of St. Peter's Catholic Church, was packed with 50 members of the football team, which included even the freshmen who didn't dress for games, dozens of townspeople and a number of invited and important guests.

The owners of the Buicks and Oldsmobiles, invited from out of town, included Fairmont sportswriters Bill Evans and Clem Hamilton. Evans, called "the dean of West Virginia Sportswriters," noted in his *Sportstalk* column a week earlier that while he had been invited to a number of banquets, "the dinner that interests us at the moment is the one being planned by the citizens of Farmington with John Manchin in the lead for the undefeated Farmers." Evans, a short, rotund, jolly old elf, was known throughout the region for his many years of sports reporting, as well as political influence. He gained the unofficial title of "Dean of West Virginia Sportswriters," not only for his many years of reporting, but his clever, well-written observation and his first hand knowledge of events that shaped the future of West Virginia athletics.

Also on hand was the banquet's guest speaker, Art Lewis, the football coach of West Virginia University, along with assistant coaches Harold

346

Lahar and Gene Corum. Evans reported in his column they would be there and also stated the reason. "The Mountaineer brain trust is pretty much interested in maintaining diplomatic relations with Farmington in the hope that Sam Huff will enroll at Morgantown next fall."

Evans was called on for brief remarks as was his fellow sportswriter, Clem Hamilton and guests, Coach Cassy Ryan of Mannington; Frank Lee, sports announcer of radio station WMMN; and Farmington High principal Joe Cotrel.

While they spoke, their words went silent to Sam's melancholy look back at all the moments that had brought him to this night. He raised his arm to touch the back of his friend Leo sitting beside him. Nobody could have meant more to him. Sam knew Leo had pushed him to this moment. All through the kid years and now as young adults, Sam was trying to keep up with his dynamic Italian buddy.

Leo felt Sam's touch and grinned at him. Leo nodded a silent gesture of warm appreciation, then looked back toward the speaker's stand.

Sam's gaze went to Blair Wolfe, the James Fork Elementary principal – and suddenly there was Leo and Sam choosing up sides and trying to outmaneuver the principal to no avail.

Sam looked at John Manchin, who had shown him the possibilities of life outside of No. 9 and beyond the culture of coal mining. He couldn't help but remember the times John had given him work when he desperately needed money and emotional support and advice for life's changes, like the time he went to him after learning of Mary's pregnancy.

Finally, Sam looked at Coach Kelly, who gave him a second chance and a third chance after he quit the team in his freshman year and his sophomore year. Sam felt his stomach turn as he realized what might have happened if Coach Kelly had said 'no' to his tearful request to get back on the team.

Now his feeling for Coach Kelly had turned into the love of a son. Looking at coach, Sam felt his eyes tear up and he quickly wiped away the tears and lowered his head to hide away his feelings.

Sam was brought back to the banquet by the applause that echoed in the church hall for the main speaker, West Virginia University football coach Art Lewis. Sam felt flushed when Coach Lewis rose to speak. He was hoping he wouldn't mention his name. Coach Lewis didn't. Instead, his remarks were general in nature, emphasizing the value of an athletic scholarship that would provide a college education. He concluded by saying, "...it is a lot better to spend four years in school at 'hard labor' than to look forward to a whole life of it without any future progress in sight."

After the banquet, Coach Lewis spoke to Sam more directly saying, "Son, either come with me or get a No. 9 shovel."

Three days later, the Mason-Dixon Conference coaches met for their annual fall meeting, which included voting for the All-Conference team. Sam was a unanimous choice and was even named 'honorary captain'. Leo was also honored with a first team selection. Four other Farmington High kids also made the mythical eleven: end Carl Gouzd, guard Don Poundstone, full-back Harry Sopuch and half-back Jack McIntyre.

The big prize for Sam – an All-State selection – came two weeks later. The selections announced by Committee Chairman Roy M. Hawley of West Virginia University were the result of a poll of coaches, officials, sports writers and radio announcers from around the state.

Finally, it was Leo now trying to catch up to Sam – Leo was named "only" second team All-State.

A week later, another banquet, this one the official Mason-Dixon Conference banquet, was held in the Farmington High School cafeteria. Conference President Larney Gump presented the Championship trophy to Farmington co-captains, Sam and Leo. It wasn't any surprise that West Virginia head coach Art Lewis attended, along with his freshman coach, Gene Corum. There was no way Sam Huff was getting away from West Virginia University.

348

The Word from New York

As the Browns were preparing for the Championship game December 23 against the Los Angeles Rams, the United Press named its' All-Pro Team for the 1951 season. On December 19 the selections were announced. The word came from New York to the Browns' public relations director, Russ Gestner, who immediately gave the information to Coach Brown.

Prior to practice, Brown was happy to be the first to congratulate the members of his team selected. He called the team together in the Browns' locker room.

"Nine members of our team were honored by the press as all-pro players." Then he smiled – a rare smile for Brown. "Nine, that's an extraordinary number considering there are only twenty-two players named. I want to congratulate you all for the year you've had. On defense we had Len Ford, Bill Willis, Tony Adamle and Warren Lahr." The players shouted and clapped in a genuine display of admiration for their teammates. Brown continued, "On the offensive side, we had five, Otto, Dub Jones, Lou Groza, Dante, and…" He paused because this last name to be mentioned pleased him most of all. It was the name of a player who had been least mentioned by the press throughout the year, yet Coach Brown knew was one of his most valuable players – a man who had been there from the very beginning in 1946 and who was finally getting the public recognition he deserved. Brown looked up from his list. "…Frank Gatski."

Immediately, Frank was dumbstruck. It was totally unexpected. He knew he had done everything expected of him but to be honored publicly for it was a shocking surprise. A second later his wide smile lit up the room. Brown shook his hand. His teammates roared their approval, pounded his back and crowded around him to let him know how happy they were for him.

Otto Graham stood back while his teammates filed out of the room to the practice field. While distant shouts of teammates still in a celebratory mood hung in the air, Otto in his quiet reserved manner, shook Frank's hand and looked him directly in the eye. "I couldn't be happier. You deserve it, Frank, more than anybody I know. I'm really happy for you."

Frank was genuinely touched by the sincere comments from the greatest player in the league. "Thanks, Otto, but you made it happen. I'm proud to be a part of it." Then Frank got back to business. "Hell, with this All-Pro crap – Let's beat the Rams."

Immediately, the <u>Fairmont Times</u> picked up on the news about the local hero. In Emlyn Thomas' column, "Sidelines," he wrote the following:

"The news that Frank Gatski has finally been chosen on the United Press All-Pro team will indeed be welcomed by those local persons who are acquainted with the big fellow. Frank had been a member of the Cleveland Browns squad since Paul Brown organized the outfit some six years ago, but other than in the lineup, his name has never been mentioned when the big name sports writers decided to sing the praises of pro stars.

In this year's roundup of the pro gridders, for example, Gatski wasn't even mentioned as one of the returning veterans. About every body else on the Browns roster was, but not Gatski.

Frank played his high school football at Farmington. If memory serves us correctly, he was a reserve center on the 1936 ball club, which swept through to the county championship.

From Farmington, Gatski moved on to Marshall College, where he played with Jackie Hunt and

350

that gang under Cam Henderson. We believe that he also played some for Auburn, shortly before signing with the Browns, but we're not too certain about that."

Browns Lose a Big One

As Frank guided the '49 Chevy off the Pennsylvania Turnpike, the curve of the ramp gently raised Ida from her sleep. She had dozed off shortly after they left Cleveland. Frank, appreciating all the sleepless hours Ida spent with their two kids, didn't make a sound while driving the two hundred miles to the Rt. 19 exit near Youngstown, Ohio. Occasionally, he would glance back at the kids in the back seat, happy that the steady drone of driving on the flat, level straight Ohio toll road put them to sleep. Three-year-old Frank, Jr. was clutching his favorite Christmas bear with his head resting on the shoulder of his little sister, Ann. On both sides of them were stacks of gaily wrapped Christmas packages destined for Benny's house in Grant Town.

The 1951 NFL Season ended on Sunday, December 23, but not the way Frank wanted it to: the Browns lost the NFL Championship game to the Los Angeles Ram 24-17.

It was different. The Browns had won four straight All-American Conference Championships from 1946 through 1949 and then followed with the National Football League Championship in 1950. Losing wasn't easy.

The team flew back to Cleveland after the game on Sunday. Players said goodbye and headed back to their off season lives.

Frank replayed the game over and over, a classic that went down to the final minute. Writer Henry Reiger began his UP story this way:

> "An amazing touchdown pass by Norm Van
> Brocklin in the fourth period gave the Los
> Angeles Rams a history-making 24 - 17 victory
> over the Cleveland Browns today for the
> National Football league championship.

352

The triumph and the title were sweet revenge for the Rams, who had the same two prizes in their grasp in last year's championship finale only to lose to the same Browns on a last-minute field goal, 30 - 28.

But more than that, the Los Angeles win marked the end of the most phenomenal streak of titles in pro football history. The Browns had won five straight pro football crowns –four in the now-defunct All-American conference and one in the N.F.L.

And the play that ended the Cleveland reign was a thriller never to be forgotten by the crowd of 59,473 at Memorial Coliseum and the millions who watched via coast-to-coast television. With the score tied at 17 - 17 midway in the final period, the Rams had the ball with a third down on their own 27 yard line. Van Brocklin, former Oregon star, passed to end Tom Fears, who caught the ball on the Browns 48 yard line and raced all the way to score."

"Damn, damn!" Frank blurted out.

Ida awoke, sat up quickly and looked at the road. "What's wrong, Frank?"

Frank, embarrassed at his outburst replied quickly, "Oh, nothin'. Sorry I woke you. I was thinking about that play."

Ida sat back, looked at the back seat at her children.

Frank checked out the kids in the rear view mirror, then laughed at himself. "I guess they don't care about the play." In the back seat the Christmas packages flashed a holiday glint. "Sure glad to get the extra money from the championship game."

353

Ida smiled. "Just in time for Christmas."

The Browns each got $1,438.12 as their share of the gate of $223,644.89; the winning Rams each took home $2018.44.

The additional championship game money had pushed Frank's take-home pay for the season to a new high, which he couldn't imagine – over $14,000.

"I'm glad to have the extra money, Ida, but you know what? I would have played for nothing."

Ida smiled. "I know!" Then she reached over and gently put her hand around his neck. "How about being named an all-pro." She laughed. "Now I can say I sleep with an all-pro; how about that?"

Frank laughed. "Finally made it, didn't I?"

"You sure did, honey!"

The Banquet

John Manchin was counting his blessings, along with the generous receipts from Christmas week at the store.

In the cramped, disheveled office in the rear of the store, he gazed at the calendar's final days of 1951. "What a year" he thought. The peace of Christmas was a reality. Finally, the war in Korea was over and soldiers were back home. The mines were working full tilt with record coal production, which meant his business was thriving. And his family was growing – he had a daughter, Janet, and two sons, Joseph and John.

And then there was his "surrogate" son, Sam Huff, an All-State football player on his way to West Virginia University on a football scholarship. He picked up the newspaper and read again the news about his good friend, Frank Gatski making the 1951 All-Pro team. He shook his head in disbelief as he sat down at his cluttered desk and pushed the invoices aside.

"Unbelievable," he whispered to himself. "So much good news." He looked up, "What a year!" He reread the Emlyn Thomas' column about Frank, "Frank played high school football at Farmington. If memory serves us correctly, he was a reserve center on the 1936 ball club…"

John stopped and read again, "…a reserve center." That's right, not even a regular in high school. "It's a miracle…how in the hell does somebody get from here…to there!"

He shook his head again, stood up and turned to the calendar on the wall. Hanging behind the 1951 calendar was the new 1952 calendar. He felt a surge of pride at knowing what Frank had accomplished, by excelling, rising to the very top of the professional football world, being named an All-Pro – and in the same year Sam Huff is named All-State!

A tingle of excitement went through him. John Manchin often felt that same "tingle" when he had a good idea. It was an alarm ringing out 'this is a good idea – go forward!'

He lifted the cover of the 1952 calendar to January then circled "Saturday, January 28". That would give him enough time. John Manchin never asked permission. He just did it, and if he circled a date on the calendar, something was going to happen. All he needed was Frank's agreement on the date, and the town – hell, the whole county would celebrate Frank Gatski Day. Nobody else needed to approve it. Why should they? John Manchin had the town's biggest grocery store, the furniture store, and the carpet store. Outside of the mines, he was the town's largest source of employment and finance – and besides, he was the mayor and father – confessor for dozens of problems – loaner of money to people in hard times and general fixer of "problem" from the student rebellion Joe Cotrel, the school principal faced, to the pregnancy of Mary Helen Fletcher Huff. No, the "good idea" alarm was ringing loudly and John Manchin was as excited as a kid at Christmas.

John Manchin sat back in his seat as the post dinner conversation – all about Gatski – filled the air. He had pulled off another celebration of extraordinary achievement, something he reveled in, especially when it came to athletes and local sports teams.

The dinner guests and news people were surrounding Frank; some to pass on a personal story and some to get their dinner invitation autographed by the All-Pro.

Sam Huff stood back waiting his turn, not knowing what to say, but trying to compose a few words that wouldn't make him sound stupid in the eyes of his hero.

John Manchin smiled. His eyes focused on Sam, who fidgeted nervously while waiting for the opening to Frank. "Damn," he thought. "I'm looking at an All-Pro football player, and an All-State kid whose trying to get in a few words to his hero and one of the greatest football players in the country. John shook his head in amazement. He mused about the rarest of possibilities that the kid could go on to ever be as good – and as honored. As much as he wanted to believe otherwise, he laughed to himself, "Not a chance!"

The End

Epilogue

Sam Huff took the advice of West Virginia University football coach Art Lewis and enrolled there in 1952. His buddy, Leo Coceano also attended the University but did not play football. The two old friends of James Fork Elementary roomed together while Sam traveled back and forth from Morgantown to Farmington to see Mary and Sam, Jr. and to continue to work part-time at Manchins.

While at West Virginia in 1952-56, Sam became one of America's top college linemen, earning All-American honors in 1955 and 1956. In 1956, he was drafted by the National Football League New York Giants.

During that period, Frank Gatski became the premier center in the NFL making the all-pro team in 1951, 1952, 1953, and 1955.

In a remarkable intersection of their destinies, Sam and Frank met on the football field at the College All-Star Game played in Soldier Field in Chicago in 1956.

The Chicago Charities College All-Star Game, played annually in August from 1935 to 1976, pitted the reigning NFL champion against a selected group of outstanding college players.

The game was the idea of Chicago Tribune sports editor Arch Ward; its purpose was to become a major source of charity contribution to the city.

In 1956 Sam was selected for the All-Star game and the NFL champion was the Cleveland Browns. Sam and Frank were on the same field and on opposing teams.

One particular play led to an interesting confrontation.

Frank leaned over the ball to snap it to the quarterback Otto Graham. "Gunner" looked up across the line of scrimmage at the College All-Star

linebacker Sam Huff. The ball was snapped. Graham handed the ball to Ed

359

Modzelewski who ran up the middle toward Sam. Frank hit Sam with a block, and both sprawled to the ground as Modzelewski ran by.

Sam screamed, "You're holding me, Frank!"

Frank rose up on his knees. "That's the only way I could get you…" Then he stood up. "Hey Sam, an all-pro would never have to hold a rookie."

Sam smiled. Frank reached down and helped Sam to his feet.

The two men played against each other in three more games, including two NY Giants/Cleveland Browns games in the 1956 season. The third and final meeting was a NY Giants/Detroit Lions exhibition game after Frank signed to play with the Lions for the 1957 season.

Sam went on to become one of the games great players, earning All-Pro honors in 1958 and 1959.

In the fifties and sixties, television was exploding the game. And Sam became the face of the NFL – and the face on the cover of TIME Magazine for November 30, 1959.

In 1960 famed newscaster Walter Cronkite featured a documentary titled *The Violent World of Sam Huff* on his popular television show "Twentieth Century." It became a sensation and made Sam a household name.

In 1964 Sam signed with the Washington Redskins where he spent five years, including one as a player-coach, with famed coach Vince Lombardi in his final season.

Frank spent eleven years with the Browns through the 1956 season. He then signed with the Detroit Lions for the 1957 season. The "forces" were still at work for Frank: in his final pro season with the Lions, his new team beat up on the Browns in the NFL championship game 59 - 14.

Frank retired from pro football in 1957 and returned to West Virginia, where he later became the football coach at Pruntytown Industrial School for

Boys, a facility for troubled boys, many of which were mentored by Frank into successful citizens.

Hall of Fame

In 1982, Sam Huff was inducted into the NFL Hall of fame with a class that included Doug Atkins, George Musso and Merlin Olson.

Three years later in 1985, Frank Gatski was inducted with one of the most noteworthy classes ever: O.J. Simpson, Joe Namath, Roger Staubach, and Pete Rozelle.

In 1985, there were only 128 members in the NFL Hall of Fame. Two were from coal camp No. 9.

Acknowledgements

Grateful acknowledgement is made to the following for their assistance:

Terry Kave, a friend of the author who managed to turn over a thousand handwritten pages into a typed manuscript, and who assisted with editing and completing the final version for publication.

Mike Arcure, a longtime friend of both Sam Huff and Frank Gatski, and fortunately the author as well. Mike's recall of facts is legendary and his contribution was invaluable in the telling of this story.

Fairmont State University for the use of the microfilm section of newspapers, which allowed the author to view past issues of the Fairmont Times, the Times-West Virginian, and the New York Times.

Michael Workman, P.h.D. of the Department of Social and Behavavorial Sciences at West Virginia State University, who reviewed the manuscript and provided information regarding coal mining.

Murvyn McDowell, a classmate of Sam Huff at Farmington High School, who provided the author with important Farmington High School yearbooks and other information.

Blair Wolfe, the principal at James Fork Elementary in the forties, for stories about Sam Huff and his buddy Leo Coceano. Mr. Wolfe passed away in 2006.

West Virginia Wesleyan College and especially archivist Brett Miller, for information on and a picture of Paul Gatski.

Lindsay Wiles, for her assistance in preparation of the manuscript for publication on Amazon.com.

Linda McClung, for her work on the cover design.

363

Others who provided pictures include:

Joan Gatski Kingery, niece of Frank Gatski

Nat DeBruin, University Archivist and Manuscripts Librarian, Marshall University

Cleveland Browns Archives

Steve Gatski, youngest son of Frank Gatski

Rick Maxwell

62295993R00212

Made in the USA
Columbia, SC
01 July 2019